Armed Conflict and Human Rights Law

This book explores developments in international law regarding the relationship between human rights law and international humanitarian law and their co-applicability in armed conflict situations.

The work examines the jurisprudence of the international human rights courts and looks at the Inter-American and European Courts of Human Rights case law in dealing with new emergencies in armed conflicts. It argues that a new interpretation and application of the law is required to deal with current needs while remaining faithful to moral commitments made in the international arena. In this way, the book deals with recent cases and their rationale to build a new understanding of law and international policy that complies with the globalization process and progress towards an enhancement of the international community's legal framework. Combining the emergencies in armed conflicts with the mutual enforcement of human rights law and humanitarian law, this book holistically develops concepts and theories to present a pragmatic solution to moral quandaries over the targeting of civilians during armed conflict situations.

The book will be a valuable resource for academics, researchers and policy-makers in the areas of international human rights and international humanitarian law.

Daniel Ivo Odon is a legal advisor on human rights at the Brazilian Ministry of Women, Family and Human Rights. He has also taught Theory of Law and Human Rights Law at several Brazilian universities.

Globalization: Law and Policy

Globalization: Law and Policy builds an integrated body of scholarship that critically addresses key issues and theoretical debates in comparative and transnational law and the principles governance and policy on which they are developed. Volumes in the series focus on the consequential effects of globalization, including emerging frameworks and processes for the internationalization, legal harmonization, juridification, and democratization of law among increasingly connected political, economic, religious, cultural, ethnic, and other functionally differentiated governance communities. Legal systems, their harmonization and incorporation in other governance orders, and their relationship to globalization are taking on new importance within a coordinated network of domestic legal orders, the legal orders of groups of states, and the governance frameworks of non-state actors. These legal orders engage a number of important actors, sources, principles, and tribunals-including multinational corporations as governance entities, contract and surveillance as forms of governance that substitute for traditional law, sovereign wealth funds and other new forms of state activity, hybrid supra national entities like the World Bank and the International Monetary Fund, and international tribunals with autonomous jurisdiction, including the International Criminal Court, the World Trade Organization, and regional human rights courts. The effects have been profound, especially with respect to the role of states, and especially of developed states as their long time position in global affairs undergoes significant transformation. Comparative and transnational law serve as natural nexus points for vigorous and sometimes interdisciplinary approaches to the study of state and non-state law systems, along with their linkages and interactions. The series is intended as a resource for scholars, students, policy makers, and civil society actors, and includes a balance of theoretical and policy studies in single-authored volumes and collections of original essays.

Larry Catá Backer is the W. Richard and Mary Eshelman Faculty Scholar, Professor of Law and International Affairs at the Pennsylvania State University. Previously he served as Executive Director of the Comparative and International Law Center at the University of Tulsa. He has published widely on comparative and transnational law.

Also in the series:

Legal and Rhetorical Foundations of Economic Globalization
An Atlas of Ritual Sacrifice in Late-Capitalism
Keren Wang

Armed Conflict and Human Rights Law
Protecting Civilians and International Humanitarian Law
Daniel Ivo Odon

For more information about this series, please visit:
www.routledge.com/Globalization-Law-and-Policy/book-series/GLOBLP

Armed Conflict and Human Rights Law

Protecting Civilians and International Humanitarian Law

Daniel Ivo Odon

Routledge
Taylor & Francis Group
LONDON AND NEW YORK

First published 2022
by Routledge
2 Park Square, Milton Park, Abingdon, Oxon OX14 4RN

and by Routledge
605 Third Avenue, New York, NY 10158

Routledge is an imprint of the Taylor & Francis Group, an informa business

British Library Cataloguing-in-Publication Data
A catalogue record for this book is available from the British Library

Library of Congress Cataloging-in-Publication Data
Names: Odon, Daniel Ivo, author.
Title: Armed conflict and human rights law : protecting civilians and international humanitarian law / Daniel Ivo Odon.
Description: Milton Park, Abingdon, Oxon ; New York, NY : Routledge, 2021.| Series: Globalization: law and policy | Includes bibliographical references and index.
Identifiers: LCCN 2021002132 (print) | LCCN 2021002133 (ebook) | ISBN 9780367773144 (hardback) | ISBN 9781003170778 (ebook)
Subjects: LCSH: International law and human rights. | Humanitarian law. | Civilians in war. | War--Protection of civilians. | Combatants and noncombatants (International law)
Classification: LCC KZ6471 .O36 2021 (print) | LCC KZ6471 (ebook) | DDC 341.6/7--dc23
LC record available at https://lccn.loc.gov/2021002132
LC ebook record available at https://lccn.loc.gov/2021002133

ISBN: 978-0-367-77314-4 (hbk)
ISBN: 978-0-367-77320-5 (pbk)
ISBN: 978-1-003-17077-8 (ebk)

DOI: 10.4324/9781003170778

Typeset in Galliard
by Taylor & Francis Books

To my parents and mi esposita.

Contents

Illustrations

Figures

Table

Abbreviations

ACHR	American Convention on Human Rights
ECHR	European Convention on Human Rights
ECtHR	European Court of Human Rights
GC I, II, III, IV	Geneva Convention I, II, III, IV
HRL	Human Rights Law
IAC	International Armed Conflict
IACommHR	Inter-American Commission on Human Rights
IACtHR	Inter-American Court of Human Rights
ICC	International Criminal Court
ICCPR	International Covenant on Civil and Political Rights
ICESCR	International Covenant on Economic, Social and Cultural Rights
ICJ	International Court of Justice
ICJS	International Court of Justice Statute
ICTR	International Criminal Tribunal for Rwanda
ICTY	International Criminal Tribunal for Former Yugoslavia
IHL	International Humanitarian Law
IMT	Nuremberg Judgement
LOAC	Law of Armed Conflict
LOW	Law of War
NATO	North Atlantic Treaty Organization
NGO	Non-Governmental Organization
NIAC	Non-International Armed Conflict
OAS	Organization of American States
PCIJ	Permanent Court of International Justice
POW	Prisoner of War
STP	Standard Temperature and Pressure
UDHR	Universal Declaration of Human Rights
UK	United Kingdom
UN	United Nations

UNGA	United Nations General Assembly
UNSC	United Nations Security Council
US or USA	United States of America
WHO	World Health Organization

1 Introduction

This work seeks to examine the effects that law provokes in society, as well as what society expects from law in answering some questions. The broad analysis of law contained herein takes into consideration connections with other branches of science, from whence we may retrieve some good analogies, hindsight and constructive ideas. It is interesting because we initially depart from a conception of law that connects itself with many other fields of knowledge – for instance, sociology and biology. There are so many questions arising from problems society faces in the natural advancement of civilization, and for each one the analysis becomes twofold: what kind of answer law provides and what kind of answer society expects from law.

The science of law has a lot of undeniable social traits, regardless of whether they are sympathetic to contractarian theory or not. Nevertheless, as science, it holds a set of methods that describes and interprets observed or inferred facts, past or present, and is targeted at testing hypothesis and building theories. At the same time, as morality is a social compass, we also understand law as a science attached to a moral background, especially in respect to human agency. For that, building theories means that the aim of this work is to explain moral constructivism through comprehensive explanations from international law provisions and cases on international human rights courts.

As defined by Durkheim, *homo sapiens* has become, through evolution and social moral configurations of modern societies, *homo duplex*, a creature who exists at two levels: as an individual and as part of the larger society. It is paramount to comprehend that nowadays all individuals bond to a social entity as a whole, which has become the purpose of contemporary international community and ideas of cosmopolitism.[1]

Therefore, moral reasoning is a cornerstone of this work and we believe that there are several layers of human knowledge that precede reason and guide humans toward true knowledge and good decisions. During this process, Hugo Mercier warns, inference comes first, then intuitions, then intuitions about representations, then intuition about reasons, then, finally, reason.[2] The rationality

1 Cited by Jonathan Haidt, The Righteous Mind: Why good people are divided by politics and religion 225 (2012).

2 Hugo Mercier and Dan Sperber, The Enigma of Reason 05–06 (2017).

DOI: 10.4324/9781003170778-1

developed here goes through this very humane process of using reason to justify ideas and opinions, starting at data-gathering observations and predictions based on international law provisions and international human rights case law and moving on to draw my own conclusions in support of the theory to be built.

Only through communicative action may civilization ascend to new levels of social enhancement and expansion of law as a moral instrument, while authorizing the democratic debate on values and providing accurate answers to real social problems. The diversity of our opinions arises not from the fact that some of us are more reasonable than others, but solely because we have different ways of directing our thoughts and do not take into account the same things. It is not enough to have a good soul; you must be able to use it righteously. The greatest minds are capable of the greatest vices, as well as the greatest virtues.[3]

Reason can be manipulated to explain or justify decisions already made and beliefs already held. This is a retrospective use of reason. On the other hand, sometimes reason is used for arguments in favor of new decisions or new beliefs. This is a prospective use of reason. Yet, when reason is used prospectively, it may be to answer an unresolved question, or to convince others of an opinion one already has. The former is inquisitive reasoning, while the latter is argumentative, or communicative, reasoning. In the production of reasons to convince others, the same reasons have both retrospective and prospective relevance. Furthermore, this work seeks to understand an argumentative kind of prospective reason, since the arguments are made in favor of new decisions and beliefs, and the aim of this argumentative exercise is to convince readers of the author's opinion about the matter, based on both the retrospective and prospective element.

To connect the dots, I combine both theoretical and pragmatic rationales. There are a lot of theories from doctrines, and just as many theories from judicial precedents on real cases. One of the most intriguing sides of law is how it changes and reacts to extreme situations, crises and emergencies that significantly challenge a great part of – or the entirety of – mankind. The different frames of law for peacetime and crisis often collide, and usually new lessons come out of it to shape a new understanding of the law operability.

The main objective of this work is to establish a deductive moral reasoning on situations of armed conflicts regulated by international law wherein targeting civilians becomes one of the most disturbing concerns for our morality of law and the use of it. The ideas developed here aim to inspire the reflective use of international law as a whole, combining especially humanitarian law and human rights law branches and their mutual relationship. Thus, the deduction method adopted here comes from observation of what international courts are testing daily in real cases where some observational and experimental truths are realized with axiomatic weight.

As a researcher, my goal is to shine a critical light on the prevailing understanding of the morality of law in order to promote an alternative containing intellectual honesty and humility, while hopefully representing a good use of

3 René Descartes, *Discurso do Método*, in Obras Escolhidas 39, 41 (1973).

reasoning. Constructing a theory requires an analytical statement with elements ranging from technical knowledge to metascientific knowledge. The former is informative and useful to our routine, while the latter builds upon concepts to construct new ideas, a technique often applied in dissertations. Therefore, this work combines some personal convictions on morality in human rights law and its interplay with other areas also covered by law. One thing that is very sensitive in lessons of hermeneutics is the importance of the interpreter's history and background in the application and insights of the law.

As observed by Michael Shermer, several decades of research in cognitive psychology has shown we are not the rationally calculating beings we would like to think we are. Conversely, we are immensely driven by our passions, blinded by our biases and moved by our moral beliefs. Reason is part of our cognitive structure and, once its capacities are in place to deduce, all data available can be put to use in analyzing problems where the objects and time elements of the reasoning process are interchangeable. This interchangeability is what enables us to adopt the perspective of another moral agent and enriches the cognitive architecture of moral reasoning.[4]

Justice is a very broad concept and it contains multiple meanings and manifestations. The most important feature in the pursuit of justice is to rationalize a reasonable theory of action. Therefore, my personal origins in South America, where discussions about law are more theoretical than pragmatic, is undeniably significant. The way law is taught in Brazilian universities is very different from the US model of learning. First, Brazil has a lineage of civil law and the strong influence of the Catholic Church in state and social politics. We've inherited a strong tradition of hermeneutics, which gives our civil law traditions and legal rigidity (*dura lex sed lex*) some flexibility, with the best resemblance of justice possible.

Second, moral values and human dignity are very important elements in the development and interpretation of law in Brazil, even while revelations of empiric hypocrisy arise every day in our society. Personally, I am agnostic, but I took a lot of moral lessons from my Catholic military father and my protestant geneticist mother. While studying in military school my whole youth and taking theology classes in parallel with law classes, I maintained my agnosticism and nurtured virtues of goodness and altruism with deep roots in Christianity, even with respect to animals, whose entitlement to basic rights I enthusiastically defend (I am a vegetarian in order to save animals' lives).

All this background certainly influences the way I think and the way I write. Diversity of background and thinking is something that American universities are used to embracing, which is one of the reasons I sought education abroad. The American inputs have helped my personal and professional growth, and in the same way I hope my inputs from this work might be part of literary materials that touch other curious souls interested in some different and plural landscape regarding the usage of law.

4 Michael Shermer, The Moral Arc: how science makes us better people 16–17 (2015). In the same sense, Ronald Dworkin, Justice for Hedgehogs 108 (2011).

That being said, the construction of this work departs from an overall vision of international law and the new design in international society from the second half of last century onwards. The promulgation of core values in human rights, a whole international system centered in human dignity instead of state interests, and the method employed to govern all these elements toward a brand-new threshold of international law and international community, are new traits that remind us that a contemporary international framework conveys high moral standards and makes mankind morally better. Some characteristics make intimate connections with the purpose of the final idea, which is a legal and moral evaluation of targeting civilians in situations of armed conflict where emergency is the reality.

Besides the proliferation of new international actors and the decentralization and universalization of international society, the legal codification process and appearance of international courts – mainly human rights courts – has brought a great shift in international values and legal framework. A very interesting phenomenon we are able to point out is the leading role played by the judicial decision-making process in defining legal contours of international law. Associated with the vertical hierarchy structure of the international legal system and several primary sources of law, the Vienna Convention and International Court of Justice (ICJ) Statute try to bring harmony and integrity to the international legal order when establishing guidelines and interpretation for the application of law.

Notwithstanding, international courts follow the good intentions of promoting humanity's core values and implementing the dynamic and ductile elements of legal provisions semantic densification into the law in order to create an alternative body of legal source that, in practice, becomes the primary source of international law. In addition, we have the opportunity to explain all the paths that human rights law has gone along, from original values to the configuration of moral reasoning, which generates a very strong conception of law, both statutorily and morally. The same proliferation of values and plurality has given human rights some moral quandaries that international courts have been settling case by case. In this regard, differences of interpretation and application of human rights provisions can be seen throughout the decisions of the Inter-American and European Courts.

By the same token, the law of war takes into account the moral component of humanity while documents are drafted to humanize the horrors of war, and a good amount of international legislation also regulates civilian immunity and care, recommending the nominal replacement of the law of war for international humanitarian law. Some international obligations upon civilians are bound in international law that demands heed is paid to principles of distinction, necessity, proportionality and, most of all, humanity. Nevertheless, civilians continue to experience the hellishness of hostilities all over the globe while international courts expound new comprehension regarding mutual applications of international humanitarian law and human rights law, setting up an eventual collision between each specific provision that will be solved by *lex specialis* criteria of the former upon the latter.

At the beginning of this century a new form of combat emerged that astonished and alarmed the international community. New terrorism does not comply with any humanitarian or human rights law, and is characterized by acts of shocking cowardice, evilness and cruelty, without value or distinction among their victims. International law, in response, progressively shapes its jurisprudence to try to overcome the evil, step by step, and restore peace and community welfare. During such process, some precedents mutate from incident to incident and worrisome considerations appear to guide a rationale that points to the logic of how international organisms and subjects respond to challenges and threats to collective survival and flourishing.

Focusing mainly on the mutual interplay between international humanitarian law and human rights law, I establish some foregrounds from which I develop thoughts on the matter. In an attempt to organize the ideas chronologically, we envision three waves of international law comprehension. The first is the official merger between international humanitarian law and human rights law, which, until that moment, were both considered two opposite branches of law. Despite placing international humanitarian law as *lex specialis* over human rights law, the compatibility between them was formally recognized. Second, human moral dignity was pushed to the centre of the interwoven relationship, interfering in acts of judgement performed during situations of armed conflict. Finally, in the third wave, we examine human moral dignity and some important human rights law provisions and considerations drawn from the relationship, which initially happened in Europe, where the effects of the fight against global terror have been felt.

Regarding this third stage, I develop a critical analysis that disagrees with the rationale employed while agreeing with the overall conclusion. Basically, I scientifically and argumentatively uphold a theory that promotes the same outcome and final understanding but with different justifications. Believing I am able to present convincing arguments, the idea is to develop a creative theory of action to change the moral overview on targeting civilians as a side effect in armed conflict situations. Taking into account all relevant international humanitarian law provisions, human rights morality, and the combination of both within the recent understanding of their mutual interplay (where not even the formal claim of derogation on human rights has to be fulfilled), we boldly present an alternative solution which complies with legal morality and rationality toward the act of targeting civilians.

The scope of the analysis of this work is narrowly related to targeting civilians in armed conflict situations, although the rationale adopted can be applied in different cases where factual analogies might be encountered. Nevertheless, the situation under the lens is the action of targeting civilians during armed conflicts wherein the factual scenario matches the consensual notion of supreme emergency or state of exception, which is also a recurrent case for international human rights courts.

The materials used to elaborate this book come from different parts of the world. I work with Brazilian theorists, Argentinian and European theories and law cases, many German scholars with their hermeneutics and sociology theories, American scholars and theorists, international documents of Inter-American human rights jurisprudence, and United Nations documents and cases from the International Court of Justice. All these materials merge upon a singular understanding of international law and its intertwined application of humanitarian law and human rights law applied to real-life cases.

Let's do it!

2 Contemporary traits of international law

Introduction

The origin of international law is closely related to the birth of the European states as political, national and sovereign unities in the sixteenth and seventeenth centuries. International law developed modern boundaries in the aftermath of the new European system of nation-states and reflects the natural development of the common human necessities of all cultures. From then on, the old idea of a state went beyond European borders, and the European system itself allowed for the appearance and coexistence of other states under the same international rules if they were "civilized" – that is to say, Christian. Subsequently, a system arose based on concepts of territorial sovereignty and equality of prerogatives among them.[1] However, international law did not regulate the issues that involved the vital interests of the states, which overlapped with the private interests of the dominant states. It means that, legally, all members of the international community were on an equal footing, while in practice, a group of Great Powers dominated the international scene.[2]

Thus, the international rules and principles embodied in old international law possessed two salient features: (i) they were the product of Western civilization based on a *laissez-faire, laissez passer* philosophy that all states were equal and free to pursue their own interests, irrespective of any economic or social imbalance; and (ii) they were mainly framed by the Great Powers, in order to serve their own interests. After the First World War this had many decisive impacts because its magnitude involved all major members of the international community. It became tough for states to keep aloof from what was happening around the world. So in 1917 a new ideology and political philosophy arose with the following fresh principles: (i) self-determination of peoples, as advocated by the USSR; (ii) the substantive equality of states instead of the old legal equality; (iii) socialist internationalism, for the first time proclaimed by a member state of the world community as a policy to disrupt capitalism, which was rapidly implemented in Mexico and Germany by the constitutions of 1917 and 1919 respectively; and (iv)

1 A. W. Brian Simpson, Human Rights and the End of Empire: Britain and the Genesis of the European Convention 91–93 (2004).

2 Guillermo R. Moncayo et al, Derecho Internacional Público 35–39 (1990).

DOI: 10.4324/9781003170778-2

the partial rebuff of international law because it was hitherto contaminated with capitalist tendencies, so only the provisions that matched with socialist interests would be endorsed.[3]

In 1919, the victors of the First World War decided to set up the League of Nations, an international institution designed to prevent the recurrence of worldwide armed conflict. The reigning belief proclaimed that the human race would grow together into a single great community in which a system of international guarantees would prevent future wars and foster democracy and the self-determination rights[4] of small nations. It was an attempt to lay the foundations for an enduring peace by replacing old diplomacy and crafting new boundaries around the notion of power balance through a system of collective security in which all nations would be part. Nevertheless, sovereign equality was shared only between member states. Thus, the League of Nations was a universal organization built on a statutory foundation whose primary mission was to preserve peace and security, as well as promote international cooperation. In parallel, there were the Permanent Court of International Justice (PCIJ), created in 1921, and arbitral tribunals.

As such, the League of Nations did not prosper. There were a lot of differences between member states, a lack of cooperation and institutional deficiencies, while Britain and France used it as a political instrument. Even in the period between the First and the Second World War, states gradually endeavored to retrieve their traditional unfettered right to use military force in international relations. The League of Nations, in this aspect, served to slow down the process and diminish the instances of armed conflict. However, the inefficiency of the League contributed to making international arbitration commonplace, which also served to prevent the eruption of new wars. But arbitration was inherently unable to restrain state power in politics. Besides these failures, some grounds were set in the international arena: the society of states gradually became more universal; the international legitimacy principle of self-determination was set in motion; and legal constraints have appeared to mold the state's freedom to engage in war, especially those based on humanitarian principles.[5]

This work departs from contemporary international law concepts since modernization theory, as once stated by Hans Joas, embeds the idea that modernity is peaceful,[6] while nevertheless not abandoning the Hobbesian view of a state that emerges from human evolution to consciously adopt the necessity of a higher power capable of defending society. In centralizing the power in the state's hands, individuals celebrate an agreement whereby they forfeit their anarchic liberty in order to prevent chaos. The state then arises as a leviathan, an opulent biblical monster that both commands its setting and protects its subjects.

3 Antonio Cassese, International Law 30–36 (2nd ed. 2005).
4 Hans Joas, War and Modernity 72–73 (2003).
5 David Armstrong et al, International Law and International Relations 58–59 (2007).
6 Hans Joas, War and Modernity 45 (2003)

Notwithstanding, John Locke has mitigated this state-centric vision as he considers that man's original freedom is not forfeited and, in this regard, serves as a limitation of state power, although sovereignty remains the absolute and undeniable state power. Nevertheless, the sole existence of a prominent figure such as the leviathan, whose subjects collectively submit to its will, allows positively unrestrained competition in economic markets or the political arena, which highlights individuality during the pursuit of personal goals, and makes possible a system centred on individual interests.[7] Also, cooperation to avoid war is easier among democracies, as it is easier if states are subject to some degree of international authority.

However, modern international law has gradually moved away from a state sovereignty-centred outlook in order to strengthen transnational forces. So, the legal international *system* or *order* has been enriched with normative elements that emphasize international social interaction, wherein a plurality of relatively independent bodies share political, economic and cultural bonds. In their mutual interactions, these bodies ought to comply with norms that are deemed to be binding on the basis of legal consciousness rooted in religious, cultural and other common shared values. International law has therefore become an elastic term set in a cosmopolitan formulation of international society that aggregates individuals and non-state groups as well as sovereign states.[8] The basis of the emerging new international law has abandoned the absolute independence of states to enforce the idea of an international community that manages multiple international subjects for the purpose of maintaining interests and common rights with and before states, forming an organic whole.[9] An international order that is to have any authority other than pure self-interest is also going to need moral resources.

War provides a lesson with great meaning for the collective. War works as a teacher because it tears collective ideas away from the feelings in which they lie and then breaks down barriers to the learning process.[10] Last century was marked by two world wars that deeply shaped the new features of modern international law. After the horrors of war, the international community came to an inexorable conclusion: international law, the international community itself and especially the law needed to change. The existing tension between the opposite poles of law and force became evident. Although we still have those scholars who advocate for the realistic need of a leviathan to regulate international relations and bring peace to an international community,[11] there is a growing movement of idealists who convey that international norms and rules must fulfill the righteous criteria of justice, which has cardinal roots in natural law.[12]

7 Hans Joas, The Creativity of Action 09–10 (2005)
8 David Armstrong et al, International Law and International Relations 36–53 (2007).
9 Stephen C. Neff, Justice Among nations: a history of international law 309 (2014).
10 Hans Joas, War and Modernity 182 (2003)
11 Michael Walzer, Just and Unjust Wars 112 (4th ed. 2006).
12 Demérito Magnoli, O Mundo Contemporâneo: relações internacionais 1945–2000 27 (1997).

In this regard the foundation of the international legal system has shifted its core from a state-centric to an individual-centric model, mostly in regard to human rights. International law has been so dramatically enhanced that new rules and principles have been stated and acted upon; a new international framework has been established with a view to place an ever-increasing number of legal restraints on state sovereignty. Peace has again become the major objective of the world community at large. In an unstable and insecure world, *humanity's law* has been constituted by the normative combination of the law of war, international human rights and international criminal justice, which has reset the paradigm of international relationships.[13] In this vein, the International Court of Justice's ruling in the case of *Nicaragua v. United States of America* asserted that the human effort to promote peace is the very cornerstone of the international community, which is so eager for peace and progress that its "non-observance could lead to disastrous consequences causing untold misery to humanity".[14]

The paradigm shift of international law and the international community

Before the Second World War the demands of individuals that were not recognized as international subjects were initially separated in two ways: in relation to policies banning the institution of slavery, or by groups of individuals whose complaints about religious, ethnic and linguistic issues were lodged with international bodies. These normative innovations were indicative of the new tendency to pay greater heed to the interests of human beings who, until then, had had no say whatsoever in the international community.[15] The establishment of mutually beneficial relations between states has become a primary goal in the new conception of international law. After all, it is within the establishment of a legal relationship between states that the preconditions required to enable every human being to live in accordance with the imperatives of reason and peace, even domestically, are created.[16]

However, new standards and human values were required following the end of the Second World War. The belief that governments themselves were not capable of safeguarding human rights was unshakable, and from that day forward people demanded international guarantees.[17] Consequently, some states lost their prerogative of self-interpretation of international law, which was collectively reconfigured to encourage only cooperative measures. Therefore, the makeup of the international community changed radically. The paradigm shift from classic to contemporary international law – designed to prevent future generations from experiencing the horrors of wars and establishing new directives to reach a

13 Ruti G. Teitel, Humanity's Law 04 (2011).

14 Case Concerning Military and Paramilitary Activities In and Against Nicaragua (Nicaragua v. United States of America), 1986 I.C.J. §§143–146 (June 27).

15 Antonio Cassese, International Law 38–39 (2nd ed. 2005).

16 Hans Joas, War and Modernity 35 (2003).

17 Luis María Desimoni, Los Derechos Humanos y La Guerra contra el Terror 35 (2009).

common good between nations and peoples – is generally divided into five waves.[18]

First came a fierce codification process of international legal order and the appearance of new institutions, regional systematization and organization of multiple branches of international law (Law of the Sea, Law of International Organizations, International Humanitarian Law, International Human Rights Law and so on and so forth). With this, there has been a continued expansion and development of areas that were formerly not subject to international scrutiny, such as transit, outer space, civil aviation, intellectual property, the Antarctic and terrorism. Alongside this expansion of the content of international law, a far deeper process of world political legislation has also taken place.[19]

Second, the legal order received a genuinely universal institutional form. The liberal-democratic theory was increasing in strength and gradually granting legal entitlements to individuals in the international arena through the human rights doctrine. Individuals have been enabled to call states to account before international bodies whenever they feel their rights are being disregarded or overlooked. It has not only resulted in the drafting of several protective international treaties (in particular the Universal Declaration of Human Rights of 1948, the European Convention for the Protection of Human Rights and Fundamental Freedoms of 1950, the American Convention on Human Rights of 1969 and the African Charter on Human and Peoples' Rights of 1981) but also created regional courts of human rights (besides the International Court of Justice, there is also the European Court of Human Rights in Strasbourg/France, the American Court of Human Rights in San Jose/Costa Rica, and the African Court on Human and Peoples' Rights in Arusha/Tanzania).[20]

A third wave can then be identified, offering international law a great deal of legal content and jurisdictional solutions for settling international disputes. As envisioned by Article 95 of United Nations Charter, there has been the gradual creation of judicial bodies with international jurisdictions to resolve controversies between parties and to directly safeguard human rights for all citizens of the world.[21] When the Permanent Court of International Justice Statute was elaborated in 1920, the dimension of international law was notably inter-state based, which led the judicial functionalism of that period to focus only on disputes between states, an option that no longer stands now that an individual person is entitled to the capacity to act (*legitimation ad causam*) and to stand (*locus standi*

18 António Augusto Cançado Trindade, Direito das Organizações Internacionais 527–528 (5th ed. 2012).

19 David Armstrong et al, International Law and International Relations 61–62 (2007).

20 Valério de Oliveira Mazzuoli, Curso de Direito Internacional Público 880–938 (5th ed. 2011).

21 Rodolfo E. Piza Escalante, *El Valor Del Derecho y La Jurisprudencia Internacionales de Derechos Humanos en el Derecho y la Justicia Internos: El Ejemplo de Costa Rica*, in 1 Liber Amicorum, Héctor Fix-Zamundio 169, 175 (Corte Interamericana de Derechos Humanos, 1998).

in judicio) before international courts.[22] Hence, international courts have acquired great importance in conciliating international conflict through their jurisprudence and have earned a major role in international law dynamics, as we shall see later.

Fourth, a communitarian law arose from the openness and universality of the international arena, henceforth making its subjects decentralized and horizontal. The openness grants the appearance of new international actors, which differ from international subjects in that the former, albeit playing a significant role in the international arena, do not have full agency in the life of international law, as do the latter, such as transnational corporations, for example. All international subjects are international actors, but not all international actors are international subjects. Decentralization grants a unique system of operability in international law, but without the monopoly of a central power. Based on self-tutelage it also consolidates juridical equality among its members, as previewed in articles 1 and 2 of United Nations Charter, and the international community enshrines the principle of non-discrimination and reciprocity among all subjects.[23]

Therefore states remain the primary actor in international law, although new players come into action bearing the same stature of states in international dialogue. New countries have been recognized following the erosion of traditional colonial empires; there was the acceptance of new subjects like international organizations, private and public, national liberation movements and individuals *per se* or in groups, transforming international society into a universal and open community. In 1945 the United Nations promptly accepted 51 new states parties,[24] as the selection criteria for international law subjects as civilized nations had to be remade. These actual subjects actively participate in foreign relations while also demonstrating the new decentralized nature of international law. This decentralization leads to a horizontal equality among its subjects, without overlap, compelling the states to support a policy of non-discrimination and reciprocity.[25]

Communitarian traits also promote a higher sense of shared values among community members. Values based on collective survival and prosperity are promoted just as much as individual values. Therefore, the formation of an international community with common shared values gives international law a great example of its moral infrastructure, even if we conceive of international society as a community of communities. In such case, the moral commitments of the community members are extended more to encompassing social or general values and entities rather than their own communities. This wider need for internalized shared values by the international community is called *embodiment*, which often proceeds collectively. Embodied common values shared among international

22 The Right to Information on Consular Assistance in the Framework of the Guarantees of the due Process of Law, Advisory Opinion OC-16/99, Inter-Am. Ct. H.R. (ser. A) No. 16, Concurring Opinion of Judge A.A. Cançado Trindade, §30 (October 1, 1999).

23 Sidney Guerra, Curso de Direito Internacional Público 48–49 (7th ed. 2013).

24 Malcolm N. Shaw, International Law 45 (6th ed. 2008).

25 A. W. Brian Simpson, Human Rights and the End of Empire: Britain and the Genesis of the European Convention 157 (2004).

society's members ought to be integrated into societal formation and help to shape behaviour. Without such embodiment, values might have reduced effects on society and a high tendency to fade.[26]

Finally, the growing significance of a global civil society, legalization and interventionism bring cosmopolitan principles into the international scenario, whose origins are found in the ideas of a great community of mankind and natural law. Cosmopolitanism enjoins moral obligations and rights as possessed equally by all individuals regardless of their bond – or no bond at all – to any specific political community. There are cosmopolitan signs spread in international treaties and customary rules of international law, especially those relating to human rights and the environment, which have coined valuable expressions like "equal and unalienable rights" and "common heritage of mankind".[27] It is now acknowledged that humans inherit inviolable rights protected by international law, which both complicates and improves the relationship among cultures in a universal community.[28] Thus, cosmopolitanism doctrines have stressed the importance of the community as defined by common history, tradition and culture, planting the seeds for the people's right of self-determination. Under the influence of collectivist doctrines, individual rights came to be viewed in terms of a community, and essentially belonging to its members.[29]

After two world wars, cosmopolitan law becomes the great hope for international community. It offers legitimate governance worldwide and is based on an "ethical-and-human-rights-law discourse" built on Kant's morality groundwork. This new discourse creates opposition to the traditional state-centric interests. International law turns into the appropriate channel to achieve peace, international security and the promotion of democracy and human rights all over the planet. The cosmopolitan landscape effectively captures the spirit that animates the proliferation of law to make it a timeless moral truth in the pursuit of justice.[30] Simultaneously, the self-interest governance and social tribalism, which gained strength in Nazi policies through social Darwinist ideas supported philosophically by Nietzsche, are overcome. Compassion is no longer a weakness, but moral solidarity; human moral dignity is no longer loathsome, but rather the new core of international law and community. Respect and sympathy become the heart of our system.[31]

Because of international legislation and the appearance of the Vienna Convention in 1969, international law codification henceforth follows general rules.

26 Amitai Etzioni, The New Golden Rule: community and morality in a democratic society 176–179 (1997).

27 David Armstrong et al, International Law and International Relations 64–65 (2007).

28 Vicente Ráo, O Direito e a Vida dos Direitos 56–57 (5th ed. 1999).

29 Maya Hertig Randall, *The History of International Human Rights Law*, in Research Handbook on Human Rights and Humanitarian Law 03, 10 (2013).

30 Ruti G. Teitel, Humanity's Law 167 (2011).

31 Jonathan Glover, Humanity: a moral history of the 20th century 327–337 (2nd ed. 2012).

Sources of law have been divided into primary and secondary, with treaties, international customs and general principles of law representing primary sources, and jurisprudence and doctrine serving as secondary sources. In addition, it has been settled that instruments stemming from neither treaties nor customs might become imperative when bearing human value, such as *jus cogens* (which is appreciated by some as the formal acceptance of natural law precepts in the international arena), since it marks the groundwork for the community as it occupies a higher level in international juridical logic and objective framework.[32] The concept of imperative norms extracted from *jus cogens* requires straightforward formulation and is not immune to the idea of limitation since it is axial to the law's understanding that everything that is legally enforced is, at same time, susceptible to certain limits. However, *jus cogens* is currently considered to be statutory law in the combined application of articles 53 and 64 of Vienna Convention, where it has received the recognition in international law as either a treaty or a custom.[33]

From this moment on, international law establishes fundamental principles regarding moral and political agendas, both of which mitigate state sovereignty. While sovereignty remains a core principle of international law, it now faces limitations set by a consensus of the international community; these are: prohibition of aggression and unilateral use of force, self-determination of peoples, and the full respect of human rights.[34] Thus, the state that overlooks the value of humanity commits grave and systematic violations of human rights and is accountable before the international community. No sovereignty permits such violations toward humanity, not even against one sole individual.[35] Hence, it seems evident today that the essential point in international law is the full protection of human rights.[36]

The major problem of our era is not finding reasonable arguments to sustain human rights, but knowing how to effectively endorse and protect them. As portrayed by David Rieff, by the beginning of the twenty-first century we had come to accept the new conventional wisdom that there are no humanitarian solutions to humanitarian problems.[37] With that being said, our problem is not of a philosophical nature, but rather juridical and political. Behind the smokescreen of human rights, international law has grappled with the safest way to ensure human rights in the face of continuous violations, independent of their nature or foundation. Besides, the Universal Declaration of Human Rights of 1948 has already

32 Hildebrando Accioly et al, Manual Direito Internacional Público 137–138 (20th ed. 2012).

33 Rodolfo E. Piza Escalante, *El Valor Del Derecho y La Jurisprudencia Internacionales de Derechos Humanos en el Derecho y la Justicia Internos: El Ejemplo de Costa Rica*, in 1 Liber Amicorum, Héctor Fix-Zamundio 169, 177–179 (Corte Interamericana de Derechos Humanos, 1998).

34 Hildebrando Accioly et al, Manual Direito Internacional Público 953–954 (20th ed. 2012).

35 Juridical Conditions and Rights of Undocumented Migrants, Advisory Opinion OC-18/03, Inter-Am. Ct. H. R. (ser. A) No. 18, §100 (September 17, 2003).

36 Samuel Moyn, The Last Utopia: human rights in history 176 (2010).

37 David Rieff, *Humanitarianism in Crisis*, Foreign Affairs Magazine vol. 81 no. 6, 111 (2002).

established the cornerstone of human rights, the foundation of which has had irrefutable value and been reached by international consensus – *consensus omnium gentium* or *humani generis.*[38]

Rules in international law

The international law codification process suggests/empowers the predominance of statutory law in international society. Thus, two major kinds of law are produced: those related to organizations and addressed to international organs within their proceedings; and those related to social behavior and values, where we have a fact and its hypothetically foreseen consequence all mingled by law to achieve the aim of promoting justice. International norms are characterized therefore by an enunciative propositional structure of certain organizations or conducts that ought to be followed objectively and mandatorily since they are formally and materially accepted by the international community's members (*praeceptum juris*), thus reinforcing the international legal system or order.[39]

The sources of law can be either formal or material. The former constitutes positive norms built up by society through a formal law-making process, while the latter reflects the phenomenic events of the world as studied by philosophy, sociology and many other fields of social knowledge. In the positive legal system, just as in the contemporary international legal order, the primary sources of law are statutes, customs and general principles of law (Article 38 of International Court of Justice Statute). There are, however, some scholars that heavily criticize positive international legal order for being contradictory since it does not have an international legislative branch, international courts with mandatory jurisdiction and sanctions centrally organized, a fact that provokes a lot of disbelief among law practitioners. From this perspective, international rules are only social structures made by primary obligations that cannot justify being called law.[40]

Notwithstanding, we acknowledge international law as a valid general branch of law. Although possessing a diminutive juridical structure, the positive norms of international law do not lack effectiveness and coercibility, which is enough to be considered law. The domestic structure of law and how it is conceived does not erode the validity of a different framework in the international arena for not reproducing it *ipsis litteris.* International law is defined by a complex system of juridical norms, built by consensus or custom, and principles that set rights and duties in international society for all its actors and then coordinates coherent, international relationships among them. As the International Military Tribunal at Nuremberg put it, "individuals have international duties which transcend the national obligations of obedience imposed by the individual State".[41] Because of

38 Norberto Bobbio, A Era dos Direitos 25–27 (2004).

39 Sidney Guerra, Curso de Direito Internacional Público 63–64 (7th ed. 2013).

40 Hebert L. A. Hart, O Conceito de Direito 230 (5th ed. 2007).

41 Cited as [I.M.T., 1 (1946), p. 223] by Joanisval Brito Gonçalves, Tribunal de Nuremberg 1945–1946 27 (2nd ed. 2004).

this there is a web of justice that affords security and effectiveness with certainty to all activities from all international figures, based on cooperation and fulfilment of multiple collective and individual interests.[42]

On this new horizon of international law, the active agency and dynamism of international organizations have done a great deal to reshape the international legal order and give it multilateral progress, regional integration and international cooperation. There have been a lot of contributions to regulating new areas of human activity and the institutional setup of a gradual valorization on international statutory law regarding concerns for humanity, issues that states were never primarily interested in regulating satisfactorily. Furthermore, this role of international organizations has enriched the process of contemporary international law universalization.[43]

By this token, the international legal system, as conceived in Article 38 of International Court of Justice Statute, is programmed into a vertical body of law, and recognizes a hierarchy among legal sources within the entire system. Thus, *jus cogens* norms are recognized as "hierarchically higher than any other rule of international law, be it general or particular, customary or conventional, with the exception, of course, of other jus cogens norms". So, it can be said that *jus cogens,* as a source of international law within a vertical legal system, basically overrides any other rule which does not have the same status. Consequently, in the "event of a conflict between a jus cogens rule and any other rule of international law, the former prevails".[44]

In accordance with articles 53 and 64 of Vienna Convention of 1969, *jus cogens* are peremptory norms set at the highest position of our vertical international legal system. In this regard, human rights law is just as appreciated as *jus cogens* norms. The International Court of Justice has held that self-determination right,[45] war crimes and crimes against humanity[46] are *jus cogens;* just as the European Court did about freedoms, life and human integrity rights[47] and as the Inter-American Court[48] and

42 Hildebrando Accioly et al, Manual Direito Internacional Público 950–951 (20th ed. 2012).

43 Antônio Augusto Cançado Trindade, Direito das Organizações Internacionais 534–537 (5th ed. 2012).

44 *Al-Adsani v. United Kingdom [GC]*, no. 35763/97 Eur. Ct. H.R., joint dissenting opinion filed by Mr Rozakis and Mr Caflisch joined by Mr Wildhaber, Mr Costa, Mr Cabral Barreto and Mrs Vajić (2001).

45 Legal Consequences of the Construction of a Wall in the Occupied Palestinian Territory, Advisory Opinion, 2004 I.C.J. §136 (July 9).

46 Case Concerning the Arrest Warrant of 11 April 2000 (Democratic Republic of Congo v. Belgium), 2002 I.C.J. §56 (February 14).

47 *Demir and Baykara v. Turkey [GC]*, No. 34503/97 Eur. Ct. H.R., §73 (2008); and *Al-Adsani v. United Kingdom [GC]*, no. 35763/97 Eur. Ct. H.R. (2001).

48 *Case of the Members of the Village of Chichupac and neighboring communities of the Municipality of Rabinal v. Guatemala*, Preliminary Objections, Merits, Reparations and Costs, Inter-Am. Ct. H. R. (ser. C) No. 328, §124 (November 30, 2016); *Caso Velásquez Paiz y Otros v. Guatemala*, Excepciones Preliminares, Fondo, Reparaciones y Costas, Inter-Am. Ct. H.R. (ser. C) No. 307, §173 (Noviembre 15, 2015); *Expelled Dominicans and Haitians v. Dominican Republic*, Preliminary Objections, Merits,

Commission[49] did about all human rights. Hence, it is widely accepted that human rights protection is a general principle of law categorized as *jus cogens* covering all international and domestic legal jurisdictions, while taking the first position in the hierarchy of international norms.[50]

In this hierarchy, decisions of international courts fill a lower position at the bottom of the verticality since they are considered an auxiliary source of law. Nevertheless, through techniques of interpretation and application of the law, we can say that international jurisprudence is endowed with plenitude and full operability as legal source, which has brought Article 38 a lot of criticism and challenges. The international community thereof interprets and applies Article 38 in broader terms. Despite this, as an auxiliary source, court decisions cannot be based only on previous courts' decisions, but rather the rationale ought to embed treaties, customs and/or general principles of law.[51] Far from being treated as an auxiliary source of international law, the decisions and opinions of international courts are treated as authoritative pronouncements upon the current state of international law. Even advisory opinions have a role of great importance.[52]

For instance, if the ICJ makes a judicial statement about some concrete case and turns it into international custom, this judicial opinion becomes binding in term of elevating that decision to a primary source of law instead of auxiliary. Therefore, in theory this decision is not mandatory to the parties involved, according to Article 59 of the ICJS, while in practice it becomes primary law,

Reparations and Costs, Inter-Am. Ct. H.R. (ser. C) No. 282, §264 (August 28, 2014); *Case of Espinoza Gonzáles v. Peru*, Preliminary objections, merits, reparations and costs, Inter-Am. Ct. H.R. (ser. C) No. 289, §141 (November 20, 2014); *Case of Norín Catrimán et al. (Leaders, Members and Activists of the Mapuche Indigenous People) v. Chile*, Merits, Reparations and Costs, Inter-Am. Ct. H.R. (ser. C) No. 279, §197 (May 29, 2014); Juridical Condition and Rights of the Undocumented Migrants, Advisory Opinion OC-18/03, Inter-Am. Ct. H. R. (ser. A) No. 18, §101 (September 17, 2003); *Case of the Ituango Massacres v. Colombia*, Preliminary Objections, Merits, Reparations and Costs, Inter-Am. Ct. H.R. (ser. C) No. 148, §47 (July 1, 2006); *Case of Caesar v. Trinidad and Tobago*, Merits, Reparations and Costs, Inter-Am. Ct. H.R. (ser. C) No. 123, §100 (March 11, 2005); *Case of Barrios Altos v. Peru*, Merits, Inter-Am. Ct. H.R. (ser. C) No. 83, §10 (March 14, 2001); and *Case of the "Mapiripán Massacre" v. Colombia*, Merits, Reparations and Costs, Inter-Am. Ct. H.R. (ser. C) No. 22, §178 (September 15, 2005) among many others.

49 *Coard et al v. United States*, Case 10.951, Inter-Am. Comm'n H.R., Report No. 109/99, OEA/Ser.L/V/II.106, Doc. 6 rev, §39 (1999); and *Jose Isabel Salas Galindo and Others v. United States*, Case 10.573, Inter-Am. Comm'n H.R., Report No. 121/18, OEA/Ser.L/V/II.169, doc. 138, §331 (2018) among others

50 German J. Bidart Campos, *Jerarquía y Prelación de Normas em un Sistema Internacional de Derechos Humanos*, in 1 Liber Amicorum, Héctor Fix-Zamundio 447, 449–451 (Corte Interamericana de Derechos Humanos, 1998).

51 Manuel Becerra Ramírez, *Las Decisiones Judiciales como Fuente del Derecho Internacional de Los Derechos Humanos*, in 1 Liber Amicorum, Héctor Fix-Zamundio 431, 432–433 (Corte Interamericana de Derechos Humanos, 1998).

52 Rosalyn Higgins, Problems and Process: International Law and How We Use It 203 (2004).

binding and *erga omnes*.[53] This can be seen in the *Mamatkulov and Askarov v. Turkey* case, where measures set by the European Court became binding through the interpretation process under Article 31 of the Vienna Convention, which points to a human rights system of protection in compliance with the principle of effectiveness.[54] Therefore, international jurisprudences are more than merely a secondary provenance for international law. The ICJ has also stressed that judicial decisions are not incapable of influencing the law-making process, and that it is not improper to function under this threshold since it gives law provisions their accurate content. The Court "states the existing law and does not legislate. This is so even if, in stating and applying the law, the Court necessarily has to specify its scope and sometimes note its general trend".[55]

The generalization of values in international law

Universalist values are produced by wars. However, they do not owe their triumph to military force and victories, but to the fact that they are capable of generalization. Although paradoxical, war succumbs to universalist values while it also curbs values and stimulates their impetus to flourish. Therefore, a generalization of values must embrace everyone, never legitimizing their use in some instances and disavowing in others, since hypocrisy is not the road to moral education.[56] History proclaims that during the universalization process of human rights, which shall be grasped in more details in the next chapter, new values were injected into international political system.[57] These common values are definitive elements of international law, and interpretations of treaties performed by states, international courts and competent organs shall constitute a relevant consideration in the resolution of cases or definition of any terms or notions.[58]

Modern humanistic values can be traced back to the visionaries of the Enlightenment who sought a more just relationship between the state and its citizens. After the American Bill of Rights and independence process and the French Revolution, human rights language was, while in its beginnings, a municipal matter, or an internal affair between the government and its citizens. International regulation regarding human values through international codification on human rights would have been perceived as interference in the domains of the state. It remained, with the exception of minority protection following the First World War, a subject of national law until after the Second World War. With the

53 Thomas Buergenthal, Manual de Derecho Internacional Público 33 (1994).

54 *Mamatkulov and Askarov v. Turkey [GC]*, nos. 46827/99 and 46951/99 Eur. Ct. H. R., §§122–123 (2005).

55 Legality of the Threat or Use of Nuclear Weapons, Advisory Opinion, 1996 I.C.J. §18 (July 8).

56 Hans Joas, War and Modernity 185 (2003).

57 Manuel Becerra Ramírez, *Las Decisiones Judiciales como Fuente del Derecho Internacional de Los Derechos Humanos*, in 1 Liber Amicorum, Héctor Fix-Zamundio 431, 434 (Corte Interamericana de Derechos Humanos, 1998).

58 *Demir and Baykara v. Turkey [GC]*, no. 34503/97 Eur. Ct. H.R., §85 (2008).

conclusion of the Second World War human rights became part of international law, starting with the adoption of the Universal Declaration of Human Rights in 1948.[59]

After the end of twentieth century, history has pointed us towards an investigation into the conditions of peace with a sober analysis of specifically modern tendencies to war. For that, there is a need to justify the normative premises underlying the modern theory and its regenerative effect of violence. Thereafter, we have clearly sensed that democracy is the yardstick of social progress – although the twenty-first century has shown an astonishing recession within democratic regimes[60] – and the social and legal reinforcement of crucial values and their foundation and development through the process of civilization.[61] It is the research on the role of war in social changes that promotes impacts and configurations in international law that allow for processes of modernization, while the jurisprudence of international courts pragmatically sets the genesis of values and the tension between them and existing institutions.[62]

Likewise, the international community has set its foundation in both individual and social values. As *homo duplex*, each individual who has gained the status of international subject acknowledges their existence at two levels: individual and as part of the larger society. This second kind of value is twofold. First, it develops social sentiments like honour, respect and fellowship. Second, it nourishes intersocial bonds, which link every single individual to the social entity as a whole. Both strands are interwoven, and they go back and forth all the time during our lives. The intersocial bond plays its role when individuals are considered as part of a whole whose actions and influences happen accordingly. On such occasions, phenomenon that shut down the self and activate the notion of collectivity are called the "*hive switch*", which follows the generalization of set values. Thus, individuals and generations are bound together by a moral law with common traditions and a mission to build a higher life founded on collective duties detached of self-interests.[63]

These intersocial bonds are basically created by sharing core human values and making a social commitment to them. Therefore, shared values rest on international bodies of law that are upheld by all international actors, mainly courts. Without necessarily embracing moral relativism, generalized shared values overlap with concepts of good by legitimating pluralism. Communitarianism, in this regard, maintains that the concept of shared values is pivotal for social thinking

59 Cordula Droege, *The Interplay between International Humanitarian Law and International Human Rights Law in Situations of Armed Conflict*, Israeli Law Review vol. 40, no. 2, 310, 313 (2007).

60 Francis Fukuyama, As Origens da ordem política: dos tempos pré-humanos até a Revolução Francesa 19 (2013).

61 Ana Paula de Barcellos, A Eficácia Jurídica dos Princípios Constitucionais: o princípio da dignidade da pessoa humana 236 (2002).

62 Hans Joas, The Sacredness of the Person: a new genealogy of human rights 86 (2013).

63 Jonathan Haidt, The Righteous Mind: why good people are divided by politics and religion 223–241 (2012).

and morality, which consequently champions the concept of a common good that eschews relying only on the good as individually formulated.[64]

The Nuremberg trials set in motion an important wave that has guided the subsequent judgments in every international court and promoted a big wave of generalization values. Basic premises were established, and a new order and human values arose. The interpretation and application of human rights therefore became the main task of the international courts and these issues were no longer centralized in States' hands. Moreover, every new subject of international law gained the faculty to participate and debate about these rights. These conditions emerged from the new framework of the world community, now universal and open to everyone. All these confluent events hugely contributed to the improvement of international law, which each day becomes an instrument to change realities. Henceforth every international actor has inherited the duty to promote legal progress while criticizing the rules and meditating on their guidelines for gradual reconfiguration through the appointment of proper and opportune reforms.[65] That is, the path towards legal stability is dynamic without being frenetic. That is the reason why Norberto Bobbio calls the twentieth century the Age of Rights. In this century, particularly, an entire new structure of law was erected and, as he has predicted, the improvement of laws has led us to experience a great challenge in the following century when the functionality of that new structure has been and will continue to be tested.[66]

Despite the revolutionary development of human rights in the United Nations era, no attempts have been made to bring to justice such gross perpetrators of crimes against humanity or genocide as Pol Pot, Idi Amin or Saddam Hussein, perhaps because the atrocities in Cambodia, Uganda and Iraq (against the Kurds) did not occur in the context of international wars. Internal strife and even civil wars are still largely outside the parameters of war crimes despite being grave breaches of provisions in the Geneva conventions.[67] As asserted by Johnathan Glover, the number of people murdered by Stalin's tyranny far surpasses those killed in the Nazi camps. The numbers of Mao's victims are yet greater. Pol Pot killed a far higher proportion of the population than Hitler did and yet, even after thinking about Stalin, Mao and Pol Pot, looking at Hitler still seems like staring into the deepest darkness of all.[68]

As such, it is post-Holocaust that a collective process enacts a community declaration drafted by a diverse group of authors and successful case of "value generalization", containing plural moral elements of individual and social nature. The world was unaware of the full extent of the Holocaust during the war, but

64 Amitai Etzioni, The New Golden Rule: community and morality in a democratic society 85–91 (1997).
65 Malcolm N. Shaw, International Law 129–130 (6th ed. 2008).
66 Norberto Bobbio, A Era dos Direitos 45–81 (2004).
67 Theodore Meron, *The Case for War Crimes Trials in Yugoslavia*, Foreign Affairs Magazine, Summer 1993, www.foreignaffairs.com/articles/yugoslavia/1993-06-01/case-war-crimes-trials-yugoslavia.
68 Jonathan Glover, Humanity: a moral history of the 20th century 317 (2nd ed. 2012).

efforts toward a human rights declaration were made before the war was over. Again, the Universal Declaration of Human Rights is a composite synthesis, the result of a dynamic process in which many minds, interests, backgrounds, legal systems and ideological persuasions played their respective determining role – the result of a successful and authentic process of value generalization. What was initially agreed on was a declaration that was entirely (or largely) nonbinding within legal contexts. Later on it became binding by successive treaties, such as the two Covenants of 1966, and regarded customary law as binding as well.[69] All human rights law frameworks, therefore, respected the cultural specificities between Western and Eastern cultures and civilizations, taking note of both differences of origins and values. Hence, the international community constructs its terms thinking of universally shared cultural assumptions and a universal validity based on generalization of values.[70]

After horrors and unnecessary suffering provoked by men and overlooked by law and nations, a generalization of values becomes necessary for dislodging human cruelty and promoting peace for humanity. As such, testimony like Fergal Keane's becomes obsolete:

> It is this immensity of evil that prompts me to speak of the 'soul of man' … . I felt there was enough decency and love around to nourish the gift of hope. There will be many who say that I was foolish, naïve to ever have had such faith in man. Maybe they are right. In any event after Rwanda I lost that optimism.[71]

The objective has not been accomplished yet, but at least we have a plurality of international actors and a legal system that can afford some good fighting. Respect for human dignity is one of the great barriers against atrocity and cruelty, which requires social cooperation and impulses.

Notwithstanding, our capacity for communicative action allows us to purport moral dialogues and communications about values. Mostly in the decision-making process of international courts, moral dialogues often appeal to an overarching value shared by the various parties involved. The idea of generalization and the definition of a common ground on moral dialogues made by courts is very important to my conclusion, since the greater good for the greatest number shall occupy a relevant role in solving some moral issues of interpreting and applying international law. After all, it is the courts' decision-making that defines when overarching values conveyed as common currency should be rejected or embraced.

Under these auspices, international courts have the mission to distinguish between descriptive definitions of morality and normative definitions. The latter

69 Hans Joas, The Sacredness of the Person: a new genealogy of human rights 182–188 (2013).
70 Xiaorong Li, *"Asian Values" and the Universality of Human Rights*, in The Philosophy of Human Rights 397, 407 (2001).
71 Fergal Keane, Season of Blood: a Rwandan Journey 185 (1996).

grasps the intent behind of the vast international bodies of law, namely those concerned to human rights. Beyond the reach of "justice, rights and welfare", decision-making process specify what legal content counts as moral and what is better suited to safeguard human dignity on international legal realm, figuring out which actions are truly right or wrong.

The communicative action on moral dialogues embedded in the decision-making process, then, shall follow Etzioni's four basic rules on values talk. First, who claims the right to dissent should assume the responsibility to debate. Second, who claims the right to criticize should assume the responsibility to comprehend. Third, who claims the right to influence should accept the responsibility not to inflame. Finally, who claims the right to participate should accept the responsibility to persuade. These rules are very important for fostering generalization of values in pluralistic communities such as international society and its designed framework. The more heterogenous a society, the greater the challenge of keeping people's autonomy bounded within an overarching society, as one community.[72]

Cooperation is the reason why we still exist and, at same time, one of our greatest challenges in building an international community based on universal and generalized values. Like all animals we have individualistic impulses, but what makes us excel in the animal kingdom is our ability to compose strong social impulses. Therefore, the survival and advancement of the international community relies greatly on our social values, while simultaneously not disregarding individuals.[73] The common use of individual and social values varies from case to case, and relies on our capability to set the overarching value through moral dialogues on communicative actions.

Complex international legal system

The contemporary international law framework is complex because it possesses a plurality of legal sources set in a vertical hierarchy. With such kinds of legal system, it is normal that some legal provisions will appear to collide with others, to be legal contradictions. For this reason, a complex legal system must include a method that manages these apparent collisions, otherwise it would not be a system, but legal disarray.

No serious system tolerates incompatible norms, which is the reason why a mechanism to eliminate incompatibility must be established. First and foremost, we need to understand that a vertical hierarchy system is endowed with three cooperating characteristics: (i) unity, meaning that all norms, from the highest part of the system to the bottom and everywhere in between, shall be connected and aligned, like an imaginary umbilical cord; (ii) coherence, meaning that all these

72 Amitai Etzioni, The New Golden Rule: community and morality in a democratic society 105–106, 193 (1997).

73 Joshua Greene, Moral Tribes: emotion, reason, and the gap between us and them 102 (2013).

norms from top to bottom must be harmonious in their purpose to guide action in a uniform way, so that from a multiplicity of norms we shall see orderly coexistence within the whole body of law just as much as between each other, working reciprocally without collision, molding a systematic and consistent bloc of law; and (iii) wholeness, meaning that the combined norms should cover all areas of human agency and interests in such a way as to leave no gap.[74]

To be clearer, the enemy of unity would be the lack of hierarchy, with a horizontal system of norms where each norm trumps another, creating legal confusion; this would be a contradiction, technically called an antinomy, or a norm prohibiting something that another allows and vice versa; and there would be legal gaps –situations for which law does not provide an answer and effectively ignores. Despite the importance of endorsing unity and coherence in a legal framework, we still lack a perfect deductive system. An interesting fact about the international legal system is that we have valid norms that are formal and written and others that are customary and mostly unwritten. This is interesting because it requires us to grapple in a certain sense with the "spirit of the system", which leads to dynamic mechanisms of interpretations and employing teleology to reach the *ratio essendi* ("raison d'être") of the law.[75]

Therefore, in the application of international law, the rational interpretation and application is imminent and essential. This is the only path to full comprehension of a complex legal system, especially when we need to extract from it the inner morality and rationality, which goes beyond literality. It is this global vision that allows us to link the past, present and future in law, guiding the interpretation and application of law as a system, not as isolated bodies of law. The legal system must convey a sense of entirety, with order created out of unity, coherence and "wholeness".[76]

Furthermore, the framework of international law is a complex one because it is made of multiple positivist and customary sources. Among primary and secondary sources of law we get international decisions that are considered a secondary source of law, as inserted in article 38 of the ICJ Statute. They are an auxiliary means of international rule in the law-making process. For that reason, article 59 makes it crystal clear that international court decisions apply only to the parties involved – that is, that precedents shall not create legal rules.

However, as Guillermo Moncayo and Thomas Buergenthal point out, international court decisions are a direct consequence of international law applicability, which means that it is court decisions that give international law its content and reach. Therefore, international court decisions should not be deemed an alien source of law irrespective of treaties. Rather, law interpretation becomes applicable to our day-to-day cases and their inner vicissitudes. This is the key to allowing the progressive development of international law.[77]

74 Norberto Bobbio, Teoria do Ordenamento Jurídico 71–80 (10th ed. 1999).
75 Norberto Bobbio, Teoria do Ordenamento Jurídico 76 (10th ed. 1999).
76 1 Hans-Georg Gadamer, Verdade e Método 444–487 (1997).
77 Guillermo R. Moncayo et al, Derecho Internacional Público 153–154 (1990); and Thomas Buergenthal, Manual de Derecho Internacional Público 33 (1994).

After all, the constructivism of moral judgments entailed by Rawls' theory of justice is constructed, not discovered, departing from an intellectual device adopted to confront practical, not theoretical, problems. Likewise, Nils Melzer considers case law and doctrine as tools to permit treaties, customs and general principles of law to be applied in practice. Treaties, which are of a statutory nature, contain indeterminacy in their expressions and concepts that need interpretation, which falls primarily to international courts and tribunals.[78]

As stated by Article 38 of the ICJ Statute, the decision-making process by international human rights courts is crucial for determining the rule of law applicable to everyday cases, although working as a subsidiary means. Despite not creating law *per se*, international decision-making on human rights law favors above all the creation, over time, of new law in the international arena, which also includes the creation of international customary rules.[79]

Therefore, three features have been relevant to the harmonization and expansion of the international legal system and its idea of *rule of law*: the prominence of general principles of law, the modern unity of law seeking justice, and international jurisdiction as a means to fulfil and pursue justice alongside domestic jurisdiction.[80] In essence, the primacy of justice becomes a foundational priority, one that bears a great deal of moral sense and outweighs political interests. Justice becomes not one value among others, but the highest of all social virtues, and the one that must be met through the interpretation and application of law on individual rights.[81]

Articles 31 to 33 of the Vienna Convention guide the rules of interpretation when it comes to determining the meaning of the terms and phrases used in the human rights bodies of law. Therefore, international courts are required to ascertain the "ordinary meaning to be given to the words in their context and in the light of the object and purpose of the provision from which they are drawn", while taking into consideration significant "supplementary means of interpretation, either to confirm a meaning determined in accordance with the above steps, or to establish the meaning where it would otherwise be ambiguous, obscure, or manifestly absurd or unreasonable". Since human rights law is first and foremost a

> system for the protection of human rights, the Court must interpret and apply it in a manner which renders its rights practical and effective, not theoretical and illusory. The Convention must also be read as a whole and interpreted in such a way as to promote internal consistency and harmony between its various provisions.[82]

78 Nils Melzer, International Humanitarian Law: a comprehensive introduction 25 (2016).

79 Valério de Oliveira Mazzuoli, Curso de Direito Internacional Público 40 (2011).

80 Antônio Augusto Cançado Trindade, *A Contribuição dos Tribunais Internacionais à Evolução do Direito Internacional Contemporâneo*, in O Direito Internacional e o Primado da Justiça 03, 12–14 (2014).

81 Michael Sandel, Liberalism and the Limits of Justice 02 (2nd ed. 1998).

82 *Demir and Baykara v. Turkey [GC]*, no. 34503/97 Eur. Ct. H.R., §§65–66 (2008); *Saadi v. the United Kingdom [GC]*, no. 13229/03 Eur. Ct. H.R., § 62 (2008); and

This advanced legislative technique reproduced in the Vienna Convention for interpreting and applying international statutes (treaties), as well as the legal, formal and written primary and most notable source of international law, gives life to their words. The principle of unity says that the law is not isolated from any of its elements, but combined with them, and, to attain the raison d'être, we need to take into consideration fact, rule and value so that each one correlates to the others in a dialectic manner. As once said by a German international law professor, Josef Kunz, "the law is a normative integration of facts in accordance with values".[83] International law is no longer conceived as a fact floating in abstraction, lost in space and time, but rather as something steeped in humanity, communicating with its agglutination of feelings and hopes. It is part of an existential process involving both individual and community. To this end, individualism gives place to social and humanistic concepts of law and, as a result of this valuative ethic, the provisions of statutes, even without textual modifications, automatically come to mean something different in accordance with the paramount principles of justice and humanity.[84]

Therefore, the provisions of law intentionally encapsulate general concepts that need interpretation at every step of human evolution and advancement of civilization. These general concepts are represented in multisemantic words called "general clauses", the vagueness of which permits the interconnection of other fields of human knowledge, like sociology, economy, religion, politics, etc., allowing them to function as true elements of connection in the legal system through judicial interpretation and application of the law. Inevitably, all kinds of concept and axiological vector from these fields come to account for the solution of social and personal issues principally related to human dignity.

Suddenly, human dignity is everywhere in law and philosophy. Almost all primary sources of international law connected to human rights movements bear some emphasis on dignity, which has become a crucial watchword. It has gone global, appearing in a number of constitutions and international treaties that wish to offer judicial guidance for the protection of basic values. It is also true that interest in dignity is everywhere in legal cases and philosophical discussions, and the current dispute among judges and commentators about how to interpret human dignity provisions is at least interesting. History matters, and it nurtures the current enthusiasm for human dignity, especially because all political and legal concepts are semantically wide open for interpretation according to the quandary presented. No other human rights concept has ever proved as malleable as human dignity.[85]

Stec and Others v. The United Kingdom, nos. 65731/01 and 65900/01 Eur. Ct. H. R., §§47–48 (2006).

83 Josef Laurenz Kunz, La Filosofía del Derecho Latinoamericana em el Siglo XX 30 (1951).

84 Miguel Reale, Teoria Tridimensional do Direito 124–126 (5th ed. 1994).

85 Samuel Moyn, Christian Human Rights 26–28 (2015).

Thus, legal provisions gain mobility through moral variables and then become an elastic tool to enact international justice and affirm community values.[86] This methodology allows for the entry of values to equip the legal system with ductile rules that can provide openness while avoiding the tension between rigid normative precepts and evolving values. Every regulatory rule becomes a vivid rule while connecting facts, norms and values of the whole legal system, which gives life and meaning to legal provisions while filling legal gaps. Both ways we satisfactorily fulfil the entirety of legal order.[87]

The International Court of Justice also incorporated a statement that diminishes gaps in the international legal system through interpretation and application of international law for the sake of unity, coherence and wholeness: "whether customary or conventional, [it] does not operate in a vacuum; it operates in relation to facts and in the context of a wider framework of legal rules of which it forms only a part".[88] Therefore, these general law clauses make for effectiveness and allow the judgment of social values directly associated with treaties, putting aside gaps and antinomies, and establishing first-level doctrines and judicial decisions.[89] Additionally, the European Court of Human Rights complements such interpretation of the wide framework of international law, which must be interpreted in the light of the rules set out in the Vienna Convention while taking into account the special nature of the Convention on Human Rights as an instrument of human rights protection. Such interpretation must be as consistent as possible with the other principles of international law of which it forms a part.[90]

Thus, in order to comply with the Vienna Convention's provisions on interpretation and application of international law, international courts must interpret in "good-faith in accordance with the ordinary meaning to be given to its terms in their context and in the light of the treaty's object and purpose",[91] and "in accordance with the principle of effectiveness" that endorses a system for the protection of human rights.[92] Yet, to maintain coherence in eventual conflicts between provisions, the principle of *lex specialis* is an accepted principle of interpretation in international law. It stems from a Roman principle of interpretation, according to which in situations especially regulated by a rule, this rule would displace the more general rule (*lex specialis derogat leges generalis*).[93]

86 Alberto Gosson Jorge Junior, Cláusulas Gerais no Novo Código Civil 10–22 (2004).
87 Norberto Bobbio, Da Estrutura à Função: Novos Estudos de Teoria do Direito 102–128 (2007).
88 Interpretation of the Agreement of 25 March 1951 Between The WHO and Egypt, Advisory Opinion, 1980 I.C.J. §10 (December 20).
89 Norberto Bobbio, Teoria do Ordenamento Jurídico 115–160 (10th ed. 1999).
90 *Mamatkulov and Askarov v. Turkey [GC]*, nos. 46827/99 and 46951/99 Eur. Ct. H. R., §111 (2005); and *Al-Adsani v. the United Kingdom [GC]*, no. 35763/97 Eur. Ct. H.R., §60 (2001).
91 LaGrand Case (Germany v. United States of America), 2001 I.C.J. §99 (June 27).
92 *Mamatkulov and Askarov v. Turkey [GC]*, nos. 46827/99 and 46951/99 Eur. Ct. H. R., §§122–125 (2005).
93 Cordula Droege, *The Interplay between International Humanitarian Law and International Human Rights Law in Situations of Armed Conflict*, Israeli Law Review vol. 40, no. 2, 310, 338 (2007).

There is an inseparability of international legal instruments and international adjudication by the courts. International jurisprudence promotes and defines the rationale and essence of international law in order to develop its terms. Judicial decisions are inherent and crucial to the workflow of the international legal system. It is a widely accepted truth that international law cannot be isolated from cases since it is fostered on a case-by-case basis. Formally, international judicial decisions are regarded as a subsidiary means for interpreting international law – and international courts and organs frequently resort to previous judicial decision and arbitral awards, which reveals the importance of jurisprudence for international law. Since international courts are responsible for settling disputes between international subjects and delivering advisory opinions to organs, they do not develop international law in the abstract as primary sources of international law (Article 38 of ICJS), while "the very determination of specific disputes, and the provision of specific advise, does develop international law". Judicial function is not simply the application of existing rules to facts, rather it is an elaboration of a norm saying that "the expansion upon uncertain materials, all contribute enormously to the development of international law".[94]

One important premise we can gather from contemporary international law is the prevalence of the rule of law to appease conflicts; to investigate relevant international facts (fact-finding proceedings); to form and strengthen judicial provisions; and to safeguard cultural plurality and diversity.[95] Modern international law, pushed by the appearance of a new human rights law regime, has been reshaped in terms of both quantity and quality, which turns the international legal system into an authentic, prolific and autonomous legal order with less sovereign state power concentration and more diluted participation of different international actors, emphasizing the sense of community.[96] In this vein, all regional human rights courts (European, Inter-American and African) have been developing a vast jurisprudence – mostly in the sphere of substantive rights – regarding the protection of human rights, which has brought about a "humanization process of international law".[97]

Alongside the positive norms of the international legal order, an international morality has arisen. A construction of international law without morality is no longer conceivable. It is fully understood nowadays that the enhancement of international law is only possible if we transcend the positivism and depart from

94 ROSALYN HIGGINS, PROBLEMS AND PROCESS: INTERNATIONAL LAW AND HOW WE USE IT 202 (2004).

95 ANTÔNIO AUGUSTO CANÇADO TRINDADE, DIREITO DAS ORGANIZAÇÕES INTERNACIONAIS 654 (5th ed. 2012).

96 Rodolfo E. Piza Escalante, *El Valor Del Derecho y La Jurisprudencia Internacionales de Derechos Humanos en el Derecho y la Justicia Internos: El Ejemplo de Costa Rica*, in 1 LIBER AMICORUM, HÉCTOR FIX-ZAMUNDIO 169, 170–171 (Corte Interamericana de Derechos Humanos, 1998).

97 Antônio Augusto Cançado Trindade, *A Contribuição dos Tribunais Internacionais à Evolução do Direito Internacional Contemporâneo*, in O DIREITO INTERNACIONAL E O PRIMADO DA JUSTIÇA 03, 35–40 (2014).

core values of social justice and solidarity.[98] Its concreteness is taken daily from general principles of law or general clauses found in international provisions, mainly in law provisions for human rights. A lot of the groundwork behind contemporary international law comes from natural law, applied in combination with positive law, as once grasped by Grotius and Pufendorf. According to this reading, it is natural law's conception of justice that gives dynamics and ductility to international positive law.[99]

The strand of international positive norms understands that bodies of human rights law regulate and value actions upon persons, individually or collectively. Its objective is based on the idea of a common welfare for international society; this rational is the fruit of a process of plural dialogue built on practical consensual reason; and it is transcendent because its scope seeks to achieve the common good of the international community, which overrides any state position of self-interest.[100] Therefore, the interpretation of international courts might go well beyond what is generally envisaged and reach some creative conclusions through innovative decisions that reflect the evolving conditions of the international community, since the drafters of international law cannot ever foreknow all possible situations. Then it is also true that international courts have indeed shaped some rudimentary legal notions into more refined and precise definitions that give the legal order some maturity. This *opinio juris* process, along with international practices, plays a significant role in crafting and ensuring unity, coherence and wholeness to contemporary international law.[101]

98 Sidney Guerra, Curso de Direito Internacional Público 70 (7th ed. 2013).

99 Stephen C. Neff, Justice Among nations: a history of international law 61–66 (2014).

100 Celso Albuquerque de Mello, Curso de Direito Internacional Público 136 (15th ed. 2004).

101 Merve Ozkan Borsa, *The Contribution of International Court of Justice to the Development of International Humanitarian Rules and Principles*, Public and Private International Law Bulletin vol. 36 no. 2, 83, 95–97 (2016).

3 Human rights law

Historical considerations

When we talk about human rights, we are talking about current politics and ethics that speak to both the international community and the histories of states, socio-economic structures, legal systems, religions and cultures. Within its legal dimension, therefore, internal state law usually mingles with international law and inter-governmental bodies in order to transform internal and international order. This "human rights movement" grapples for universal validity throughout the body of law, which has both horizontal and vertical strands that are equally important to legal concepts and moral development. The horizontal strand involves the widening process of constitutionalism among states through comparative law, while the vertical refers to the binding effect of international treaties on human rights held by international institutions.[1]

In this sphere, however, we must draw a line in human history from the Second World War onwards, which reveals a change in approach. A bridge is usually built between the American and French revolutions in the eighteenth century and 1945. Despite several documents that are related to human rights historiography, we ought to focus our attention initially on the eighteenth century, when declarations of human rights were proclaimed in America and France, and then move forward.

Although it is common to find some declarations of rights within the English Declaration of Rights of 1689, most human rights advocates do not cling to this. This declaration might be deemed the first declaration of rights, but it nevertheless remains attached to the medieval tradition and lacks the core elements of the ones that follow. Although influenced by the rationalism of the revolution that prompted it, it is still related to Middle Age precepts and the English parliamentary monarchy.[2] This bill of rights, for instance, considers that royal dignity is only attainable for the nobility – which was later broadened to all humanity, as we shall see.

1 Henry J. Steiner et al, International Human Rights in Context 58–59 (3rd ed. 2007).

2 Ricardo D. Rabinovich-Berkman, Derechos Humanos: una introducción a su naturaleza y a su historia 150 (2007).

DOI: 10.4324/9781003170778-3

The same must be said about older instruments, such as the Magna Carta of 1215 (usually cited as one of the first human rights precedents), the Petition of Rights of 1628 (in which the English Parliament offers King Charles I the constitution of distinct rights) and the Habeas Corpus Act of 1679.[3] All of them represent an human rights historical commitment and each one carries meaningful content according to their epoch. Whilst being human rights ballasts, they have no use today but historical reminiscence. They lack the rationalism and pluralism ideals from Enlightenment. Even though they comprise human rights historic ballast, they do not fit the purpose of this work, which sees human rights as reflecting, in the first instance, the rationalism and pluralism of the Enlightenment epoch. Therefore, we begin the current approach from the eighteenth century's declaration onwards.

The American Declaration of Independence of 1776 and the French Revolution Declaration of the Rights of Man and Citizen of 1789 were the first documents to bear the idea of unalienable rights regarding life, liberty and happiness. Moreover, the French Declaration also brought the promise of universal human rights, as indicated by Article I: "men are born and remain free and equal in rights".[4] At that time, the terms were "rights of man" (in France) and "natural rights" (notably in the US); there was no reference to "human rights".[5] Both instruments laid out general principles of justice that were retrieved from ideas of natural law, such as the belief that law should be the same for everyone and nobody should have his liberty constrained arbitrarily.

However, the eighteenth-century breakthrough of universal rights encompassed political and social exclusion of women, children, slaves and religious minorities, among others. The connotation of "rights of men" – so-called self-evident – did not insist upon equality of rights, which also puts their naturalness in doubt. Therefore, the meanings of these emancipatory declarations were not full-fledged but rather restricted. Nonetheless, they inaugurated the first generation of rights, strengthening the notion of liberty and individual rights – which contains concepts of enlightened human autonomy and the human capacity to discern good from evil.[6]

Notwithstanding, recent historians have repeatedly noted that the human rights we have today do not resemble the rights of man or natural rights conceived of in the eighteenth century. Even the thinking of the abolitionist movement – which Jenny Martinez claimed was foundational to human rights[7] – has been challenged by the suggestion that abolitionists did not rely on a conviction of rights, but rather on ideas based on Christianity, humanitarianism or other ideologies. Rights were never a cornerstone of the sought-after freedoms.[8]

3 Carlos S. Fayt, Derechos Humanos y El Poder Mediático, Político y Económico: su mundialización en el siglo XXI 56–70 (2001).
4 Lynn Hunt, Inventing Human Rights 15–17 (2007).
5 Samuel Moyn, Human Rights and the Use of History 05–06 (2014).
6 Lynn Hunt, Inventing Human Rights 19–27 (2007).
7 Jenny S. Martinez, The Slave Trade and the Origins of International Human Rights Law 15, 134–135 and chapter 8 (2012).
8 Samuel Moyn, Human Rights and the Use of History 58–59 (2014).

The same is true of the second generation of rights that were constructed the following century, when political rights were not enough to embrace society's need to improve the welfare of its worse-off members. The socialism derived from the nineteenth century emphasized solidarity and the need for positive rights supported by state intervention in order to fight economic inequality and to protect certain members of society who were considered vulnerable, especially to cruel industrial labor exploitation. Nevertheless, the breakthrough of international human rights as we know them today occurred in the twentieth century, as a revival of natural law and a redesign of human rights as moral.[9]

Between the declarations of the eighteenth century and those of the mid-twentieth century, human rights remained a domestic concern. It was only after the Second World War that they became an international concern. New values and commitments seemed to appear quite suddenly before the international community's eyes, a shift regarded as one of the great transformations in this process of modernization.[10] The idea of universality came up again , but this time it was universal in the sense that any state of the world could join – a result of the open character of the new international society's framework. The human rights movement arose alongside the creation of the United Nations. It was not just a systematic ordering of fundamental postulates, ideologies and norms, it was also an organization of institutions – national and international, governmental and nongovernmental.[11]

Therefore, in 1947 the UN General Assembly gathered representatives of all states that were members in order to draft a universal declaration of human rights that would serve as moral exhortation to state politics, but not as a legally binding instrument. The promotion of human rights was the main motivation of the UN, which makes it clear in its Charter Preamble that human rights are linked with human dignity, and it is therefore self-evident that neither need either justification or guidance. Then, at the end of 1948, the UDHR was adopted as a "common standard of achievement of all peoples and all nations".[12]

Right after the Second World War, human rights were minimal, individual and fundamentally moral. So, in order to pass in the UNGA, the Declaration of 1948 had to be essentially non-binding, and was approved by 48 states voting in favor and eight abstaining.[13] The truth is that states were not prepared "to derogate from the established character of the international system by establishing law and legal obligation that would penetrate Statehood in the radical way".[14]

Although deemed a mere moral instrument, the UDHR emerged, linking itself to the Enlightenment and the French Declaration of 1789. Using the same

9 Maya Hertig Randall, *The History of International Human Rights Law*, in RESEARCH HANDBOOK ON HUMAN RIGHTS AND HUMANITARIAN LAW 03, 09–10 (2013).

10 HANS JOAS, WAR AND MODERNITY 78 (2003).

11 HENRY J. STEINER ET AL, INTERNATIONAL HUMAN RIGHTS IN CONTEXT 133–134 (3rd ed. 2007).

12 Maya Hertig Randall, *The History of International Human Rights Law*, in RESEARCH HANDBOOK ON HUMAN RIGHTS AND HUMANITARIAN LAW 03, 16 (2013).

13 SAMUEL MOYN, HUMAN RIGHTS AND THE USE OF HISTORY 82 (2014).

14 HENRY J. STEINER ET AL, INTERNATIONAL HUMAN RIGHTS IN CONTEXT 139 (3rd ed. 2007).

language, the UDHR made references to "inherent dignity", "equal and unalienable rights", freedom and reason. However, there was no mention of natural law or any other philosophy, which has kept the moral foundation of human rights undetermined. Nevertheless, the cultural influence of philosophies that shaped the American and French revolutions remains undeniable, chiefly with regard to democracy and the rights of men. Philosophically, several concepts have shaped the features of the modern age and our thinking on human rights, but their mainstay is still the idea of reason achieved in the Enlightenment era.[15]

Moreover, as argued by Samuel Moyn, the idea of human dignity as part of human rights became current mostly after 1945. The previous declarations of rights of man did not take into account dignity in order to establish their standards. The notion of human dignity was only conceived of and encoded in the United Nations Charter, the Universal Declaration of Human Rights of 1948 and the German Grundgesetz – the constitutional Basic Law of 1949. Until that time, dignity was not a key element of human rights, or inviolable. It was during the middle of the last century that human dignity and democracy were translated into human rights. In that period, the notions of human dignity and its non-negotiable character emerged largely from Catholic doctrine. Despite the Catholic origin of human dignity framed in international human rights bodies, the expression has acquired new interpretations over time as secular policies have advanced in Western cultures, making human dignity inviolable and a vivid standard for guiding further human rights disputes and conflicts.[16]

In spite of the non-binding character of UDHR, nowadays we have a tenacious blend of international bodies that make human rights enforceable as hard law – even though many people considered the declaration enforceable from day one as part of customary international law. Straight after the adoption of UDHR in 1948, UNGA decided to split its provisions between two core treaties, one on civil and political rights and the other on economic, social and cultural rights. Despite being conceived of in 1952, the project was only approved in 1966 with the creation of the two major covenants on human rights: the International Covenant on Civil and Political Rights (ICCPR) and the International Covenant on Economic, Social and Cultural Rights (ICESCR). Only ten years later, in 1976, the number of ratifications was met and both instruments of positive law entered into force, shifting the soft law structure of human rights to a hard law imposition.[17]

The division of UDHR into two covenants was for both ideological and legal reasons, although they have an equal structure and both refer to the inherent dignity of the person as a foundation of the proclaimed rights. The ideologies underlying both covenants reflected the division between East and West in the Cold War. Their legal significance came through the codification of Article 2 of the UDHR they represented, which made the dispositions legally binding. Besides, the covenants hold to the universality and equality of their provision, now

15 Patrick Hayden, The Philosophy of Human Rights 03 (2001).
16 Samuel Moyn, Human Rights and the Use of History 20–33 (2014).
17 Henry J. Steiner et al, International Human Rights in Context 136 (3rd ed. 2007).

added to by the so-called third generation of rights – a person's right to self-determination. Together they form the International Bill of Rights, which has been enlarged by other human rights instruments that represent a treaty-based enforcement mechanism of the contemporary international human rights regime.[18]

Therefore, to enforce Article 103 of the UN Charter, international jurisprudence puts states' commitment to human rights before any conflicting national obligation or any other international agreement. Human rights have become the ultimate promise that trumps any other obligation, no matter what. As upheld by the Inter-American Court of Human Rights, in *Sawhoyamaxa Indigenous Community v. Paraguay*, human rights are currently peremptory norms of international law and cannot be circumvented by any state, not even by a parallel treaty.[19]

Summing up, the law of human rights is deeply rooted in moral philosophy. Even after the Second World War, modern international law of human rights has been indissolubly linked with moral concerns.[20] All conflicts addressed by human rights are also moral conflicts, and through the development of the modern international community, which accounts for plural subjects and sources of law dynamism, human dignity has served as a guide for human rights conflict resolutions appeasement. Both old and new human rights frameworks have had the same overall aim to construct a world that is more peaceful and humane, which would lead to the vanishing of war and all forms of human cruelty and barbarism.[21]

The rise of human rights morality

As stated in Article 1 of UDHR, "all human beings are born free and equal in dignity and rights". Since the birth of human rights in the American Declaration of Independence in 1776 and the French Declaration of the Rights of Man and Citizen of 1789 (where the correlated statement was "men are born and remain free and equal in rights"), the words *equality in dignity and rights* have been added. This subtle change encompasses a substantial reform of what we conceive as human rights and, most of all, who we perceive as human beings.

A context of value is merged with human rights comprehension – considered human values acquired through the history of mankind – to comprise the *juridical inventory of humanity.* [22] Although the process of modernization might seem to

18 Fernando R. Tesón, *International Human Rights and Cultural Relativism*, in THE PHILOSOPHY OF HUMAN RIGHTS 379, 382–383 (2001).

19 Case of the *Sawhoyamaxa Indigenous Community v. Paraguay*, Merits, Reparations and Costs, Inter-Am. Ct. H.R. (ser. C) No. 146, §§137–140 (March 29, 2006).

20 Maya Hertig Randall, *The History of International Human Rights Law*, in RESEARCH HANDBOOK on HUMAN RIGHTS AND HUMANITARIAN LAW 03, 09–10 (2013).

21 JONATHAN GLOVER, HUMANITY: A MORAL HISTORY OF THE 20TH CENTURY 06–07 (2nd ed. 2012)

22 FLÁVIA PIOVESAN, DIREITOS HUMANOS E O DIREITO CONSTITUCIONAL INTERNACIONAL 28–30 (2007).

bring a decline or erosion of values, in fact it has proven the opposite. Too many atrocities and cruelty were perpetrated during the building process of human rights. In general, human rights transgressions are diminishing, while ***human dignity*** is being emphatically advocated, which might be due to several reasons.[23] However, one of the most important is that the notion of human dignity embraced by human rights encompasses human values related to religious and cultural traditions. These values are associated with a general duty to help people who are suffering, independent of who or where they are. Thinking around human dignity therefore emphasizes (i) the sacredness of human life, (ii) an ethos of love and (iii) universal respect.[24]

The sacredness of human life

Georg Jellinek was the first to conceive the idea that human rights in the French Revolution were not developed solely during the Enlightenment. The concept of natural law could never have led to the codification of human rights by itself. There was another, equivalent, force, which had Christian roots. Human rights – or the "rights of man" and "natural rights", as they were called initially – as binding metanorms turned into positive law could never stem from a philosophy based only on reason, not even natural law or Kant's theory, for instance. The *dignity* of all human beings also had deep roots in the Christian tradition.[25]

According to this view, the idea of legally establishing unalienable, inherent and sacred rights of men has not a political but a religious foundation. For Jellinek, this is the source of all other rights of individuals within and against the state. The rise of abolitionism, while the fight against the slave trade continued, for example, was built upon the laws of God and the rights of men, which details that every human being is entitled to the fruits of his own labor and also his liberty.[26] Although it was not the only source for the abolitionist movement (as slave owners also based their ownership rights of humans on God's law), Christianity undeniably contributed to the argument.[27]

Therefore, the core liberty rights of the first dimension of human rights actually have Christian roots, just like the American (and later the French) declaration. What was needed was a cognitively secular language that was understandable on all sides, wherein the promise of a wide allegiance could be fulfilled, since the

23 For instance, the international proliferation of NGOs and their recognition as international subjects; the establishment of international courts on human rights; the enactment of new international treaties among international cooperation of states; the replication of human rights on domestic level, in national constitutions, and so forth.

24 Hans Joas, The Sacredness of the Person: a new genealogy of human rights 09 (Alex Skinner trans., 2013).

25 Georg Jellinek, The Declaration of the rights of the man and citizens 53–55 (2018).

26 Jenny S. Martinez, The Slave Trade and the Origins of International Human Rights Law 17–20 (2012).

27 Joshua Greene, Moral Tribes: emotion, reason, and the gap between us and them 156 (2013).

"rights of man" were vigorously declared as self-evident. Although there has been a lack of self-evident truths, this does not mean a loss of a common vocabulary that we may use to attain a consensus on values.[28]

Considering this, analyzing the background of human rights might give us the confidence to state that such rights have features of both Enlightenment rationalism and Christian canons. These two components are effectively in balance in the understanding of human rights, and this duality contributes to a process that has been called *the sacralization of reason*.[29] The rationalism of the Enlightenment conveys the autonomy and the cultivation of reason that grants human beings the cardinal instrument of independence, in which Kant's theory plays a major role – since Kantianism has been regarded as the most compelling theory on human rights and the modern philosophy of justice that is part of it.[30]

The eighteenth-century philosophy of human rights reflected a restrained notion of human dignity, since its political and social applicability ignored women, children, slaves and religious minorities. However, it existed under a self-evident moral power that initiated welcome social changes. The UN Charter, the Universal Declaration of Human Rights of 1948 and the German Grundgesetz revisited the notion of human dignity ("inherent dignity" that leads to "equal and unalienable rights"), but in quite a different way. Human dignity now involves respect for other people as a form of recognition of their moral standing, and this duty of respect, so broadly upheld nowadays, is what Kantian ethics and moral rights are based on – the inobservance of which entails a denial of humanity itself.[31]

Accordingly, both rationalism and religious tradition encompass the sacralization of reason, which delivers a significant cultural twist to the process by which a human person becomes a sacred object. Human rights and universal human dignity become the "religion of humanity".[32] The sacredness of the person exceeded the limits of religion to find itself at the center of human reason during the Enlightenment period, mostly through Kant's theory that detaches our likeness to God from the notion of dignity and replaces it with an individual's moral autonomy.[33] This means that the holiness of the person, which is grasped by most (if not all) religions in the world, descends to human beings as *dignity*, bound to us all due to the humanity we share. As rational beings, only our humanity can carry moral law, which gives us autonomy and dignity.[34] Thus, the notion of dignity that comes from our humanness and reason merges with the inalienability of inner human value prevailing in the precepts of any religion.

28 Hans Joas, The Genesis of Values 09 (Gregory Moore trans., 2000).
29 Hans Joas, The Sacredness of the Person: a new genealogy of human rights 27–32 (Alex Skinner trans., 2013).
30 Michael Sandel, Justiça: o que é fazer a coisa certa 135 (2012).
31 Jonathan Glover, Humanity: a moral history of the 20th century 28–49 (2nd ed. 2012).
32 Émile Durkheim, *Individualism and the Intellectuals*, in Durkheim on Religion 59, 64 (1994).
33 Bernardo Gonçalves Fernandes, Curso de Direito Constitucional 216 (3rd ed. 2011).
34 Michael Rosen, Dignity: its history and meaning 22–26 (2012).

Human rights and human dignity therefore arise as an expression and part of the process of the sacralization of the person, which constitutes, as Durkheim has stated, the religion of humanity where "man is at the same time both believer and God".[35] The godliness and inward faith of the individual are now set up to be fundamental to the social cohesion of modern society. But this endless process of sacralization of the person, despite having Christian roots, also means overlapping old tradition in the sense that it has to continue to be as broad and pluralistic as possible in order to transcend Christianity, which is merely acknowledged as having paved the way to this new stage.[36]

From Christianity we borrowed the idea that we are made in the image of God or are the children of God. The former gives us a divine essence, the soul, while the latter carries the idea that our life (with its soul) is a gift that demands a measure of restraint. The former also encompasses the metaphysical sacred core of every human being, while the latter involves a sense of the indispensability of our lives. The sacralization of the person embedded in human rights and dignity has become a challenge for religions (in general) as it represents secular value that is interpreted over and over during the process. The articulation of this process presents the values in a language that is accessible to believers and nonbelievers alike. The concept of the soul is translated into that of the "self", endowed with reason; and the gift of life turns into a rational argumentation where we are not a fact of mere existence, but a non-random offering that, for reasons of gratitude and logic, we cannot dispose of as we might desire.[37]

Therefore, through the novel process of sacralization of the person we understand the concepts of inalienability, inviolability and indispensability of rights and human dignity without embracing any religious dogma regarding the sanctity of human life. Likewise, we comprehend the notion of life as a gift and the moral weight it contains, whether or not we credit God as the source.[38] The rational recognition of our finitude turns out to be the precondition for the genesis of human life; the self's awareness of its own finitude becomes the main point validating the giftedness of life.[39] Hence these ideals constitute the formation of human rights and dignity throughout time and the history of mankind.

Ethos of love

The notion of love has always been the central canon of Christianity. The concept of *goodness* descends from divine love. All rational human principles, rules and notions of justice came afterwards. Love is anchored in the heart of social behavior

35 Anthony Giddens, Durkheim on Politics and the State 81 (1986).
36 Émile Durkheim, *Individualism and the Intellectuals*, in Durkheim on Religion 59, 68 (1994).
37 Hans Joas, The Sacredness of the Person: a new genealogy of human rights 143–162 (Alex Skinner trans., 2013).
38 Michael Sandel, The Case Against Perfection: ethics in the age of genetic engineering 95 (2007).
39 Hans Joas, The Genesis of Values 80 (Gregory Moore trans., 2000).

that guides human agency and sets its values. Nevertheless, both religion and emotion have been present in the process of constructing the morality of law, namely the morality of human rights law. The moral code contained in all religions has joined with human empathy throughout the history of values, which framed and keeps framing the understanding of human rights and dignity.[40]

Historians trace the uprising of emotions in the mid-eighteenth century back to novels (mainly Samuel Richardson's and Jean-Jacques Rousseau's) and new notions of bodily integrity. Therefore, the comprehension of "bodily integrity" and "empathetic selfhood" served as principle elements in the history of human rights and their development.[41] For example, Russeau's book *Julie ou La Nouvelle Héloïse* (1761) prompted a worldwide reaction against bodily punishment and marriage freedom, a reaction similar to the one provoked by Harriet Beecher Stowe's *Uncle Tom's Cabin* (1852) against the cruelty of slavery in the United States. All kinds of violence – such as torture, or cruelty directed at women, children, slaves and animals – gradually began to wane, particularly in Western societies. The rise of compassion for human suffering brought to light the need for a revolution in political rights.[42] The Law of the Seas, for instance, was a pioneer branch of international law in ruling against piracy, which had served as *hostis humani generis* in human rights history for so many years, and exemplified the will to deter crimes against humanity by subjecting perpetrators to punishment and vastly intensifying their pursuit.[43]

Likewise, a renewal of collective ideas, especially after a great social trauma such as war, can only be achieved when the theory of learning is anchored in emotions. The need to uproot collective ideas and replace them with new ones – also anchored in emotions – assists in a process of change that cannot be carried out simply through the non-violent coercion of superior arguments. Hence, war has an important teaching effect over those involved and allows the overcoming of barriers that might otherwise block the rise of collective ideas that have significant emotional associations.. Thus, a multiplicity of collective experiences in war is juxtaposed by the common existential experience of many individuals who share empathy on the basis of association and cohesiveness strengthened by the trauma of war.[44]

Empathy (which guides a rational process in which we put ourselves in another's place) has stimulated a sense of shared identity among people and served as a touchstone in the foundation of human rights. Lynn Hunt attributes the awakening of inward feelings to novels, which give rise to empathy and a sense of equality through emotional attachment to the narrative. Although empathy is not a new human feeling, it found a new way to express itself through fiction, which creates the "ideal presence" whereby the reader puts him/herself into the story as

40 Hans Joas, The Genesis of Values 26–47 (Gregory Moore trans., 2000).
41 Lynn Hunt, Inventing Human Rights 30 (2007).
42 Samuel Moyn, Human Rights and the Use of History 04–05 (2014).
43 Ekrem Korkut, Turkey and the International Law of the Sea 166–172 (2017).
44 Hans Joas, War and Modernity 182–184 (2003).

a subject of imaginative identification, with this trancelike state nurturing morality. People become more interested in performing "acts of generosity and benevolence" and at the same time find evil doings and immoral acts more reprehensible. These new experiences have shaped new social and political concepts.[45]

Thus, comprehension of human rights eclipses the traditional relationship between aggressor and victim – at domestic and international level – and puts humanity at the forefront of the relationship. Human rights violations concern all mankind. This notion of humanity has to do with "understanding and kindness towards other people".[46] Empathy and compassion have deep roots in Christianity and came out of a desire to rediscover human dignity. The Enlightenment blended feeling and reason in order to foster the value of humanity.[47]

In Christianity we have the interplay between the principles of love and justice. All in all, love works as a moral dimension that combines with reason to apply and organize the social milieu. As love empowers us to act morally, it also engenders endless reinterpretation of justice, since love and justice together pose a "relationship of indissoluble tension".[48] This duality is what we see as the morality of law; this duality governs the world, nature and mankind, science and consciousness, logic and moral, economy, politics and history; and it is the semantic of all human rights.[49]

The key, however, is the balance between the two elements. Emotions engaged in empathy and love cannot create moral judgments all by themselves, and neither can reason. Empathy and love would rule a system permitting impersonal validity criteria that lead to moral disagreements and manipulative social relations.[50] Reason in turn cannot sustain moral axioms based on self-evident truths because there is no such thing; no substantive moral conclusion is entirely capable of appeasing moral disagreement in the real world.[51] The idea that a genuine moral action, in order to be regarded as moral, can only be motivated by what is morally right no longer has standing in contemporary law philosophy.

Joas and Durkheim criticize Kant when he states that only duty based on reason constitutes a necessary factor in the definition of moral rules. According to Kant, rational duty cannot be compromised by inclinations, which means that goodwill and good deeds do not have moral value if inspired by emotions.[52] Actually, human agency is unable to perform solely from a sense of duty. We must also add common goodness – human will to perform good acts – and empathy, which are

45 Lynn Hunt, Inventing Human Rights 32–39, 56–65 (2007).

46 Jenny S. Martinez, The Slave Trade and the Origins of International Human Rights Law 135 (2012).

47 Samuel Moyn, Human Rights and the Use of History 05–09 (2014).

48 Hans Joas, The Sacredness of the Person: a new genealogy of human rights 169 (Alex Skinner trans., 2013).

49 Jonathan Glover, Humanity: a moral history of the 20th century 401–402 (2012).

50 Alasdair MacIntyre, After Virtue chapter 3 (3rd ed. 2007).

51 Joshua Greene, Moral Tribes: emotion, reason, and the gap between us and them 183–184 (2013).

52 Immanuel Kant, Fundamentação da Metafísica dos Costumes 23 (2006).

both just as much a part of morality. Goodwill and good deeds, in fact, possess as much moral value as *love*. Accordingly, there must be coexistence between rational duty and goodness, so that the two factors might interplay to establish human obligations.[53]

In this regard, Bernard Williams grasps that there is no need to deem an action or a perspective moral if only guided by reason. There is no exclusive relationship between morality and reason.[54] Behind the smokescreen of our moral duties, our emotional life gives us access to ideal values. As glimpsed by Joas, the feeling-state of pain unites all mankind, since we all share sensitivity to pain, not only physical but also psychological, often in the form of humiliation. The struggle for human protection and welfare is the common ground for shaping public life and the meaning of solidarity that we achieve through our shared empathy. This is actually the element that surfaces not from abstraction but from real life. In this regard, the prevention of cruelty is the essence of an ethos of love that exceeds the spell of imperative morality of duty and formalism to break through to a new non-formal conception of values based on a *phenomenology of value-experience*.[55]

Universal respect

The principles of justice and love form a complex interweaving formula of morality. Taking the Christian notion of love and the principle of reciprocity it implies, our life is a gift. This reciprocity encompasses the idea of life's inalienability, inviolability and indispensability, and a duty to respect it, even against our own will. Moreover, this central idea has become politically and morally shared among all peoples, independent of religious belief. It is now simply part of the human rights tradition. The notion of life as a gift has also reached the world of reason, as belief and reason are complementary.[56]

In fact, the value we have given to life since the Enlightenment era would never have endured if based solely upon human reason. The idea of life as mere existence and the randomness it suggests requires the support of belief in an immortal soul. That is why Lynn Hunt states that humans by themselves "cannot overcome their inner propensity to apathy or evil". The idea of life as a gift gives life its metaphysical *raison d'être*.[57] In this vein, the concept of life as a gift may arise from either religious or secular sources. According to Michael Sandel, holding a religious belief is unnecessary for revering the gift of life. Its inalienability and inviolability have a moral weight independent of any sense of religious sanctity.[58]

53 Hans Joas, The Genesis of Values 65–87 (Gregory Moore trans., 2000).
54 Bernard Williams, Moral: uma introdução à ética 107 (2005).
55 Hans Joas, The Genesis of Values 92–93, 158–159, 166 (Gregory Moore trans., 2000).
56 Hans Joas, The Sacredness of the Person: a new genealogy of human rights 168–170 (Alex Skinner trans., 2013).
57 Lynn Hunt, Inventing Human Rights 211 (2007).
58 Michael Sandel, The Case Against Perfection: ethics in the age of genetic engineering 92–95 (2007).

In secular terms, the giftedness of life sheds a light on human dignity, highlighting the inner value of each human being as acknowledged by our common reason. Therefore, the sacredness of modern human rights can be seen in societies that uphold the principles of unalienable rights and the dignity of the individual – not dignity as social status, as upheld by the Catholic Church and religious societies before the eighteenth century. Actually, human dignity comes from the democratization of high social status once reserved exclusively for the well-born. It entails a gradual levelling-up process whereby more and more people are treated as equal and deserving of social respect. Human rights hold that "everyone becomes a king where claims that basic human dignity is non-negotiable".[59] Thus, dignity turns out to be the mainstay of human rights morality. That said, the estimate of reciprocal human dignity that a rational being must make comes through the universal duty of *respect.*

During the Enlightenment, as the notion of dignity lost its link to religion and moved closer to reason, the connection between human autonomy and dignity was made for the first time in Kant's *Groundwork*. In essence, autonomy is the idea that the moral law that governs us all also gives us the agency to be an end in ourselves, since the moral law is self-given. Dignity in turn is our priceless inner value, incomparable in nature. As dignity is something we all possess due to our humanity, the moral law that drives us to autonomously treat each other as an end in its own right involves in equal measure the duties of respect and self-respect.[60]

Our rational capacity is what makes humans special. According to Kant, rationality dictates our autonomy, which in turn means we are endowed with the freedom to act according to the moral law we give ourselves. Contrariwise, heteronomy is the force that bends us before desires we have not chosen for ourselves. It is the autonomy, by this means, that gives human life its special dignity, which regards persons not just as a means, but also as an end in themselves. Thus, our rationality grants us the autonomy that makes us worthy of dignity and respect. It is the way we face human dignity that defines our current conception of universal human rights and our entitlement to respect, since we are all rational beings completely capable of thinking and acting autonomously and choosing freely.[61] Alongside acknowledging our own specialness, we need to recognize the same dignity in each and every individual. In this regard, Article 1 of the UDHR treats us all without discrimination, no matter how reasonably and sensitively we differ from each other. We are all endowed with reason and conscience and we should interact among ourselves in a spirit of brotherhood.[62]

Michael Rosen discusses respect as a new strand of dignity, distinguishing "respect-as-observance" from "respect-as-respectfulness". The former implies a duty to respect human dignity, albeit not necessarily justifying or matching it with

59 Samuel Moyn, Human Rights and the Use of History 19–20 (2014).
60 Immanuel Kant, Fundamentação da Metafísica dos Costumes 65 (2006).
61 Michael Sandel, Justiça: o que é fazer a coisa certa 136–139 (2012).
62 Erin Daly, Dignity Rights: courts, constitutions, and the worth of the human person 14 (2013).

genuine acts. That means that our respect comes from an automatic setting coming from social rules rather than judgement. In the latter the duty to respect others derives from the moral action of treating someone with dignity, which occurs irrespective of positive law commanding you to do so.[63] This version of respect touches the morality of aspiration asserted by Lon Fuller, for whom the morality of law comprised both morality of duty and morality of aspiration. While the first maintains respect via the minimum social duties required for a civilized society to function, the second goes beyond to reach the highest point of human moral behavior, which, regardless of mandatory minimum rules, responds with respect in the context of the humanity and equality we universally share.[64] This morality of aspiration is deeply linked to a communitarian mainframe found in contemporary international law. When promoting human values as the centerpiece of human rights law and international humanitarian law, the framework envisions that social conduct must be regulated by reliance on a moral inner voice in addition to the law.[65]

In Kantian terms, human rights are universal in the sense that we are free to act autonomously in accordance with a moral law that is self-given, from whence the duty to respect each other flows. In the case of acting heteronomously – that is, by inclination – the universality and equality of human dignity is overlooked and turned into an instrumental value. Utilitarianism in turn holds that all human beings are worthy of respect because in the long run this provides the greatest happiness to the greatest number. Even a modern kind of utilitarianism values human rights as a kind of calculation that portrays the maximization of utility (overall happiness) in society. Hence, respect for human dignity remains instrumental since it is not based on the respect of human life, but on the ultimate goal of making things better for the greatest number of people.[66]

Nevertheless, as asserted above, the duty to respect another's dignity must merge with inclinations without compromising the meaning of human rights law. Goodwill and doing good have moral value even when inspired purely by emotion. It does not matter whether acts are motivated by inclination or by duty (although Kantian theory acknowledges only those acts performed by duty). Motive and consequence of human agency are both equally important in human rights morality.[67] Moreover, not all actions and practices based on self-interest are immoral because they are founded on egoism.

For example, someone who gives money to charity in order to enhance his/her social reputation is moved by ego – and considers the beneficiaries a means to an end; however, people taking advantage of the donation are truly better off for it. Although the beneficiaries were not treated as an end but as a means, we can

63 Michael Rosen, Dignity: its history and meaning 57–58 (2012).
64 Lon Fuller, Morality of Law 04–06 (1969).
65 Amitai Etzioni, The New Golden Rule: community and morality in a democratic society 139 (1997).
66 Carlos S. Fayt, Derechos Humanos y El Poder Mediático, Político y Económico: su mundialización en el siglo XXI 109 (2001).
67 Michael Sandel, Justiça: o que é fazer a coisa certa 143–144 (2012).

clearly see that there is a difference between this donor and someone who chooses to spend the same amount of money on a jet ski for their own amusement and completely disregards those in need. According to Kant, both men are equally and morally wrong. Nevertheless, we do not all dispute that the action of the donor is far better than the *bon vivant*'s action – even though the donor did not have respect-as-respectfulness for those he was assisting, he complied with respect-as-observance in order to maximize the morality and benefit of human welfare. So, the donor is not entirely approved by morality, but he possesses something that is akin to the notion of morality.[68]

Hence, we cannot conclude that moral actions only come from moral reason. Neither can we conclude that moral actions solely arise from behaviors that have a moral aim or principles. To Kant, the person who behaves honestly for their own sake is morally reprehensible because this action is based on inclination, but this behavior has, indisputably, a moral aftermath. There are actions that, based on the outcome they intend to implement or modify, are morally relevant as an observance – not because of their motivation or individualistic outlook, but because of the benefit they provide to others.[69] Thus, the interplay between strict duty to respect and respect stemming from doing good represents exactly the interwoven relationship between respect-as-observance and respect-as-respectfulness – or, we should also say, the morality of duty and the morality of aspiration. Together they make the overall morality of human rights endorsable.

Fuller suggests there are some corners of morality that not even the law can reach. There is and always will be a gap between morality of duty and morality of aspirations, and all human agency inspired by aspiration – even based on goodwill and doing good – integrates the morality of law.[70] Therefore, there are some empirical elements around human rights that not even international law can reach, and this grey zone comes very clearly to the surface in wartime. As Michael Walzer once said, "war is hell". In a war, human cruelty usually arises as the facade of our civilization slowly gives way.[71]

Yet human agency sometimes reveals aspiration and respect-as-respectfulness even when law does not pursue it. For instance, in Robert Graves' memoir of his experience in the Second World War he describes watching a frontline post and seeing a German soldier some yards away from him taking a shower behind the German line. Graves had him on target but chose not to shoot, passing the rifle to his sergeant, who shot him. Both men were following the same law and knew that that death was lawful. The difference between them existed on another level, one that law does not reach. Graves said he refused to shoot because when that man was taking a shower, he did not see a soldier, but a simple man, like any one of us.[72] This is aspiration, respect-as-respectfulness, empathy, love and sacralization

68 Bernard Williams, Moral: uma introdução à ética 108–109 (2005).
69 Bernard Williams, Moral: uma introdução à ética 111–113 (2005).
70 Lon Fuller, Morality of Law chapter 1 (1969).
71 Michael Walzer, Just and Unjust War 142 (2006).
72 Robert Graves, Good-bye to All That 132 (2014).

of life, all combined together. This is what launched human rights in the first place, and the same elements remain precious nowadays. It is contained in the morality of law, whether it comes from inclinations or not – whether it encompasses utilitarian calculation or not.

This interplay between human rights, Kantian human dignity and utilitarian calculation will be further explored in the following chapters. However, it brings to light the necessity for human agency to comply with the moral philosophy of utilitarianism, which reveals to us its valuable contribution to disciplining human inclinations by framing acts as rationality through clearly defined interests. The duty to respect human dignity as an inviolable, unalienable and indispensable right is not absolute, which makes inclinations and utilitarian calculations equally relevant.[73]

Human dignity

When we talk about morality, we refer to what is valuable to us as social beings. As suggested by sociobiology, our common reason shapes societies as an aggregation of its collective approvals and disapprovals, and evolves in an expanding circle, which denotes our constant enhancement via good deeds and virtues.[74] Besides social evolutionism, we also commit to values that come from experience of violence and injustice (known as *trauma*) that has transformed our relationship with ourselves, the world, and our understanding of values. These experiences can be recollected from the historical process of constructing human rights, especially by the central role played by human dignity in the recent international human rights bodies and modern constitutions – for which it has served as an "epistemic foundation".[75]

Notwithstanding, the history of human rights has demanded three interlocking qualities. Human rights have to be natural (as an inheritance of human beings), equal to everyone and universal. As a moral urging to humanity, all people in the world must possess them equally while sharing the common status of human beings. However, the naturalness is more commonly shared than equality and universality, as rights of men vis-à-vis each other.[76] Since the Enlightenment, the equality and universality of human rights have been the unfinished elements of the equation. They have been easier to endorse than to enforce because there is a permanent tension between practices and values.

The very notion of dignity has significantly changed throughout human history. As an essential value for humanity, its conception has evolved and is still evolving, especially following the Universal Declaration of 1948 and the international framework it launched. Thus, the modern understanding of human dignity applies

73 Hans Joas, The Creativity of Action 23 (Jeremy Gaines and Paul Keast trans., 1996).

74 Peter Singer, The Expanding Circle 94 (2011).

75 Hans Joas, The Sacredness of the Person: a new genealogy of human rights 69–77 (Alex Skinner trans., 2013).

76 Lynn Hunt, Inventing Human Rights 20–21 (2007).

equally to all people, instead of just a few (replacing the notion of dignity in the English Bill of Rights of 1689 and approaching the naturalness, universalism and equality of the declarations of the eighteenth century). The starting point is the idea that everyone is "subjected to the same obligations and entitled to the same benefits under the law",[77] and its validity stems from international treaties and postwar constitutions, applied and enforced by both domestic and international courts.

Dignity can be regarded as a right or a value, or even both. The preamble of the UN Charter of 1945 establishes dignity as a value while reaffirming its "faith in fundamental rights, in the dignity and worth of the human person". As a value, it guides the interpretation and application of positive fundamental rights but does not constitute a right *per se*. Rather, it helps international courts set their jurisprudence based on interpretation of human dignity and embeds it into rights assured by human rights treaties. Additionally, the UDHR of 1948 offers the statement that "all human beings are born free and equal in dignity and rights", which sets a new moral paradigm requiring the equal and respectful treatment of all people simply by virtue of being human. At the back of these documents rests the hope that the acknowledgment of human dignity can bring abuse and cruelty to an end.

As observed by Erin Daly, the interpretation of human dignity comes with enormous cultural baggage all around the world and dignity does not transform into a right at first glance.[78] On the UDHR's behalf, the preambles of the International Covenant of Civil and Political Rights (ICCPR) and International Covenant of Economic, Social and Cultural Rights (ICESCR) recognize dignity as the inheritance of all humanity and assert the "equal and unalienable rights of all members of the human family as the foundation of freedom, justice and peace in the world, recognizing that these rights derive from the inherent dignity of the human person". From that moment on, dignity is not a mere value, but the centrepiece that roots all fundamental rights, the *cardinal value*.[79] This was exemplified at the Convention on the Elimination of All Forms of Discrimination against Women of 18 December 1979, when the preamble emphasized in particular that discrimination against women "violates the principles of equality of rights and respect for human dignity". It becomes a *supervalue* placed in between law and morality in such a way that the former can only be founded on the latter as a legitimate rationale.[80]

Due to its multiple irradiating effects, human dignity has been established by international courts – and some domestic courts – as the epicenter of all human rights, and it has also been interpreted and applied as literally not treating man as a

77 Erin Daly, Dignity Rights: courts, constitutions, and the worth of the human person 12 (2013).

78 Erin Daly, Dignity Rights: courts, constitutions, and the worth of the human person 15 (2013).

79 Ana Paula de Barcellos, A Eficácia Jurídica dos Princípios Constitucionais: o princípio da dignidade da pessoa humana chapter 1 (2002).

80 Bernardo Gonçalves Fernandes, Curso de Direito Constitucional 219 (3rd ed. 2011).

means but as an end in itself. As a cardinal value (or supervalue), it has been coined a tiebreaker in human rights conflict resolutions, like liberty versus life. Thus, human dignity has been held to be inviolable, inalienable and indispensable for ourselves and others.[81] Despite the intention of implementing UDHR essential human rights through the enforcement of human dignity, international bodies subsequent to UDHR have galvanized a "ubiquity of dignity in current legal discourse" that masks a "great deal of disagreement and sheer confusion"[82] – the moral quandaries.

To sustain human dignity, states and the international community have the power to enforce the duty to respect others and us. Following Article 1 of the UDHR, the Federal Republic of Germany reconstructed its constitutional framework according to the new international law standards, particularly those concerned with human rights. In 1949 Germany enacted its basic constitutional law, the Grundgesetz. More than any other country, Germany had a moral obligation to fulfill the human rights positivation process and affirm the sacrosanct nature of human dignity, as affirmed in Grundgesetz's first article:

> human dignity is inviolable. To respect it and protect it has been the duty of all state power. The German people therefore acknowledge inviolable and unalienable human rights as the basis of every community, of peace and of justice in the world.

In one way or another, since the UDHR all domestic constitutions have been redrafted in such a way that nowadays almost all national constitutions refer to human dignity – some as a value, some as a right, and some as both. The Grundgesetz turned out to be a pioneer, and German constitutional philosophy and theory have inspired and guided the constitutional law and jurisprudence of numerous civil law systems. As highlighted by Samuel Moyn, the UDHR and Grundgesetz put dignity into politics and turned it into a watchword in philosophy and political theory. Before that, he reminds us, dignity was not even considered an inviolable value.[83]

In this regard, many scholars grasp that both the UDHR and Grundgesetz have built the concept of dignity and modern international human rights largely on Immanuel Kant's theory[84] (although the drafting process gathered several moral philosophies from both the West and the East), especially his categorical imperative of humanity as an end, not a means – also called the formula of humanity – and the connection between the dignity and autonomy of human nature. There are several precedents from international human rights courts that mention this quite overtly.

81 Daniel Sarmento, Livres e iguais: estudos de Direito Constitucional 60–61 (2006).
82 Michael Rosen, Dignity: its history and meaning 67 (2012).
83 Samuel Moyn, Human Rights and the Use of History 21 (2014).
84 Michael Rosen, Dignity: its history and meaning 19 (2012); Jonathan Glover, Humanity: a moral history of the 20th century, 23–24 (2012); Michael Sandel, Justiça: o que é fazer a coisa certa, 135–137 (2012); Samuel Moyn, Human Rights and the Use of History 23 (2014); and Joshua Greene, Moral Tribes: emotion, reason, and the gap between us and them 108–116 (2013).

The preamble to the Charter of the United Nations (1945) stresses the determination of the peoples of the United Nations "to reaffirm faith in fundamental human rights, in the dignity and worth of the human person, in the equal rights of men and women and of nations large and small". The concept of dignity, as mentioned, is also embedded in the UDHR preamble, which explicitly recognizes the inherent dignity and equal and unalienable rights of humanity, as does the preamble of the Convention against Torture and Other Cruel, Inhuman or Degrading Treatment or Punishment (1984). The preambles of the International Covenant on Civil and Political Rights and International Covenant on Economic, Social and Cultural Rights of 16 December 1966 make reference to principles proclaimed in the Charter of the United Nations, recognizing that the rights enlisted therein derive from the inherent dignity of the human person: Article 10 asserts that all persons deprived of their liberty shall be treated with humanity and respect for the inherent dignity of their human person, while Article 13 recognizes the right to education for the full development of the human personality and its sense of dignity. The preamble of the Charter of Fundamental Rights of the European Union (2000) affirms that being "conscious of its spiritual and moral heritage, the Union is founded on the indivisible, universal values of human dignity, freedom, equality and solidarity", while Article 1 states that human dignity is inviolable and must be respected and protected.

Although all its human dignity references are contained in the preamble, Article 31 of the Vienna Convention (1969) sets out the general rules of interpreting a treaty that would occur in "good faith in accordance with the ordinary meaning to be given to the terms of the treaty in their context and in the light of its object and purpose". For that, the preamble is unambiguously included in the purpose of interpretation of a treaty – Article 31, §2. All regional human rights conventions also put human dignity at the centre. The African Charter on Human and Peoples' Rights (1981), in Article 5; the American Convention on Human Rights (1969), in articles 5, 6 and 11; and the European Convention on Human Rights, in Protocol 13 and Article 4 of Protocol 4. Similarly, almost all the great treaties that contain the body of law for international human rights expressly consider human dignity as a value and right. The list below is not exhaustive, but serves to make the point:

- i the preamble and articles 23, 28, 37, 39 and 40 of the Convention on the Rights of the Child (1989) all refer to the spirit of peace, dignity, tolerance, freedom, equality and solidarity;
- ii the preamble and articles 3, 8, 16, 24 and 25 of the Convention on the Rights of Persons with Disabilities (2006) condemn discrimination against any person on the basis of disability as a violation of the inherent dignity and worth of the human person;
- iii the Convention on the Elimination of All Forms of Discrimination against Women (1979) emphasizes that discrimination against women "violates the principles of equality of rights and respect for human dignity";
- iv the preamble of the Second Optional Protocol to the International Covenant on Civil and Political Rights on the abolition of the death penalty (1989) says

that "abolition of the death penalty contributes to enhancement of human dignity and progressive development of human rights";

v Article 18 of the Oviedo Convention for the Protection of Human Rights and Dignity of the Human Being (1997), with regard to the Application of Biology and Medicine, establishes that States' Parties "shall protect the dignity and identity of all human beings and guarantee everyone, without discrimination, respect for their integrity and other rights and fundamental freedoms with regard to the application of biology and medicine";

vi the International Declaration on Human Genetic Data (2003) sets its purposes as ensuring the respect for human dignity and protection of human rights and fundamental freedoms in the collection, processing, use and storage of human genetic data, human proteomic data and of the biological samples from which they are derived, in keeping with the requirements of equality and justice;

vii the United Nations Declaration on Human Cloning (2005) forbids all forms of human cloning in as much as they are incompatible with human dignity and the protection of human life, and the application of genetic engineering techniques that may be contrary to human dignity; and the Universal Declaration on Bioethics and Human Rights (2005) proclaims the need for scientific research to occur within the framework of ethical principles and to respect human dignity, human rights and fundamental freedoms; the fundamental equality of all human beings in dignity and rights is to be respected so that they are treated justly and equitably; and no individual or group should be discriminated against or stigmatized, in violation of human dignity, human rights and fundamental freedoms;

viii the preamble and articles 6 and 16 of the Council of Europe Convention on Action against Trafficking in Human Beings (2005), in which human trafficking constitutes a violation of human rights and an offence to the dignity and the integrity of the human being.

The Inter-American Human Rights Court has expressed the broadest conception possible of human dignity, with the protection of private life encompassing a series of factors associated with the dignity of the individual. This includes the ability to develop his/her own personality and aspirations, determine his/her own identity and define his/her own personal relationships; also aspects of physical and social identity, including the right to personal autonomy, personal development and the right to establish and develop relationships with other human beings and with the outside world.[85] Moreover, it has endowed human rights and dignity with such importance that they are often opposed to state policy or action even when expressing collective interest for the entire international community.[86]

85 *Artavia Murillo et al. (In Vitro Fertilization) v. Costa Rica,* Preliminary Objections, Merits, Reparations and Costs, Inter-Am. Ct. H.R. (ser. C) No. 257, §143 (November 28, 2012); and *Rosendo Cantú et al. v. Mexico,* Preliminary objection, merits, reparations and costs, Inter-Am. Ct. H.R. (ser. C) No. 216, §119 (August 31, 2010).

86 Case of the *Members of the Village of Chichupac and neighboring communities of the Municipality of Rabinal v. Guatemala,* Preliminary Objections, Merits, Reparations and Costs, Inter-Am. Ct. H.R. (ser. C) No. 328, §124 (November 30, 2016); *Expelled Dominicans and Haitians v. Dominican Republic,* Preliminary Objections, Merits, Reparations and Costs, Inter-Am. Ct. H.R. (ser. C) No. 282, §267, 463 (August 28, 2014); and *Contreras et al. v. El Salvador,* Merits, Reparations and Costs, Inter-Am. Ct. H.R. (ser. C) No. 232, §112 (August 31, 2011).

In *Pretty v. United Kingdom*, the European Court of Human Rights overruled Diane Pretty's personal and private family decision to end her life because of an untreatable and incapacitating disease that caused great suffering. After accusing the United Kingdom of ill treatment and torture for the denial of her "right to die", she took her case to the European Court. The court upheld the indispensability and inviolability of her human dignity, which does not give her the right to treat herself as a means in order to "deny the principle of sanctity of life" protected under human rights bodies. The right to life cannot entail a negative form, not even when the victim consents. There is no "self-determination in the sense of conferring on an individual the entitlement to choose death rather than life". To the court, assuring the inviolability and indispensability of her life emphasizes her human dignity rather than the alleged "lack of respect" for diminishing her human dignity by letting her degenerate and suffer at the pace of the disease.[87]

The European Human Rights Court has established that the very essence of the Human Rights Convention is respect for human dignity and human freedom. In other words, human rights like liberty and life are intimately linked to human dignity, and this intimate link has been repeatedly stated in numerous international documents, with frequent references to General Comment No. 12 and General Comment No. 15 adopted by the United Nations Committee on Economic, Social and Cultural Rights at its twentieth and twenty-ninth sessions.[88] Therefore, Europe also requires broad human rights protection in the name of human dignity.[89]

In *Manuel Wackenheim v. France*, the International Court of Justice upheld France's decision to terminate Mr Wackenheim's job in order to maintain his human dignity. Mr Wackenheim was hired by a French entertainment company that presented an event known as dwarf tossing, and he was one of several dwarves who had been tossed. For reasons of human dignity, the activity was banned by the local mayor, at which point Mr Wackenheim fought to overrule the ban, arguing that he had not had his dignity diminished at all but, rather, been glad to have a nice, fun job. To him, the violation was that he could not continue working as he wished, which constituted a violation of his freedom, employment rights and right to respect for private life. Moreover, he emphasized, "there is no work for dwarves in France and this job does not constitute an affront to human dignity since dignity consists in having a job".[90]

In the *Wackenheim* case, France upheld the ban on dwarf tossing, basing its arguments on the legitimacy of human dignity upon the alleged discrimination against dwarves. Therefore, France deemed it a question of upholding the public order, furthermore suggesting that "human dignity is part of public order", "despite the consent of the individual concerned". In response, Mr Wackenheim

87 *Pretty v. United Kingdom [Fourth Section]*, no. 2346/02, Eur. Ct. H.R., §§ 37–39, 52 and 65 (2002).

88 *Lambert and Others v. France [GC]*, no. 46043/14, Eur. Ct. H.R., §§ 142–143 (2015).

89 *Vo v. France [GC]*, no. 53924/00, Eur. Ct. H. R., §§ 75, 82, 84–85 (2004).

90 *Manuel Wackenheim v. France*, Communication No. 854/1999, U.N. Doc. CCPR/C/75/D/854/1999 (2002).

asserted that "employment is an element of human dignity and depriving an individual of his employment is tantamount to diminishing his dignity".[91] Both sides were basing their arguments on human dignity and both sides were citing human rights – such as Mrs Pretty and her self-right to die without suffering. This and several other quandaries regarding human rights and human dignity have been settled by international courts using the Kantian formula of humanity.

The reason why modern human dignity and its moral bounds are related to Kant is because the language used nowadays, mostly by scholars and international/domestic jurisprudence,[92] tends to emphasize the Kantian categorical imperative and notion of dignity as an inherent value. Dignity shows itself in different strands, such as status, behavior and inherent value. The third was developed by Kant and is encompassed by modern international human rights, also unfolding and carrying within it the universal duty of self and mutual respect. Through human autonomy, each human being contains a humanity core that is greater than the exercise of personal choice (inclinations); humanity, in this sense, sets boundaries on what human beings may do.

Such a value transcends the human person and his own will. For example, in *Parrilo v. Italy*, the European Court of Human Rights recognized the dignity of an unborn human life. With respect to dignity, as a value and right, the potential to be born is enough. In such terms, "human embryos must be treated in all circumstances with the respect due to human dignity", and not even genetic science shall prevail "over the respect for human dignity" since "scientific progress must not be built upon disrespect for ontological human nature", and the "scientific goal of saving human lives does not justify means that are intrinsically destructive of that life".[93] The same transcendental sense of dignity was also upheld by the Inter-American Court when it credited human dignity to human remains, especially in relation to liturgy and the religious beliefs of the dead.[94] Likewise, as stated in the *Wackenheim* case, France's ban on dwarf tossing had "reasonable grounds". Not every differentiation of treatment between people constitutes discrimination, which would occur when not based on objective and reasonable grounds. The Human Rights Committee thus endorsed France's policy, saying it was "necessary in order to protect public order, which brings into play

91 *Manuel Wackenheim v. France*, Communication No. 854/1999, U.N. Doc. CCPR/C/75/D/854/1999 (2002).

92 For instance, in 2006 the German Constitutional Court held unconstitutional the statute enacted by parliament regarding Homeland Security, which asserted that aircraft taken by terrorists could be lawfully shot down in order to save the lives of those who would be on the ground. The Court rationale was that such provision erodes the human dignity of those who are inside the plane, even considering their death a certain outcome. Check on case 1BvR 357/05 of the German Constitutional Court.

93 *Parrilo v. Italy [GC]*, no. 46470/11 Eur. Ct. H.R., §47 (2015).

94 *Velásquez Paiz y Otros v. Guatemala*, Excepciones Preliminares, Fondo, Reparaciones y Costas, Inter-Am. Ct. H.R. (ser. C) No. 307, §173, 220 (Noviembre 15, 2015); *Caso Bámaca Velásquez Vs. Guatemala*, Reparaciones y Costas, Inter-Am. Ct. H.R. (ser. C) No. 91, §81 (Febrero 22, 2002); and *Caso Blake Vs. Guatemala*, Fondo, Inter-Am. Ct. H.R. (ser. C) No. 36, §115 (Enero 24, 1998).

considerations of human dignity that are compatible with the objectives of the Covenant"[95] – Article 26, ICCPR.

Kantian theory is very appealing in the modern international arena, emphasizes Martha Nussbaum. It puts ethical content into international politics and general relationships, forcing all nations to sign up to certain moral mandatory statements. This approach puts upholding universal equality and enhancing the value of human life and dignity above any other interest, including economic power (as in the case of the *Sawhoyamaxa Indigenous Community v. Paraguay*). However, Nussbaum highlights that it has not been enough to establish international social cooperation that grants equal respectfulness to all human beings.[96]

The reasoning behind these agreements is guided by the categorical imperative of the formulation of humanity as an end, in which there is an invisible (but not untraceable) power requiring us to be respectful to others and ourselves. Human dignity, therefore, serves as a mediator for moral quandaries, since every rational being exists as an end in themselves, not merely as a means for arbitrary use by this or that will.[97] However, as warned by Michael Rosen, treating human beings as an end leads to open questions which are unanswered by the formula of humanity, particularly because Kant does not forbid treating humans as a means totally. Rosen explains that the formula of humanity condemns treating humans as *means only*, which prompts a variety of semantic differences in which some kinds of means treatment may be acceptable, leading to a grey zone of uncertainties about what is and what is not morally permissible in human rights practice.[98]

Human dignity has become the foundational norm that guides all fundamental rights just as much as it settles conflict between them, even though human rights morality is not entirely derived from Kantianism. Suddenly, all other values and rights become instrumental.[99] For those constitutions and international treaties that treat human dignity as a value, it also becomes an undeniable right through constitutional and international jurisprudence in courts of human rights. For them, using the value of dignity to override an individual's personal choices and behavior makes sense because what this protects is "respect for the dignity of the human person". The UDHR and the Grundgesetz both turn on the Kantian conception of dignity as an essential value and also as the central principle guiding state actions.[100]

Taken piecemeal, human dignity reveals itself as at one and the same time a universal value and a contextualized right. It is thus both a principle that leads the interpretation of law and a right that is judicially, legally and politically

95 *Manuel Wackenheim v. France*, Communication No. 854/1999, U.N. Doc. CCPR/C/75/D/854/1999 (2002).

96 Martha C. Nussbaum, Fronteiras da Justiça: deficiência, nacionalidade, pertencimento à espécie, 334–337 (2013).

97 Immanuel Kant, Fundamentação da Metafísica dos Costumes 68 (2006).

98 Michael Rosen, Dignity: its history and meaning 83–86 (2012).

99 Carlos S. Fayt, Derechos Humanos y El Poder Mediático, Político y Económico: su mundialización en el siglo XXI 109 (2001).

100 Michael Rosen, Dignity: its history and meaning 125–126 (2012).

enforceable.[101] However, far from being a universal and self-evident concept, the right to dignity has created an enduring tension that neither positive law nor judicial interpretations have been able to settle. As remarked by Erin Daly, any effort to find a single, unifying theory of dignity will ultimately be thwarted by "the vast range of unconnected instances of its use",[102] which requires human rights to be regarded in the context of a "dynamic and evolving process of international norm-setting" that takes into consideration plurality and different historical, cultural and religious backgrounds.[103]

Human rights (wannabe) universalism

As we have mentioned, the American Declaration of Independence and the French Revolution's Declaration of the Rights of Man and Citizen borrowed the essence of natural law theories. The philosophy originates from Hugo Grotius and establishes rights that are fundamental to human nature, irrespective of God. Human rights, which unite rationality with the idea that each person has rights simply by being human, have animated the modern era by making the right to life, liberty, happiness and property "natural" to any human being, independently of political society. These precepts went deep into the Enlightenment and the social transformations of the eighteenth century they prompted in accordance with the idea that universal natural rights are inalienable. They cannot be taken away or conferred by society since they are "self-evident" and of a moral quality – thinking that came up again during the revival of human rights in the second half of the last century.[104]

However, from the beginning of the UN human rights movement, the delimitation of universality has been a great problem. The diversity of philosophies in the UDHR drafting process represents very well the unraveling nature of simple questions regarding basic human values. The philosophers gathered together had to trace a "*common conviction*" because the perspectives of human rights varied, just like Western and Eastern culture and philosophy.[105] Hence Hans Joas advocates a duty of *value generalization* in order to maintain the constitutive patterns of the system's identity.[106]

101 Ana Paula Barcellos, A Eficácia Jurídica dos Princípios Constitucionais: o princípio da dignidade da pessoa humana chapter 2 (2002); Nelson Rosenvald, Dignidade Humana e Boa-fé no Código Civil 07–62 (2005); and Luis María Desimoni, Los Derechos Humanos y la Guerra contra el Terror 41 (2009).

102 Erin Daly, Dignity Rights: courts, constitutions, and the worth of the human person 20 (2013).

103 Maya Hertig Randall, *The History of International Human Rights Law*, in Research Handbook on Human Rights and Humanitarian Law 03, 20 (2013).

104 Patrick Hayden, The Philosophy of Human Rights 04–05 (2001).

105 Mary Ann Glendon, A World Made New: Eleanor Roosevelt and the Universal Declaration of Human Rights 221–222 (2002).

106 Hans Joas, The Sacredness of the Person: a new genealogy of human rights 179–182 (Alex Skinner trans., 2013).

International human rights law has been broadly attacked and criticized for being unfit for universalism in a pluralistic world. Some believe universalism comes from the capability of autonomy and reason that all humans share. Jenny Martinez points to the no-dissent ratification of the UDHR in 1948 (the "positivist credentials") and its morally exhortative force regarding right and wrong.[107] Lynn Hunt offers the claim that the moral rules framed in human rights are universal because they are "self-evident".[108] Actually, neither of them is right.

Positivist credential

International law has traditionally sought to establish universality by configuring the related juridical positivism to its standards. The international community has always been represented by states – even nowadays, with the openness of the international arena, states remain the prime subjects – and their will can only be granted and visualized via positive international instruments. In this regard, the positivist tradition of international law can be traced back to state sovereignty, the only source of legal power where human beings could find protection.[109]

As cited before, the UDHR entered international law as a soft law instrument. Only later did it become hard law by the enforcement of parallel treaties, such as the two covenants of the 1970s. Nowadays, several international bodies constitute the global human rights bloc, each one with its own scope. Despite the positivist movement, transgressions of human rights become ever more frequent, meaning that universal respect is not the universal value it was once portrayed to be. Hence, international subjects and courts struggle every day to establish a minimum of morality for human rights, taking into account the generalization of values and the sustenance of world plurality.

Once again, we face the chasmic gap between positivism and human behavior, and state policy. Beyond the reach of the positivist movement, however, we find goodwill and doing good – and whether these come from moral duty, religious principles of love or pure prudence (reason), they are very welcome. What has really mattered so far, and will always matter to the morality of law, is the content of international actions, including the judgment, practices and principles involved, whatever their motivation. Throughout the process of distinguishing facts from values, we face the objective value of human welfare (objective in the sense that welfare does not mean the good of one individual but the good of countless individuals). The value of human welfare as an international moral compass ought to be debated at a broader level where "welfare" meaning might be interpreted in general terms. This would mean that values, practices and institutions could be

107 Jenny S. Martinez, The Slave Trade and the Origins of International Human Rights Law 161 (2012).
108 Lynn Hunt, Inventing Human Rights 19 (2007).
109 Antônio Augusto Cançado Trindade, A Humanização do Direito Internacional 13 (2006).

approved by more generally understood terms in order to arrive at a global understanding of human welfare without a dispute over meaning.[110]

Therefore, the generalization of human rights – and the vagueness this implies – has given international courts enlarged powers to set the jurisprudence of the court. During this process of stating value, the pluralism of international society makes consensus over the core value hard to achieve.[111] The current sense of humanness, as a secular and anti-religious term, has embedded in it connotations of human happiness. But moral philosophies disregard happiness as a fundamental notion as it contains multiple meanings about the nature of welfare which no one looks at in general terms.[112]

Self-evidence

To proclaim human rights as self-evident, three intertwined and inseparable qualities are required. First, human rights must be natural, that is, inherent to all human beings; second, they must be equal, which means being the same for everyone; and third, they must be universal and applicable everywhere. In sum, human rights ought to pertain to all mankind because of our shared status of "human being". Of these qualities, the naturalness has been easier to embrace than equality or universality. Beyond this, to make these qualities meaningful we have to add the political content. Since they are human rights in society – domestically or internationally – states must engage with them.[113]

Samuel Moyn agrees with Hunt about the need for political engagement. For him, the advances in human rights have been minimal since 1945. They have a moral foundation but lack political enforcement, since the United Nations at that time insisted on its nonbinding character in order to make the Universal Declaration pass in the General Assembly. Only in the 1970s did the human rights movement gain strength and scope beyond government institutions, thanks mostly to NGOs. Only then were human rights positioned as a moral alternative to the near-sightedness of politics.[114]

Notwithstanding, Hunt still believes the universality of human rights lies in our universal "effort to dislodge cruelty", which has been part of mankind's history from the beginning. This common effort originates from our empathy, which has become a "more powerful force for good than ever before"; this makes human rights our bulwark against evil. Accordingly, human rights are better defended by the sentiments, convictions and agency of people who seek answers to their outrage – and this goes beyond law, which sometimes serves as an instrument of oppression. This characteristic is enough to make them self-evident and have the potential for universality.[115]

110 Bernard Williams, Moral: uma introdução à ética 117–124 (2005).
111 Alberto de Amaral Júnior, Curso de Direito Internacional Público 113–128 (2nd ed. 2011)
112 Bernard Williams, Moral: uma introdução à ética 133–134 (2005).
113 Lynn Hunt, Inventing Human Rights 20–21 (2007).
114 Samuel Moyn, Human Rights and the Use of History 82–83 (2014).
115 Lynn Hunt, Inventing Human Rights 212–214 (2007).

The outlook of the Inter-American Court of Human Rights is very akin to Hunt's. In Advisory Opinion OC-18/2003 it endorsed that human rights emanate from "human conscience" rather than the will of states. They come from a consensus of all the subjects of international law – *opinio juris communis* – in which conscience occupies a bigger stage than will. The court acknowledges that human rights are ostensibly and flagrantly violated every day and everywhere. However, against these transgressions, which are an affront to the juridical conscience of mankind, international courts contribute to the ongoing process of international law humanization, where lie universality and the unity of mankind.[116]

Along the same lines, the international human rights movement has gradually enforced its validity over the uneasy arguments of cultural relativism. To overcome the alleged cultural specificity and difference of origins and values, the international community has been focusing on a few universally shared cultural assumptions that are easily invoked to foster and implement a universal validity based on the generalization of values.[117] To arrive at these minimal shared values, we must follow the Habermas discursive dialogue process based on public and democratic reasoning which, in turn, allows us to constantly revise, interpret and apply human rights morality.[118]

Moral and political philosophy from the twentieth century onwards has overcome the prevailing ideas of early modern philosophy and natural law theory. Contemporary human rights justifications have to be more sophisticated to move beyond the moral reasoning and idea of self-evidence, especially in the face of the world's moral, political and religious pluralism.[119] A global demand for human rights generalization seems more and more necessary.

Universalizability

Human rights, self-evident and potentially universal, have many faces and multiple uses. Hunt asserts that rights cannot be defined once and for all because their emotional element keeps them in permanent flux, just as our sense of right and wrong varies through time, while Moyn thinks otherwise. According to him, it is a fiction that human rights convey an inviolable consensus shared by all. In fact, their interpretations and applications are inevitably partisan and, just like anything that calls itself universal, human rights are violated every time they are interpreted and encoded into a specific program.[120]

116 Juridical Condition and Rights of the Undocumented Migrants, Advisory Opinion OC-18/03, Inter-Am. Ct. H. R. (ser. A) No. 18, Concurring opinion of Judge A. A. Cançado Trindade, §§21–30 (September 17, 2003).

117 Xiaorong Li, *"Asian Values" and the Universality of Human Rights*, in The Philosophy of Human Rights 397, 406–407 (2001).

118 1 Jurgen Habermas, Direito e Democracia: entre facticidade e validade 190–210 (2nd ed. 2012).

119 Patrick Hayden, The Philosophy of Human Rights 07 (2001).

120 Samuel Moyn, Human Rights and the Use of History 84 (2014).

ICJ Justice Cançado Trindade, in his turn, believes that moral excellence is acquired by practices and experience over time, giving shape to human behavior bit by bit. This process is part of what he calls the "common right of mankind" (tantamount to Flavia Piovesan's "juridical inventory of mankind"), which represents the evolution of the *jus gentium*. To him, rather than the positive law, the common rights of humanity – as a *jus gentium* evolution – disregard legislative authority because they are understood by natural human reason gathered from human consciousness throughout history, which also gives them their universal validity.[121] International human rights courts seek to rescue the universalism of human rights and place it above the will of states and politics by recognizing that the essential rights of man are derived not from being a national of a certain state but rather from attributes of the human personality, and therefore justify international protection.[122]

This historical evolution and universal ethical compilation common to every man, which together create "universal juridical conscience", has the singular aim of realizing the common welfare within international society and law. In a world marked by human and cultural diversity, plurality of ideas and cosmopolitan visions, the *jus gentium* becomes a *societas gentium* where its unity is protected by the universal juridical conscience. In this regard, while placed above positive law, it has revealed itself as unable to protect humanity.[123]

In addition, Helio Gallardo explains that since the rise of the second dimension of human rights in the nineteenth and early twentieth centuries, the alleged universalism has been shown to be false. The expression of human rights takes into account the socio-historic place of groups, nations and individuals, which means humaneness is always observed in a particular way, not universally as abstractly envisaged by the drafter and supporters of the first dimension of human rights in the eighteenth century. For him, the difficulties in uniformly establishing social, economic and cultural rights throughout the world serve as evidence of the fallibility of universalism, alongside an inner tension in human rights integrity, which he portrays as the permanent conflict between capitalism and the workforce that impairs the general right of life.[124]

Although Gallardo is right in his observation, this relativist anti-universalization and human rights inefficiency has already been responded to by modern sociological theories. Beyond positivism, universalizability is grounded in morality,[125] even when progressing its terms and scope from tribal concerns to larger questions

121 Antônio Augusto Cançado Trindade, A Humanização do Direito Internacional 08–10 (2006).

122 The Effect of Reservations on the Entry into Force of the American Convention on Human Rights, Advisory Opinion OC-2/82, Inter-Am. Ct. H. R. (ser. A) No. 2, §31 (September 24, 1982).

123 The Right to Information on Consular Assistance in the Framework of the Guarantees of the due Process of Law, Advisory Opinion OC-16/99, Inter-Am. Ct. H. R. (ser. A) No. 16, §§03–04 (October 1, 1999).

124 Helio Gallardo, Teoria Crítica: matriz e possibilidades de direitos humanos 50 (2013).

125 Bernard Williams, Moral: uma introdução à ética 37 (2005).

of humanity. The moral perfectionism of law that requires unconditional and universal validity for human dignity no longer exists. Like Joas' and Habermas' criticism of Kant's theory, no philosophical development can be dealt with via morality, irrespective of history. Conversely, a moral legal universalism must take into account historical and cultural sources that may merge arguments for universality with the genesis of values.[126] A universalistic morality cannot be based only on pure practical reason; it must also account for religious beliefs, emotions and cultural traumas.

The fact is that true universality does not apply to mankind. In the real world, there is no such thing as a universal and identical form of autonomous, enlightened reason. The larger a society is – ultimately, an international society – the harder it is for it to achieve homogeneity of practices, mainly because of the historical and cultural inputs. Kant's rationalism, therefore, is the secularized echo of religious absolutism.[127] Humanity does not need to be – nor is it pragmatically conceivable to be – morally perfect. But we need to pursue moral improvement, just as Singer envisioned with his expanding circle.[128] Our moral values and progress are and always will be in motion.

We do have too many relativist arguments attempting to erode the universalizability of human rights: basically, they comprise cultural differences and shifts of empowerment between individual and social rights. But, as asserted by Fernando Tesón, "the place of birth and cultural environment of an individual are not related to his moral worth or to his entitlement to human rights".[129] Likewise, Xiaorong Li argues that the origin of an idea in one culture does not necessarily mean its unfitness to another.[130] Bernard Williams, in his turn, calls this misunderstanding a "relativist error", in which no injustice can find comfort in subjective morality, nor can it provoke a complete absence of protest. This kind of relativism and subjectivism is more than incoherent – it is false.[131]

The difference in perspective of Western and Eastern cultures on human rights also fails to illuminate the situation. The idea that Eastern philosophy places community over the individual in opposition to Western individuality is also a fallacy. The so-called Western rights (first dimension of human rights), such as political and civil rights, are actually inseparable from Eastern social, economic and cultural rights (second dimension rights). They are, however, represented in two covenants, which together make part of the whole body of international human rights. Each one of them is indispensable for the effective exercise of the other. Nowadays, political and civil liberty and the rule of law improve social and

126 Hans Joas, The Genesis of Values 174–175 (Gregory Moore trans., 2000).
127 Hans Joas, The Sacredness of The Person: a new genealogy of human rights 128–129 (Alex Skinner trans., 2013).
128 Peter Singer, The Expanding Circle 118–123 (2011)
129 Fernando R. Tesón, *International Human Rights and Cultural Relativism*, in The Philosophy of Human Rights 379, 386 (2001).
130 Xiaorong Li, *"Asian Values" and the Universality of Human Rights*, in The Philosophy of Human Rights 397, 401 (2001).
131 Bernard Williams, Moral: uma introdução à ética 42–43 (2005).

economic opportunities, especially because history has shown that what begins as endorsement of the value of community and social harmony ends in support for authoritarian regimes, where anything that opposes the "community interest" is erased.[132]

As warned by Samuel Moyn, if human rights do not offer a "more realistic and politicized utopia, something else will take its place". The multipolarization that has prevailed in the international arena is no longer supported by morality above politics.[133] Similarly, Jürgen Habermas asserts that human rights values are inevitably particular and cannot be subjected to universal validity through normative processes.[134] Both Habermas and Moyn believe we might attain universalism, but it must not be the product of international law. The claim for universalism of human rights by normative validity is unsuited to a plural and cosmopolitan environment like the international community. As Hans Joas states, "the only hope of universalization lies in the spheres of law and normative morality"; communication about values ought to have as its starting point our own commitment, our own moral sense that enables us to differentiate good from evil.[135]

As grasped by Jonathan Glover, respect and sympathy are at the heart of our humanity and the cornerstone of all human values, regardless of its codification in positive law. This immanent morality is the main source of the process of universalization and value generalization.[136] As an illustration, he cites some instances when morality prevailed over law – for example, when Sargent Anton Schmidt, who was in charge of a German army patrol in Poland, gave forged papers and the use of military trucks to the Jewish underground until he was arrested and executed.[137] We could also add the German anti-Nazi students who were executed for distributing subversive pamphlets in Munich, their leader a young girl named Sophie Scholl who today has schools and streets named after her[138]; and the village of Le Chambon which hid several Jews in French homes occupied by Nazi's forces.[139] These acts of "civil courage" took place in several different places and among different people, and this is the morality that might reach universalization, unrelated to any binding normative process.

Although reality does not support universalistic claims, a human rights utopia must endure. What is needed, in fact, is not a blind belief in universal values for the moral perfection of humanity. Rather, we need a new process of language that fits human rights morality in a real geopolitical and plural world, where humanity

132 Xiaorong Li, *"Asian Values" and the Universality of Human Rights*, in The Philosophy of Human Rights 397, 403–405 (2001).

133 Samuel Moyn, Human Rights and the Use of History 146–147 (2014).

134 1 Jurgen Habermas, Direito e Democracia: entre facticidade e validade chapter 3 (2nd ed. 2012).

135 Hans Joas, The Sacredness of the Person: a new genealogy of human rights 176 (Alex Skinner trans., 2013).

136 Jonathan Glover, Humanity: a moral history of the 20th century 337 (2nd ed. 2012).

137 Jonathan Glover, Humanity: a moral history of the 20th century 382–383 (2nd ed. 2012).

138 Sophie Scholl, The final days (2005).

139 Weapons of the Spirits (1990).

takes steps forward in moral improvement while not ignoring the generalization of values and process of developing common and shared beliefs (a common currency). We do not need to be morally *perfect* but morally *better* – even though a desire for moral perfection must exist to keep us moving forward. We will reintroduce this subject in chapter 6 when we discuss the main themes of the book.

Apparent conflicts

Each legal system constituted of multiple sources of law is deemed a complex system. Therefore, each complex system must possess unity, completeness and coherence to keep itself strong and sustainable. Therefore, from the highest norm to the lowest, all must be logically linked and appropriately content-based; all situations occurring in day-to-day practice must have an answer in law; and all legal instruments, no matter how diverse they are, must maintain coherence in order not to create legal contradictions. During this process of eschewing contradictions, multiple scenarios of conflict between legal instruments occur, among higher and lower statutes (in hierarchical systems), older and newer norms, general and special norms, domestic and international laws, and so on and so forth. Thus, all these situations must have solutions within the system and reasons why they are called apparent conflicts – otherwise, if they were real, the only solution would be to eliminate one of the conflicting norms.[140]

The same dynamic flow happens in modern international law, especially following article 38 of the ICJ Statute and its plural sources of international law. Moreover, we still have conflicts inside this international treaty and the international bodies it belongs to, such as human rights.[141] Likewise, the inclusion of new participants in international politics through the new international community framework has contributed to a rich and endless building process in human rights. International courts, organizations and treaties have been shaping solutions and interpretations that guide human rights applicability on international and domestic politics in order to solve apparent conflicts that appear every single day. All international subjects follow the development of the case law that has been built upon human rights courts and treaties, leading towards a particular interpretation and application that has the legitimacy to form a consistent *jus commune* among nations.

Marcelo Neves mentions a transconstitutionalism, but that does not mean an international constitutionalism. The concept refers to a process for relieving and solving juridical problems that are common to all legal systems. Therefore, a transconstitutionalist problem involves states, international, transnational courts just as much as local legal institutions, all committed to dealing with the problem. What this encompasses nowadays are the problems related to fundamental human rights, which goes way beyond any modern constitution.[142]

140 Norberto Bobbio, Teoria do Ordenamento Jurídico chapter 1 (10th ed. 1999).
141 Norberto Bobbio, A Era dos Direitos 58–60 (2004).
142 Marcelo Neves, Transconstitucionalismo 21–22 (2009).

For Marcelo Neves, the challenges we currently face do not necessarily have an internal solution; they are not solely a constitutional problem. Rather, the key is to identify the problems that emerge in all democratic legal systems and draw up a solution that can settle all of them equally, running the response through systems so it can be called universal. For this, the members of the international community need to cooperate in order to settle their conflicts and reach mutual appeasement.[143]

In the process of settling apparent conflicts over human rights, the constitutional and international concepts depart from the same place: human dignity. This is simply because dignity is the universal boundary and, when it is crossed, the state and international communities are called upon to intervene. Thus, the governing rule becomes a formula to affirm human dignity, while understanding that deprivation of dignity does not mean disappearance of dignity – since dignity cannot be detached from our humanity – but the denial of rights. However, this general rule applied to the interpretation and applicability of human rights is not sufficiently powerful in the face of modern conflicts that have entrenched moral quandaries.

That being said, it would usually be argued that any particular value should override the claims of inferior values. However, with human rights all claims are of the same kind because all of them derive from human dignity. Attempts to impose a hierarchy would lead us to a dead end. How can we settle the competing dignity claims of life and safety, liberty and privacy, for instance? Rosen shrewdly observes that in such cases, human dignity has not been balanced since it is the core of each of the conflicting rights. Dignity is the foundation of rights, and it is rights that can be weighed, not dignity. This means that the inviolability of rights and the inviolability of dignity are not the same thing.[144]

Thus, the idea of transconstitutionalism has embedded in it the idea of universalizibility of human rights. When you have the same problems and moral values, the solution should be the same. However, reality is different. As stated by Bernard Williams, there is no one way to see human nature and morality; there is no universal and unique moral ideal.[145] This becomes very clear when we cross-examine the rationale employed in the case of the Princess of Monaco. When accusing the paparazzi of invading her private life, the German Constitutional Tribunal held that as a public figure she is not entitled to the full guarantee of privacy that ordinary citizens enjoy.[146] But when the case reached the European Court of Human Rights, with the same facts and moral values, the legal solution was entirely different. The Court concluded that no freedom of press or expression can erode the princess's human right to family privacy.[147] Same facts, same human rights law, same moral values, but two completely different outcomes.

143 Marcelo Neves, Transconstitucionalismo 121 (2009).

144 Michael Rosen, Dignity: its history and meaning 108–109 (2012).

145 Bernard Williams, Moral: uma introdução à ética 101 (2005).

146 Bundesverfassungsgericht [German Constitutional Court] December 15, 1999, Case of *Von Hannover v. Germany*, BverfGE 101, 1 BvR 653/96, 1999 (Ger.).

147 *Von Hannover v. Germany [Third Section]*, no. 59320/00, Eur. Ct.H.R. (2004).

Incommensurability

When we deal with social values and their penetration into the legal decision-making process, we shed light on social goals based on reason around individual and collective welfare. Morality and welfare, by this token, are not two independent areas; one does not exclude the other; and there is no collision between them. Therefore, there is no specific prior tendency governing their demands.

If we have two co-existing values, such as liberty and equality, we might deliberate that liberty prevails over equality or the other way around, or even that they have equal potency. It is within this zone of inaccuracy that the relativist judgment develops according to the strength of two co-existing values. However, in the field of social science we dare to go further. By delving deeper into the relativist interplay between two values, we grasp the idea of the *incommensurability* of these two values, and how they are rooted so fiercely in human rights history.

Thus, incommensurability departs from two premises: (i) that no value overrides another; and (ii) at same time, they are both unequal. So, X and Y are incommensurable when neither of them is better than the other or equal in value. Incommensurability is then defined in the sense that only what possesses intrinsic value (or negative value) is incapable of being measured by or compared with another competing value.[148] Claiming that one value outweighs another raises a multitude of issues and, in the end, conflates the category of the *incommensurable* with the category of the *incomparable*. There is no common scale where X and Y can be put together in such way that Y can be seen as proportionate in value to X, but they can also share comparability without proportionality.[149] For instance, freedom of press and individual privacy; security and liberty – they are all incommensurable in essence.

When we work on the idea that X is not better than Y and Y is not better than X and they are also unequal in terms of value gradation, we enter a second stage of reasoning where this statement does not present itself as false or true because their values are immeasurable. Moral quandaries are part of human sociology. When we grasp apparent conflicts inside lists of human rights, we are facing moral quandaries that have a sociological background. As there is no hierarchical relationship or equality between them, to find a solution for the conflict we must examine the social value dimension, which will illustrate the prevailing right. As long as we organize ourselves like a pluralist society, there is no prevailing understanding of rights. The prevailing right is going to be revealed after robust debate, using communicative action skills that drive us away from static pre-comprehension of values.[150]

This formula is based on the rationale of jurisprudence, in which normativity and rationality mingle to make a reconstructive theory of society based on

148 Joseph Raz, The Morality of Freedom 322 (1986).
149 Larry S. Temkin, Rethinking the Good: moral ideals and the nature of practical reasoning 53 (2015).
150 Eduardo Ribeiro Moreira, Critérios de justiça 25 (2014).

communicative reasoning.[151] It does not constitute an axiom because morality does not contain self-evident truths, not to mention that substantial moral conclusions are incapable of settling moral disagreement in the real world. This means that a certain action might be wrong under certain circumstances and right under others.[152] For example, we can readily say that it is wrong to kill a person, but there is no crime in killing a murderer trying to kill other people if that is the only way to spare victims' lives. In this vein, the killer who murders to prevent other deaths does not choose to act wrongly but is acting under circumstances that make it correct to commit what is usually deemed a wrongdoing. This explains how in each conflicting situation there is at least one option where no error can be found, and this does not encompass the erosion of any social value encapsulated in content norms. The reason that guides the choice made in conflicting situations, whatever it is, will be linked to some social value because all human action is embedded in values that drive rational human agency. The social value behind the action will surface regardless of the agent's ability to choose under certain circumstances.

All the same, international law has given some cardinal values hierarchical status in order to secure the sacredness of the person and the new set of human values that foster human rights enforcement. Appearing as acknowledged, indisputable and international values, the international community frames these values as *jus cogens*, with a *erga omnes* nature because of the importance of the values that need protecting. Under article 53 of the Vienna Convention on the Law of Treaties (1969), *jus cogens* appertains to the area of international enforcement related to the hierarchy of rules in the international normative order, and enjoys a higher rank in the international hierarchy than treaty law and even "ordinary" customary rules. The most conspicuous consequence of this higher rank is that states cannot derogate the principle at issue through international treaties or local or special customs, or even general customary rules not endowed with the same normative force.[153]

Moral actions are not dogmas or mathematical axioms. Human agency can be wrong in some circumstances and right in others. For example, it is wrong to kill for pleasure, but it is right to kill a murderer who is attempting to kill someone else. In such case, there is no choosing between two wrongs. The latter action is right, but the act it requires is normally wrong. What is interesting in a plural society like the international community is that we have a lot of values coming and going and a lot of moral quandaries. So, two lessons emerge: moral pluralism asks for reasons for action, and incommensurability creates conceptual room for wrongdoing as a justification for acts that become right according to circumstances. They are moral

151 1 Jurgen Habermas, Direito e Democracia: entre facticidade e validade 21 (2nd ed. 2012).

152 Joshua Greene, Moral Tribes: emotion, reason, and the gap between us and them 184 (2013).

153 *Prosecutor v. Anto Furundzija [Trial Chamber]*, Case No. IT-95–17/1-T, 1998 I.C. T.Y. §153 (December 10); and Case of *Al-Adsani v. United Kingdom*, no. 35763/97, §60, ECHR (GC), 2001.

dilemmas because "they are cases in which the act which is morally required of one is wrongful".[154]

Basically, we have two driving forces that are incommensurable to each other but regulate international law morality and statutes. In consequence, moral dilemmas arise. Deontology and individual welfare advocates take opposing sides to teleology and social welfare advocates. However, the survival of incommensurable social values is essential to the very notion of community. The selection process that will prevail in an apparent conflict shall be guided by moral reasoning that grapples with democratic discourse, creativity of action and communicative performance of rational morality and positive law.[155]

Closing considerations

Human rights have been deemed a body of hard law that enshrines morality through the force of law. Human rights composition takes into account multiple human values that – regardless of religious and cultural traditions and idiosyncrasies – have been upheld globally by several international and national institutions and subjects. The main scope of this brand of international law, however, depends on the inefficiency of human rights to settle real conflicts and solve moral dilemmas.

Human rights from a Kantian perspective assume a moral perfection ruled by the categorical imperative of humanity as an end. However, there is no room for absolutism in applicability within the international arena, as pointed out by Michael Rosen. The question of whether to treat human beings as an end is an open question that remains unanswered by the formula of humanity where the prohibition seems to exclusively embrace the idea of treating human as *means only*, which generates a variety of semantic differences within a grey zone of uncertainties.[156] Moral perfection would only be possible if we achieve universal moral standards – which we have been unsuccessful in establishing since the Enlightenment.

The multiplicity of human rights dimensions – Neves' transconstitutionalism – brings about a moral quandary that is becoming commonplace in our globalized and complex international law. For this, Neves defends a transverse rationality that allows a constructive dialogue among legal systems in order to sustain the pluralism and respect for diversity without commeasuring and outweighing values that are, for the sake of pluralism and diversity, incommensurable, as outlined by Hans Joas and Jürgen Habermas. According to Neves, the world's plurality ought to be made up of identity and otherness. Each state should give a self-solution to your problem in order to build an identity that is gradually intertwined with those of other states from the core notion of otherness. Only through permanent exchanges can the international

154 Joseph Raz, The Morality of Freedom 361–365 (1986).
155 Hans Joas, The Creativity of Action 160–161 (2005); and 1 Jurgen Habermas, Direito e Democracia: entre facticidade e validade 139–140 (2nd ed. 2012).
156 Michael Rosen, Dignity: its history and meaning 83–86 (2012).

community build a constructive dialogue among nations and enhance its human rights decisions and articulations.[157]

Joas and Habermas, in their turn, propose a constructive and democratic dialogue over social values as well. For them, the universalizability of human values to set human behavior will come from a process of value generalization where the society will openly and democratically discuss ideas for social enhancement and moral improvement. For this to happen, however, it is first necessary to set the social values, put them into social practices, and only then permit them to become a social institution.[158] Moreover, during this process of values generalization, we might find a common currency, as espoused by Bernard Williams and Joshua Greene – a core of minimal shared beliefs through which humanity might cultivate universal understanding, interpretation and application of law and the morality it entails. In contrast to Kantian premises, this approach does not mean a denial of human rights, but a new densification of them on common-sense, moral grounds.[159]

The search for this universal common value must not diverge from the universal principle borne within the rationale of human rights – the universal effort to dislodge cruelty. Empowering good against evil has unquestionably been a common goal for humanity, as well as the aim of all morality of law.[160] Especially in the international arena, where plurality and cosmopolitanism prevail, there must be a thriving process of communicative action over values, and an enforcement of their universalizability based on the generalization and adoption of common ground.

157 Marcelo Neves, Transconstitucionalismo 264 (2009).

158 Hans Joas, The Sacredness of the Person: a new genealogy of human rights 140 (Alex Skinner trans., 2013); and 1 Jurgen Habermas, Direito e Democracia: entre facticidade e validade 158–159 (2nd ed. 2012).

159 Bernard Williams, Moral: uma introdução à ética 117–134 (2005); and Joshua Greene, Moral Tribes: emotion, reason, and the gap between us and them 306–345 (2013).

160 Lynn Hunt, Inventing Human Rights 212–214 (2007).

4 The law of armed conflict

Historical background

The understanding of a just war arose very early in the history of international law. The crowning achievement of the *jus gentium* in the Middle Ages, the just war doctrine is a body of law that stipulates when armed force may be justified in order to stop some kind of evildoing. The main concern then was the permissibility of resorting to force, not the methods by which the hostilities were conducted. In this regard, it has been noted that the just war doctrine had no specific rules about the conduct of war, but rather one general prohibition against purely gratuitous violence that became its cornerstone, which said that irrespective of the rules regarding methods of combat, acts that are nihilistically, needlessly violent should not be tolerated.[1]

Even liberals, whose discourse aims for the limitation of state power and enhancement of individual agency, consider all wars equally immoral, unjust and harmful. Wars cause too much damage in the economic sphere and to domestic and foreign free trade policy. The depopulation of entire tracts of land, the destruction of capitals, the increased burden of taxes, the growth of government debt, the shrinking of international trade and general impoverishment are just some of the clear and devastating impacts that wars have upon economies.[2] Therefore, the Pact of Paris (or Kellogg-Briand Treaty) of 1928 represented a major gain for international law because war was finally put outside the borders of law (outlawry of war), with the intention of eliminating acts of aggression – only defensive war was acceptable.[3]

The Pact of Paris of 1928 became the most prominent treaty on the subject of armed conflict and the prohibition of war as an instrument of national policy.[4] Nevertheless, the following years showed that a simple declaration, no matter how solemn, is not enough to prevent new – and bloody – wars. The rise of fascism and National Socialism and their relationship to a spirit of national aggression

1 Stephen C. Neff, Justice Among nations: a history of international law 67–83 (2014).
2 Hans Joas, War and Modernity 34 (2003).
3 Hildebrando Accioly et al, Manual Direito Internacional Público 1.206-1.207 (São Paulo: Saraiva, 20th edition, 2012).
4 Stephen C. Neff, Justice Among nations: a history of international law 361 (2014).

DOI: 10.4324/9781003170778-4

created the idea that war would have a revitalizing effect on society. More than a continuation of old-fashioned militarism, this idea was conceived as modern hindsight. War itself was deemed a modern revolution. Therefore, violence and terror were not only practiced against enemies but also encouraged in cases where there was no instrumental purpose.[5]

As some scholars point out, the reality is that it is barbaric totalitarian regimes that invariably pursue, destroy and humiliate ethnic groups or peoples through war that prompt foundational changes in international law. In wartime law is silent. War interrupts peace – which is, more than just time without fighting, peace-with-rights that represents liberty and safety. The outcome always turns out to be a union of nations and peoples committed to establishing new moral guidance based on ideas of democracy, liberty, equality and justice just as much as fostering the necessity to preserve peace in the face of destruction from the enhancement of technology and modern war methods. Nowadays there is a strong conviction and shared consensus among nations that human dignity and fundamental liberties and rights must endure and be indivisibly and universally attained by all.[6]

With the downfall of the colonial empires, the framework of the growing international community was designed to make armed clashes exceptional events alongside their constant control and dissolution by means of international institutionalized cooperation. The Charter of the United Nations then banned the use of threat of force and simultaneously granted power to the Security Council of the United Nations to issue sanctions and proper measures including the use of force against any state breaking that ban. For the first time an international instrument expressly prohibited not just war but any threat of resorting to the use of military force. From that time on, the fundamental principles of international relations were: (i) the substantive equality of states; (ii) non-intervention in the internal or external affairs of other states; (iii) prohibition of the threat or use of force; (iv) peaceful settlement of disputes; (v) respect for human rights; and (vi) self-determination of peoples. Creating the new order became a peaceful aim and the international protection of human rights came to be presented as such an aim, principally by those who placed primary importance on individualism, political freedom and the furtherance of democracy.[7]

Since the end of the twentieth century, history has pointed us towards an investigation into the conditions of peace together with sober analysis of specifically modern tendencies to war. For that, there is a need to justify the normative premises underlying the modern theory and its regenerative effect of violence. We have clearly stated that democracy is the yardstick of social progress – although there has been an astonishing decline in democratic regimes in the twentieth-first

5 Hans Joas, War and Modernity 49–51 (2003).

6 Rodolfo E. Piza Escalante, *El Valor Del Derecho y La Jurisprudencia Internacionales de Derechos Humanos en el Derecho y la Justicia Internos – El Ejemplo de Costa Rica*, in 1 Liber Amicorum, Héctor Fix-Zamundio, 169, 174 (1998).

7 Antonio Cassese, International Law 46–59 (2nd ed. 2005).

century[8] – and the social and legal reinforcement of crucial values and their foundation and development through the process of civilization is of extreme importance.[9] It is research on the role of war in social change that prompts impacts and configurations in international law, which then allows modernization processes, especially through the jurisprudence of international courts that pragmatically sets in motion the genesis of new values as well as the tension between them and existing institutions.[10]

From the law of war comes a type of international law characterized by its use of the principle of humanity to underlie the application of principles of necessity and proportionality in situations of armed conflict. Therefore, a strong preoccupation with victims of the conflict – civilian or military – drives a desire to regulate the means and methods of engagement in war. These new traits intensify from the first half of the twentieth century and become increasingly entwined in moral questions.

The morality inquiry is brought to light for two core reasons, one reflecting a change in the world, the other a change in the way international law understands its subjects. From this perspective, humanity's codifications have basically been developed in the Hague, Geneva and New York, and this international humanitarian law is configured by primary international law sources for the sake of human dignity and the flourishing of mankind. It is compatible with the contemporary international legal order and maintains the unity, coherence and wholeness of the system even in wartime. The Hague statutes regulate *jus in bello* and its methods combat the use of force. Geneva and New York are then more relevant, since the former deals with the victims of armed conflicts and the latter with human rights within armed conflicts.[11]

Subsequently, international humanitarian law (IHL) became a specialized branch of international law applied in armed conflicts. This may be understood in a very broad sense, such as covering a rule of international law, applicable in both peace and war, which has a humanitarian purpose. This would include branches of international law such as human rights law, refugee law, international criminal law and so on. There are different expressions used to designate this body of law. The "Law of War" (or "Laws of War") (*jus in bello*) is the oldest expression, still used today. However, the "Law of War" is not really an appropriate expression, since in terms of this work we see it as a central piece of international humanitarian law. After the Second World War, when the material and objective notion of armed conflict replaced the formal and subjective notion of war, another expression was used: the law of armed conflict (LOAC). However, the term international humanitarian law is used to cover the whole body of rules regulating all aspects of armed conflicts, including those rules that regulate the conduct of hostilities.[12]

8 Francis Fukuyama, As Origens da Ordem Política: dos tempos pré-humanos até a Revolução Francesa 19 (2013).
9 Ana Paula de Barcellos, A Eficácia Jurídica dos Princípios Constitucionais: o princípio da dignidade da pessoa humana 236 (2002).
10 Hans Joas, The Sacredness of the Person: a new genealogy of human rights 86 (2013).
11 Joanisval Brito Gonçalves, Tribunal de Nuremberg 1945–1946 207–208 (2004).
12 Nils Melzer, International Humanitarian Law: a comprehensive Introduction 56 (2016).

International humanitarian law: contemporary traits

The main sources and subjects of IHL are the classical sources and subjects of international law. The extent to which those rules apply depends upon whether the armed conflict in question qualifies as an international armed conflict or a non-international armed conflict. This means that treaties and customary law are the most important sources, while states, as well as international organizations, are the most important subjects. The inclusion of armed groups in the study of IHL is becoming ever more important because classical international armed conflicts, between two or more states, have become relatively rare in comparison to what we call internal or non-international armed conflicts, which are contested by a state and an armed group or between armed groups.

IHL is the result of a delicate tension between two major preoccupations: on one hand military necessity, which means that belligerents must have enough freedom to fight the war; and on the other, humanitarian considerations, which seek to minimize unnecessary suffering. Furthermore, IHL is the result of an equilibrium between two fundamental principles: the principle of military necessity and the principle of humanity. IHL seeks to achieve this equilibrium by regulating two aspects of warfare. The first aspect concerns the protection of individuals under the control of the enemy. It is often referred to as the Geneva Law, which regulates a wide range of issues that arise in armed conflict such as the treatment of prisoners of war, medical aid for wounded soldiers and the detention of civilians. A significant part of the Geneva Law also deals with the issue of occupation of a state's territory by another state. This is the law of occupation. The law of occupation sets the duties and rights of the occupying power in relation to the occupied population. It is particularly relevant in relation to the occupied Palestinian territories. The second part of IHL concerns the actual conduct of hostilities. To regulate the conduct of hostilities means setting the rules regarding who or what can be lawfully targeted and which arms or methods of warfare can be used (the Hague Law).

We should always keep in mind that international humanitarian law was conceived of as the legal regime that limited the behavior of parties in war-like situations. In the respective treaty laws, war-like situations are referred to as armed conflicts. Thus, IHL limits the behavior of parties in armed conflicts. IHL only applies to situations that have reached a special threshold of armed violence either between states, between states and certain non-state actors, or even between non-state actors. Therefore, IHL does not apply to internal disturbances or tensions falling below that threshold, such as riots, isolated and sporadic acts of violence, or acts of terror. In these latter situations, human rights law and domestic law applies. International humanitarian law recognizes two types of armed conflict: international armed conflicts (IACs) that occur between two or more states and non-international armed conflicts (NIACs) or civil wars, which usually occur within a state. As you might already know, both international and non-international armed conflicts are governed by a different set of rules as a result of political history.[13]

Traditionally, states expressed their intention to start a war through a formal declaration. Today, however, international armed conflict is presumed to exist as soon as a state uses armed force against another state, regardless of the reasons for the confrontation, the intensity of the violence or the existence of a formal declaration of war. The rules of IHL governing situations of international armed conflicts have been codified primarily in the 1907 Hague Regulations, the four 1949 Geneva Conventions, and the 1977 Additional Protocol I supplemented by customary international law. Armed conflicts derive their international character from the fact that they occur between states. Common Article 2 of the Geneva Conventions provides that "The present convention shall apply to all cases of declared war or of any other armed conflict which may arise between two or more of the high contracting parties. Even if the state of war is not recognized by one of them". An armed conflict exists whenever situations occur marked by armed force between states; protracted armed violence between governmental authorities and organized armed groups; or between such groups within a state. International humanitarian law applies from the initiation of such armed conflicts and extends beyond the cessation of hostilities until a general conclusion of peace is reached – or until, in the case of internal conflicts, a peaceful settlement is achieved. Until that moment, international humanitarian law continues to apply across the whole territory of the warring states or, in the case of internal conflicts, the whole territory under the control of a party, whether or not actual combat takes place there.[14]

The insights and practices of the human rights movement and the placing of humanitarianism within the context of international humanitarian law creates an important connection to human rights law and their interwoven moral revalidation, since the language of rights proves attractive in war-like zones. The convergence of interests between IHL and HRL has restored human dignity at large and allowed charitable work to be done, especially by NGOs. The moral code that underlies such a bond is impregnable.[15] There is a process of humanization driven by human rights norms and the principles of humanity. Although both branches have specific traits and scopes, it is undeniable that they also share a common nucleus of non-derogable rights and a common purpose of protecting human life and dignity, which makes their provisions mutually reinforcing.[16] Despite their

13 Nils Melzer, International Humanitarian Law: a comprehensive introduction chapter 2 (2016).

14 *The Prosecutor v. Dusko Tadic [Appeal Chamber]*, Decision of the Defense Motion for Interlocutory Appeal on Jurisdiction, Case No. IT-94–1, 1995 I.C.T.Y. §70 (October 2).

15 David Rieff, ***Humanitarianism in Crisis***, 81 Foreign Affairs Magazine no. 6, 113–114 (2002).

16 ***Juan Carlos Abella v. Argentina***, Case 11.137, Inter-Am. Comm'n H.R., Report No. 55/97, OEA/Ser.L/V/II.95, doc. 7 rev. at 271, §158 (1997); ***Prosecutor v. Anto Furundzija** [Trial Chamber]*, Case No. IT-95–17/1-T, 1998 I.C.T.Y. §183

divergences, these two branches share the same essence. "Under the influence of human rights, the law of war has been changing and acquiring a more humane face: the inroads made on the dominant role of reciprocity; the fostering of accountability; the formation, formulation and interpretation of rules".[17]

Universal human rights law, on the other hand, protects all persons against "arbitrary" deprivation of life, thus suggesting that the same standards apply to everyone, irrespective of their status under IHL. In such cases, the respective provisions are generally reconciled through the *lex specialis* principle, which states that the law more specifically crafted to address the situation at hand (*lex specialis*) overrides a competing, more general law (*lex generalis*). Accordingly, the ICJ has held that, while the human rights prohibition on arbitrary deprivation of life also applies in hostilities, the test of what constitutes arbitrary deprivation of life in the context of hostilities is determined by IHL, which is the *lex specialis* specifically designed to regulate such situations. Similarly, the question of whether the internment of a civilian or a prisoner of war by a state party within an international armed conflict amounts to arbitrary detention prohibited under human rights law must be determined based on the third and fourth Geneva Conventions, which constitute the *lex specialis* specifically designed to regulate internment in such situations.[18]

Geneva Conventions: rules and development

Wars have destructive consequences that go on long after they have come to an end. During the postwar period, there is not only mourning for human lives lost to violence but also social relations torn apart, cities and countryside torn to pieces. Even survivors bear eternal scars of destruction and violence. It is true that social life is never entirely free from violence or the threat of violence, but in war the degree of this threat and the accompanying fear surpass any imagination of it entertained by people who grow up in peacetime.[19]

The Geneva Conventions were conceived of after the 1862 publication of *A Memory of Solferino* by Henri Dunant, in which he wrote of the horrors he had witnessed in that battle. To alleviate them, he proposed the creation of neutral relief groups to provide humanitarian aid in time of war. In this way the Red Cross was born and the First Geneva Convention for the protection of wounded and sick soldiers on land in time of war was passed in 1864. The Second Convention, enacted in 1907, extended those protections to those who needed it on the sea. The Third Convention, guaranteeing decent treatment for prisoners of war, was

(December 10); and Report on Terrorism and Human Rights, Inter-Am. Comm'n H. R., OEA/Ser.L/V/II.116, doc. 5 rev. 1 corr., §108 (2002).

17 Merve Ozkan Borsa, *The Contribution of International Court of Justice to the Development of International Humanitarian Rules and Principles*, 36 Public and Private International law Bulletin no. 2, 83, 87 (2016).

18 Legality of the Threat or Use of Nuclear Weapons, Advisory Opinion, 1996 I.C.J. §25 (July 8).

19 Hans Joas, War and Modernity 111 (2003).

concluded in 1929. In 1949, all three Conventions were updated, and a fourth Convention was created, the basic purpose of which was to protect innocent civilians by deterring violations of the laws of war. To that end, the Convention also offered protection to combatants who followed the laws of war.[20] The First and Second Geneva Conventions, therefore, deal with the sick and wounded of armed forces on the field and on shipwrecks at sea, while the Third takes care of prisoners of war, and the Fourth protects civilians.

Nowadays, it is the Geneva Conventions that lead the way in international humanitarian law. The Common Article 2 of Geneva Conventions establishes that their provisions shall be implemented in peacetime and applied to all cases of declared war or of any other armed conflict that may arise between two or more states, even if the armed conflict is not recognized by one of them. It is also applied to all cases of partial or total occupation of the territory of a state, even if the said occupation meets with no armed resistance. Furthermore, an armed conflict exists "whenever there is a resort to armed force between States or protracted armed violence between governmental authorities and organized armed groups or between such groups within a State". As addressed by ICTY, the standard rule on international humanitarian law is that it covers all facts from the beginning of such armed conflicts to the termination of hostilities and when a general conclusion of peace is reached. In this case, no peace means that international humanitarian law continues to apply across the whole territory of the warring states.[21]

The difference between international armed conflict (between two states) and non-international armed conflict (between states and non-governmental armed groups or between such groups only) follows political history (rather than military necessity or humanitarian need), with rationales that are essentially the same for both types of conflict. The incorporation of the concept of non-international armed conflict (NIAC) in Common Article 3 of the 1949 Geneva Conventions was a landmark in the development and codification of this branch of international law. From that moment forward, organized armed groups, such as terrorist groups, have been considered "parties" to an armed conflict, with their own obligations under international law. Although the historical retrospective of international armed conflict is more extensive, non-international armed conflicts are the main concern in contemporary international law.[22]

Non-international armed conflicts are considered so because they occur between on the one hand the government forces of a sovereign state and on the other hand what are known as organized armed groups. Yet, in certain cases, a non-international armed conflict can also exist between two or more organized armed groups without the involvement of the state. This is because treaties applicable to non-international armed conflicts are much more limited than those

20 William Shawcross, Justice and the Enemy: Nuremberg, 9/11, and the Trial of Khalid Sheikh Mohammed 54 (2011).

21 *The Prosecutor v. Dusko Tadic [Appeal Chamber]*, Decision of the Defense Motion for Interlocutory Appeal on Jurisdiction, Case No. IT-94–1, 1995 I.C.T.Y. §70 (October 2).

22 Nils Melzer, International Humanitarian Law: a comprehensive introduction 53 (2016).

applicable to international armed conflicts. The behavior of the parties in a non-international armed conflict is limited mainly by the rules laid down in Common Article 3 of the 1949 Geneva Conventions and the 1977 Additional Protocol II. The inclusion of this provision in the Geneva Conventions after World War II was a major achievement. This provision contains a series of rights and duties that ensure a minimum level of protection to civilians and other persons who did not take, or are no longer taking, an active part in hostilities. The International Court of Justice has even held that Common Article 3 embodies elementary considerations of humanity. This implies that respect for Common Article 3 is supposed to make situations of war more humane.

Meanwhile, Protocol I of 1977 and Protocol III of 2005 deal with victim protection in international armed conflicts and the Adoption of an Additional Distinctive Emblem, respectively. Even the law of war is currently centered on humanity. This shift of values between the old and the new regime endeavors to build a bridge between power (generally assumed to reside in the hands of states) and transpolitical moralism. Thus, the legal humanity discourse provides an entire body of law full of principles and values as a global governance alternative.[23]

As is well known, the international community has banned the separatism between the law of armed conflicts and human rights law, which for a long time – throughout the 1940s and 1950s – were largely considered mutually exclusive. Their core reasoning was the non-binding force of the UDHR of 1948 and the different material scope – human rights law is applied in peacetime and international humanitarian law in times of armed conflict. However, after the adoption of the Fourth Geneva Convention on civilian protection during hostilities, a humanitarian element was added to the equation, and this principle of humanity has been enough to change the approach. Likewise, the two covenants of 1966 have designated human rights obligations as positive international law, further eroding the older understanding of human rights as a non-binding law (simply a moral exhortation to states). These humanitarian features have gradually established the common ground of HRL for the protection of the human person, shifting the IHL military-oriented and state-centered outlook to a person-oriented law.

One of the great advances of the last century in international law is the Fourth Geneva Convention, which came into play to create a legal regime to protect civilians in wartime and therefore improve upon the Fourth Hague Convention of 1907. The treaty sees civilians as either those who are in the hands of an adversarial element of the conflict or nationals of a belligerent state who are in the territory of the adversary, and also extended its reach, in Article 4, to protected persons – that is, those who "at a given moment and in any manner whatsoever, find themselves, in case of a conflict or occupation, in the hands of a Party to the conflict or Occupying Power of which they are not national". The principle of distinction between combatants and civilians became extremely important in international humanitarian law, the strength of which comes from a comprehensive framework made up of the Fourth Geneva Convention, Common Article 3,

23 Ruti G. Teitel, Humanity's Law 35 (2011).

the additional protocols and customs, all combined to ensure the protection of civilians in armed conflicts and occupations. Adopting a binary concept, Article 50 of Additional Protocol I considers a civilian anyone who is not legally defined as a combatant. If any doubt arises, the person's status is deemed civilian in order to afford as much protection as possible. Also, the civilian population does not lose its civilian character in the case of a combatant hiding or otherwise living in its midst.[24]

This understanding gives way to the assumption that civilians include all those who are innocent in the sense that they do not present a current threat or are not part of a recognized fighting group. F. M. Kamm adds that even if civilians take up arms and become a threat to combatants, they do not thereby acquire combatant status unless they are part of a recognized fighting group.[25] In this respect, the Inter-American Commission on Human Rights has specified in Common Article 3 that customary law principles applicable to all armed conflicts require the contending parties to refrain from directly attacking the civilian population and individual civilians, and to distinguish, when targeting, between civilians and combatants and other lawful military objectives. In order to spare civilians the effects of hostilities, other customary law principles require the attacking party to take precautions to avoid or minimize loss of civilian life or damage to civilian property incidental or collateral to attacks on military targets.[26]

Article 51 of Additional Protocol I includes the provision that forbids military attack on civilians. Such a situation is only admissible if the civilians take part in a military hostility. Under this provision, the principle of proportionality prohibits "attacks which may be expected to cause incidental loss of civilian life, injury to civilians, damage to civilian objects, or a combination thereof, which would be excessive in relation to the concrete and direct military advantage anticipated". However, precedents from the International Criminal Tribunal for the former Yugoslavia make an addendum, detailing that targeting civilians is an offense when not justified by military necessity. Therefore, attacks on civilians are forbidden when launched deliberately in the course of an armed conflict without military necessity as justification.[27] The principle of necessity justifies only those measures of military violence not specifically forbidden by international law that are relevant and proportionate to securing the rapid submission of the enemy with the least possible expenditure of human

24 Laurie R. Blank and Gregory P. Noone, International Law and Armed Conflicts: fundamental principles and contemporary challenges in the law of war 277–283 (2013).

25 Frances Myrna Kamm, The Moral Target: aiming at right conduct in war and other conflicts 83 (2012).

26 Report on Terrorism and Human Rights, Inter-Am. Comm'n H.R., OEA/Ser.L/V/II.116, doc. 5 rev. 1 corr., §101 (2002); and *Juan Carlos Abella v. Argentina,* Case 11.137, Inter-Am. Comm'n H.R., Report N° 55/97, OEA/Ser.L/V/II.95, doc. 7 rev. at 271, §177 (1997).

27 *Prosecutor v. Blaskic [Trial Chamber]*, Case No. IT-95–14-T, 2000 I.C.T.Y. §§180, 510 and 544 (March 03); and *Prosecutor v. Galic [Trial Chamber]*, Case No. IT-98–29-T, 2003 I.C.T.Y. §§42–44 (December 05).

and economic resources.[28] Military necessity means "doing what is necessary to achieve a war aim", and it acknowledges the potential for unavoidable civilian death and injury.[29]

Common Article 3 and the rule of civilian immunity

Despite the lack of a legal definition, it is widely accepted that non-international armed conflicts governed by Common Article 3 are those waged between state armed forces and non-state armed groups, or between two or more non-state armed groups.[30] Two criteria are considered indispensable for classifying a situation of violence as a Common Article 3 armed conflict, thus distinguishing it from internal disturbances or tensions that remain below the threshold. First, the existence of parties in the conflict, with a minimum requisite of organization entailing, at least, a command structure, disciplinary rules and mechanisms within the armed group; the existence of headquarters; the ability to procure, transport and distribute arms; the group's ability to plan, co-ordinate and carry out military operations, including troop movements and logistics; its ability to negotiate and conclude agreements such as ceasefire or peace accords; and so forth. Second, the intensity of violence involved, which is measured by the number, duration and intensity of individual confrontations, the type of weapons and other military equipment used, the number and caliber of munitions fired, the number of persons and types of forces partaking in the fighting, the number of casualties, the extent of material destruction, and the number of civilians fleeing combat zones.[31]

Common Article 3 simply identifies a number of key duties and prohibitions providing a minimum of protection to all persons who are not, or who are no longer, taking an active part in the hostilities. In return, each party to any armed conflict that is not of an international character must apply the provision minimally. To this end, some acts are prohibited at any time and in any place whatsoever with respect to the above-mentioned persons: (a) violence to life and person, in particular murder of all kinds, mutilation, cruel treatment and torture; (b) taking of hostages; (c) outrages upon personal dignity, in particular, humiliating and degrading treatment; (d) the passing of sentences and the carrying out of executions without previous judgment pronounced by a regularly constituted court affording all the judicial guarantees which are recognized as indispensable by civilized peoples.

Common Article 3 permeates all four Geneva Conventions and defines certain rules to be applied in the armed conflicts of a non-international character. It is

28 Report on Terrorism and Human Rights, Inter-Am. Comm'n H.R., OEA/Ser.L/V/II.116, doc. 5 rev. 1 corr., §110 (2002).

29 Laurie R. Blank and Gregory P. Noone, International Law and Armed Conflicts: Fundamental Principles and Contemporary Challenges in the Law of War 312 (2013).

30 Jelena Pejic, *The Protective Scope of Common Article 3: More than Meets the Eye*, 93 International Review of the Red Cross no. 881, 189, 191 (2011).

31 *Prosecutor v. Ramush Haradinaj et al [Trial Chamber]*, Case No. IT-04–84-T, 2008 I.C.T.Y. §§49–60 (April 3).

unquestionable that, in the event of international armed conflicts, these rules form a minimum yardstick to be added to other rules that also apply to international conflicts. Also, this article incorporates rules that reflect "elementary considerations of humanity".[32] Therefore, it has been settled by international courts that Common Article 3 is as binding as international customary law regardless of the character of the armed conflict (non-international/international), and it is not restricted to the territory of a single state, confirming its extraterritoriality effect.[33]

International humanitarian law has put great importance on protecting civilian populations caught up in conflict zones and suffering the horrors of war without being part of the combat. This protection involves both positive and negative obligations. One example of a negative obligation is the British army's bombing policy at the beginning of hostilities in the Second World War. Initially, it was not directed at civilians – the targets were military – but the bombing was inaccurate and civilians who lived or worked near military installations were often hit. However, inevitable civilian casualties were accepted as a reasonable price to pay for helping to defeat Hitler. This situation amplified to the point when a conscious decision between abandoning bombing altogether or intentionally continuing to bomb civilians had to be made. The bombing of Germany killed 593,000 non-combatants, Churchill being an advocate of the bombing strategy.[34] While we still have the double effect doctrine, this scenario would no longer be acceptable according to Common Article 3 and Geneva Conventions provisions on civilian protection. States now have the negative obligation to refrain from hitting civilians in military operations.

The harm that civilians experience is unimaginable, and the discourse of peace in contemporary international law can never justify suffering or eliminate its enduring burden. In addition, ignoring the misery experienced by civilians is also forbidden in Common Article 3, which requires states to take action to end such suffering. In fact, the word "peace" arouses disdain and uneasiness among people who have gone through wars and its hellishness. This is because "peace" has so often been employed to justify foreign policies that are not defensive at all. The word has become devalued in such a way that people do not necessarily pay attention to discourses about interruptions to peace – or threats of it.[35]

For this reason, in the 1990s, when the United Nation Security Council made the statement – intended to be of ground-breaking importance – that violations of international humanitarian law constitute a threat to international peace and security and that the establishment of the war crime tribunal for Yugoslavia would contribute to the restoration and maintenance of peace, the community was not impressed. After all, as stated by a Bosnian woman who had been raped,

32 Case Concerning Military and Paramilitary Activities In and Against Nicaragua (Nicaragua v. United States of America), 1986 I.C.J. §218 (June 27).

33 *The Prosecutor v. Jean-Paul Akayesu [Chamber I]*, Case No. ICTR-96-4-T, 1998 I.C.T.R. §608 (September 2); and *The Prosecutor v. Dusko Tadic [Appeal Chamber]*, Decision of the Defense Motion for Interlocutory Appeal on Jurisdiction, Case No. IT-94-1, 1995 I.C.T.Y. §155 (October 2).

34 Jonathan Glover, Humanity: A Moral History of the 20th Century 70–77 (2nd ed. 2012).

35 Hans Joas, War and Modernity 125 (2003).

> In the end, I get a bit tired of constantly having to prove. We had to prove genocide, we had to prove that our women are being raped, that our children have been killed. Every time I take a statement from these women, and you journalists want to interview them, I imagine those people disinterested, sitting in a nice house with a hamburger and beer, switching channels on TV. I really don't know what else has to happen here, what further suffering the Muslims have to undergo … to make the so-called civilized world react.[36]

Not doing anything is also inadmissible under Common Article 3.

To overcome the suffering that occurs in true combat zones, the moral exhortation to relentlessly repudiate vile actions becomes a central part of the fabric of humanitarian law and human rights law.[37] The principle of distinction plays an important role in this. It is based on the recognition that "the only legitimate object which States should endeavor to accomplish during war is to weaken the military forces of the enemy", whereas "the civilian population and individual civilians shall enjoy general protection against dangers arising from military operations." Therefore, the parties to an armed conflict must "at all times distinguish between the civilian population and combatants and between civilian objects and military objectives and accordingly shall direct their operations only against military objectives". Accordingly, parties to the conflict must distinguish between military objectives and civilians and launch attacks only against the former. Likewise, it must distinguish between persons who, by their actions, constitute an imminent threat of death or serious injury, or a threat of committing a particularly serious crime involving a grave threat to life, and persons who do not present such a threat. Force is only justified against the former.[38]

Basically, in international armed conflict, all persons who are neither members of a party's armed forces during a conflict nor participants in a *levée en masse* are entitled to protection against direct attack unless they take a direct part in hostilities. In non-international armed conflict, all persons who are not members of state armed forces or organized armed groups of a party to the conflict are civilians and therefore entitled to protection against direct attack unless they take a direct part in hostilities.[39]

Principles of necessity and humanity

The fundamental principles of international humanitarian law are universal directives to nations and binding on states since they stem from the basic standards of the Geneva Conventions and the additional protocols. These principles determine,

36 Jonathan Glover, Humanity: A Moral History of the 20th Century 05 (2nd ed. 2012).

37 Legality of the Threat or Use of Nuclear Weapons, Advisory Opinion, 1996 I.C.J. §83 (July 8).

38 Report on Terrorism and Human Rights, Inter-Am. Comm'n H.R., OEA/Ser.L/V/II.116, doc. 5 rev. 1 corr., §§99, 111 (2002).

39 Jelena Pejic, *The Protective Scope of Common Article 3: More than Meets the Eye*, 93 International Review of the Red Cross no. 881, 189, 222–223 (2011).

limit and channel the conduct of international actors in armed conflicts. By this token, a proper interpretation of them is required in order to show how they complement each other within the scope of a refraining act that might endanger the life and integrity of the civilian population and their property.[40]

International humanitarian law is based on a balance between considerations of military necessity and of humanity. On the one hand it recognizes that, in order to overcome an adversary in wartime, it may be necessary to cause death, injury and destruction and to impose more severe security measures than would be permissible in peacetime. On the other hand IHL also makes it clear that military necessity does not give the belligerents carte blanche to wage unrestricted war. Rather, considerations of humanity impose certain limits on the means and methods of warfare and require that those who have fallen into enemy hands be treated humanely at all times. The balance between military necessity and humanity finds more specific expression in the core principles of humanitarian law. The principle of humanity complements and inherently limits the principle of necessity by forbidding those measures of violence that are not necessary, relevant and proportionate to the achievement of a definitive military advantage.[41]

The first principle is that military necessity does not detach its actions from the scrutiny of law. Consequently, all military conduct should be controlled, the necessary spectrum understood as achieving, as quickly as possible, the complete or partial submission of the enemy. The military action that does not seek to fulfill this objective is deemed unlawful, especially when it involves wanton killing and destruction. Necessity has been a bulwark for the law of war since before the world wars of the last century, and now it has to be applied in accord with concerns for humanity. Hence, the principle of military necessity exists in delicate balance with the second core principle of international humanitarian law, the principle of humanity.[42]

It is necessity that generally allows the use of violence and its justification to the limit of their acceptability in order to achieve the end of the conflict or a great advantage. The interesting thing about the principle of necessity is that it was applied at the Nuremberg trials as a defense maneuver. Not only did German defendants use it to justify their hideous acts, but the United States also cited it in its decision to bomb Hiroshima, arguing that it was a necessity to save uncountable human lives, and saying that eschewing Japan's invasion would lead to another significant number of military casualties. Since the Nuremberg trials rejected the justification, a new foundation of international law of war was established that stressed the imperative approach of the principle of humanity. Nevertheless, necessity is still a core principle of law in armed conflicts, even if the recent statute of the International Criminal Court offers it as an exculpatory feature of

40 *Jose Isabel Salas Galindo and Others v. United States,* Case 10.573, Inter-Am. Comm'n H.R., Report No. 121/18, OEA/Ser.L/V/II.169, doc. 138, §§342–345 (2018).

41 Report on Terrorism and Human Rights, Inter-Am. Comm'n H.R., OEA/Ser.L/V/II.116, doc. 5 rev. 1 corr., §110 (2002).

42 Laurie R. Blank and Gregory P. Noone, International Law and Armed Conflicts: Fundamental Principles and Contemporary Challenges in the Law of War 37 (2013).

international criminal justice (Article 31).[43] Yet, the United Nations conveyed in its annual report on Afghanistan in 2010 that when a

> raid by military forces is conducted against a legitimate military objective, such as combatants, it is largely governed by the same standards of international humanitarian law that govern other attacks, including rules and principles pertaining to the verification of the target as a military target, proportionality, precautions in attack and military necessity.[44]

Common Article 3 of the Fourth Geneva Convention conveys the principle of humanity, which enshrines the minimum applicable to all armed conflicts. The Geneva Conventions, by discussing civilians, slowly opened the door to new connections because of the inevitable link between "civilians" and "human beings". "Elementary considerations of humanity" are "illustrative of a general principle of international law" and "should be fully used when interpreting and applying loose international rules" of treaty law.[45] Nevertheless, the principle reference occurred long before in the preamble to the Hague Convention IV of 1907, and also later in Article 1 of Additional Protocol I of the Geneva Conventions.

Humanity implies a moral force. In international law, humanity is interpreted in terms of people's security and well-being. Therefore, a universally applicable and objective definition of humanity is proposed to help clarify the complex relationships between humanity, inhumanity, the capacity for armed violence, the restraint of armed violence, and international law. The word humanity has rather vague associations. Nevertheless, there is general agreement as to its principle element of active goodness –its *ethos* of love deeply connected to the sacredness of human life and universal respect for all fellow human beings.[46] Not only is it crucially about the elimination or mitigation of unnecessary suffering to any human being, it also affirms the immunity of civilian populations and serves as an essential counterbalance to the principle of military necessity.[47]

Regarding these two intertwined principles, humanity does not always govern necessity as the theory suggests. Daily, reality and pragmatism determine the decision-making process in international politics. Even so, some scholars argue that international pragmatism should be mitigated by idealism, especially in wartime when necessity should be overshadowed by the general principle of law, *salus populi suprema lex esto* – the welfare of the people should be the supreme law.[48]

43 Joanisval Brito Gonçalves, Tribunal de Nuremberg 1945–1946 210–212 (2004).
44 United Nations, Afghanistan Annual Report on Protection of Civilians in Armed Conflicts, 2010, 29 (March, 2011).
45 *The Prosecutor v. Kupreskic et al. [Trial Chamber]*, Case No. IT-95–16-T, 2000 I.C. T.Y. §524 (January 14).
46 Robin Coupland, *Humanity: What Is It and How Does It Influence International Law?*, 83 IRRC, December, 971–972 (2001).
47 Laurie R. Blank and Gregory P. Noone, International Law and Armed Conflicts: fundamental principles and contemporary challenges in the law of war 41 (2013).
48 Hildebrando Accioly et al, Manual Direito Internacional Público 448 (São Paulo: Saraiva, 20th edition, 2012).

Therefore, between necessity and humanity we shall insert a third principle that serves to moderate necessity based on humanity – the principle of proportionality. The concept of proportionality is intrinsic to the complementary and customary law principles of necessity and humanity that underlie the law governing the conduct of all armed conflicts.[49]

Proportionality is also a very relevant principle in international humanitarian law. To fight justly (*jus in bello*) two points are considered: civilian immunity and proportionality, both serving as a means to reduce or eliminate excessive harm and save as many civilian lives as possible. Proportionality is weighed by considering the misdeed (immediate harm and permanent injury to the interests of humanity) and the contribution that this misdeed makes to ending the armed conflict. This is a difficult criterion to apply. It is a calculation of costs and benefits in terms that suggest civilians might have lesser value than the victory that is being sought, since it is imperative for soldiers to try to win the wars they are fighting with all the assets at their disposal.[50] After all, the legal provision on targeting civilians does not extend to an entire prohibition of civilian casualties, and the law, interestingly, has always tolerated some civilian deaths as a consequence of military maneuvers.[51]

The principle of proportionality has its modern formulation inscribed in Additional Protocol I of the Geneva Conventions. Envisaging the protection of civilians in general, it forbids any "attack which may be expected to cause incidental loss of civilian life, injury to civilians, damage to civilian objects, or a combination thereof, which would be excessive in relation to the concrete and direct military advantage anticipated". Subsequently, some provisions of the Protocol raise a flag to precautions that must not be overlooked by military activities. There are restrictions on what can be considered indispensable in order to achieve a desirable military gain during an attack operation, for instance. It can be said that the principle of necessity looks to the lawful military objectives of the armed conflict, while proportionality looks to humanitarian protections of noncombatants, which means that the balance of the two is a central concern of international law.[52]

Contemporary international humanitarian law vigorously applies the combination of these three principles, especially with regard to military responses to terrorism in the international arena. The Inter-American Commission Report on Terrorism underpins that international humanitarian law

> imposes a general limitation on military operations by requiring that parties to an armed conflict respect the principles of necessity, distinction, proportionality and

49 Report on Terrorism and Human Rights, Inter-Am. Comm'n H.R., OEA/Ser.L/V/II.116, doc. 5 rev. 1 corr., §110 (2002).

50 Michael Walzer, Just and Unjust Wars 129 (2006).

51 Laurie R. Blank and Gregory P. Noone, International Law and Armed Conflicts: Fundamental Principles and Contemporary Challenges in the Law of War 51 (2013).

52 *Jose Isabel Salas Galindo and Others v. United States,* Case 10.573, Inter-Am. Comm'n H.R., Report N° 121/18, OEA/Ser.L/V/II.169, doc. 138, §§360–364 (2018).

> humanity. These principles seek to limit the sufferings of the victims of armed conflicts, including the unnecessary loss of lives.[53]

The rule of proportionality applies in peacetime as well as in situations of armed conflict. It has a different meaning and different implications in each context, though.

Contemporary wars and their *hostis humani generis*

In 2002, the Council of Europe issued some guidelines regarding terrorism, a contemporary form of warfare: "States are under the obligation to take the measures needed to protect the fundamental rights of everyone within their jurisdiction against terrorist acts, especially the right to life." "All measures taken by States to fight terrorism must respect human rights and the principle of the rule of law." "In their fight against terrorism, States may never act in breach of peremptory norms of international law nor in breach of international humanitarian law, where applicable."[54] In 2001, the United Nations Security Council issued Resolution 1373, which called upon all states to comply with all obligations under international law pursuant to taking "the necessary steps to prevent the commission of terrorist acts".[55]

Paul Butler once asserted that there is a big difference between terrorism and traditional war. The former is illegal while the latter is legal; the perpetrators and the intended victims of the former are often civilians, whereas in the latter the perpetrators and victims are both soldiers.[56] But the legal and practical difficulties that have arisen as a result of changes in the contemporary security environment have caused confusion and uncertainty not only about the distinction between armed conflict and law enforcement but also about the traditional categorization of persons as civilians and combatants and the temporal and geographic delimitation of the "battlefield". The most urgent humanitarian need, however, is not to adopt new rules but rather to ensure compliance with the existing legal framework.[57]

Although terrorism might be efficient according to detached consequentialist analysis, the fundamental critique turns on ground that is central in the law of humanity: morality. Terrorism may be rational, but it is also evil. The immorality of terrorism lies in the risk that it poses to the public at large; the powerlessness of people put at risk; and the instrumentality of attacking innocent people in pursuit of an alleged political goal. Nevertheless, it is important to separate immorality and the killing of innocent people because they are not always mutually inconsistent.

53 Report on Terrorism and Human Rights, Inter-Am. Comm'n H.R., OEA/Ser.L/V/II.116, doc. 5 rev. 1 corr., §§99, 110 (2002).

54 The Council of Europe, Human rights and the fight against terrorism 09–13 (2005).

55 S.C. Res. 1373 (2001), U.N. Doc. S/RES/1373, 2(b) (September 28, 2001).

56 Paul Butler, *Terrorism and Utilitarianism: Lessons From, and For, Criminal Law*, 93 Supreme Court Review no. 1, 04 (2003).

57 Nils Melzer, International Humanitarian Law: a comprehensive introduction 46 (2016).

There are cases in which taking innocent lives in pursuit of an urgent objective may be warranted. Moral standing in this regard is about legitimacy and not about right. In the context of international law, politics and morality matter.[58]

While killing combatants is still a huge point of controversy between human rights and humanitarian law, the main focus is on a more advanced perspective of killing noncombatants, which in two sorts of situation is tolerable in the law of war. Generally, when military necessity demands a conduct of double effect directed at military and nonmilitary targets, we have to use utilitarian arguments to legitimize it. To perform an act with evil consequences (noncombatant casualties), the good effect ought to be sufficiently good to compensate for the evil effect. However, in the modern understanding of humanitarian law, the double effect theory is defensible only when the good end is achieved and the evil consequence is reduced as much as possible. Despite the utilitarian grounds of the theory, there must be some kind of commitment to save as many civilian lives as possible, since the principle of proportionality demands moral maneuvering to make it appropriate.

There is a second situation where the killing of innocent people can occur fairly. It is when we have the ongoing self-determination of a group or people. As stated in the Protocol of 1977 of the War Convention and United Nations Resolutions 1514 and 2908, the armed struggle is justified against (i) alien occupation, (ii) colonial domination and (iii) racist regimes. Thus, these causes are just causes for a fight and they must observe the same rules of proportionality and civilian immunity as an armed conflict. However, if deliberation and a nonviolent approach can go no further and the oppression is such that it justifies turning to violence as a last resort, then the moral issue establishes that the weak have the right to fight dirty in order to have a chance against the strong. If we oblige the weak to fight clean, the strong will always win. The only tactic that converts weakness into strength is terrorism – that is, hitting the enemy at its most vulnerable point, its civilian population.[59]

This second scenario presents the lesser evil argument. In order to overcome the greater evil of injustice and oppression, the weak must be entitled to resort to the lesser evil of terrorist violence, otherwise the weak will be condemned to an eternity of subjugation. However, that justifiable targeting of innocent people is restricted to the right of self-determination of a people or group under alien occupation, colonial domination or a racist regime. The lesser evil argument does not apply to nihilist terrorism. This aims to attack the enemy, but it intentionally chooses to attack noncombatants rather than combatants in order to have more humiliating impact and destroy national morale. There is no commitment to spare civilian lives: the method is the random murder of innocent people.

58 Paul Butler, *Terrorism and Utilitarianism: Lessons From, and For, Criminal Law*, 93 Supreme Court Review no. 1, 07–13 (2003).

59 G.A. Res. 1514 (XV), *Declaration on the Granting of Independence to Colonial Countries and Peoples*, U.N. Doc. A/RES/1514 (XV) (Dec. 14, 1960); and G.A. Res. 2908 (XXVII), *Implementation of the Declaration on the Granting of Independence to Colonial Countries and Peoples*, U.N. Doc. A/RES/2908 (XXVII) (Nov. 02, 1972).

It has become commonplace to argue that contemporary wars, especially the global war on terror, hinder a new balance being found between liberty and security. The moral liability we share on our actions supports a moral claim that undermines individual rights we normally respect for the sake of collective protection against terrorist menace. Political convictions start to overlap with personal ones so that although we may not subject strangers to risks of grave injury we would not accept for ourselves, we may tolerate it in the political policies we endorse.[60]

Closing considerations

The systematic use of remote-controlled drones for counterterrorist operations in countries such as Afghanistan, Pakistan and Yemen raise questions as to the applicability of IHL to these operations and, consequently, the rules governing the use of lethal force against the persons targeted. Where IHL is applicable, the systematic use of drones raises concerns with regard to the reliability of the targeting information used, the exposure of the civilian population to incidental harm, and the inability of the attacker to care for the wounded or to capture rather than kill. Another relatively recent development is the expansion of military operations into cyberspace, the so-called "fifth domain of warfare", beyond land, sea, air and space. While it is generally uncontested that IHL would also apply to cyber operations conducted in relation to an existing armed conflict, it is unclear whether cyber operations, in and of themselves, could give rise to an armed conflict and, thus, trigger the applicability of IHL. Also, once cyber operations are governed by IHL, questions arise as to what exactly amounts to "attacks" – defined in IHL as "acts of violence" – in cyberspace, and how the proportionality of "collateral damage" to civilian infrastructure should be assessed, particularly in view of the fact that military and civilian computer networks are generally interconnected. This ongoing process, however, should not lead to the perception of a legal void in this "fifth domain" but must build on the premise that existing international law fully applies in cyberspace. In situations of armed conflict, that includes all relevant rules and principles of IHL.[61]

International humanitarian law and human rights law emerged on the international arena at different times, under different circumstances and with different aims. Even the recent editions of the UDHR and Geneva Conventions were clearly not inspired in the same way. Although sharing common ground – a principle of humanity and all it entails – there was an understanding that they would have overlapping areas of application: in effect, that human rights would not be applied in situations of armed conflicts, but in times of peace, since peace was what the United Nations has struggled to achieve.[62]

60 Ronald Dworkin, Justice for Hedgehogs 99–106 (2011).
61 Nils Melzer, International Humanitarian Law: a comprehensive introduction 42–43 (2016).
62 Robert Kolb, *Human Rights Law and International Humanitarian Law Between 1945 and the Aftermath of the Teheran Conference of 1968*, in Research Handbook on Human Rights and Humanitarian Law 35, 39–40 (2013).

Yet there is a resounding recollection of war in the debates on the Universal Declaration. Since then, the international community has acknowledged that human rights are relevant in armed conflict, as ascertained by the United Nations General Assembly of December 3, 1953, when Resolution 804 invoked human rights in the context of the Korean armed conflict[63]:

> *Having considered* the item "Question of atrocities committed by the North Korean and Chinese Communist forces against United Nations prisoners of war in Korea" [...], *Recalling* the basic legal requirements for humane treatment of prisoners of war and civilians in connection with the conduct of hostilities are established by general international law and find authoritative reaffirmation in the Geneva Convention of 1929 and 1949 relative to the treatment of prisoner of war and in Geneva Convention of 1949 relative the protection of civilians in times of war, *Recalling* that these Conventions also embody precise and detailed provision for giving effect to the basic legal requirements referred to above, and that these provisions, to the extent that they have not become binding as treaty law, have been accorded most general support by international community, *Desiring* to secure general and full observance of the requirements of international law and of universal standards of human decency, (1) *Express its grave concern* at reports and information that North Korea and Chinese Communist forces have, in a large number of instances, employed inhuman practices against the heroic soldiers of forces under the United Nations Command in Korea and against the civilian population of Korea; (2) *Condemns* the commission by any governments or authorities of murder, mutilation, torture, and other atrocious acts against captured military personnel or civilian populations, as a violation of rules of international law and basic standards of conduct and morality and as affronting human rights and the dignity and worth of the human person.

The same happened a few years later when the Soviet army invaded Hungary and the United Nations General Assembly, on December 12, 1958, issued Resolution 1312 invoking human rights boundaries in ongoing armed conflict:

> *Again calls upon* the Union of Soviet Socialists Republics and the present authorities in Hungary to desist from repressive measures against the Hungarian people and to respect the liberty and political independence of Hungary and the Hungarian people's enjoyment of fundamental rights and freedoms.[64]

63 G.A. Res. 804 (VIII), *Question of atrocities committed by the North Korean and Chinese Communist forces against United Nations prisoners of war in Korea*, U.N. Doc. A/RES/804/VIII (Dec. 3, 1953).

64 G.A. Res. 1312 (XIII), *The Situation in Hungary*, U.N. Doc. A38/49 (Dec. 12, 1958).

Not least, on 19 December 1968, the United Nations General Assembly designated 1968 as the International Year for Human Rights by Resolution 2441 and, by Resolution 2442, confirmed and endorsed the Final Act of the International Conference on Human Rights held at Teheran some months earlier. Thereafter, Resolutions 2443 and 2444 received edits that embodied respect for and implementation of human rights in occupied territories and armed conflicts, respectively. These United Nations resolutions therefore expressly reflect the provisions of the Geneva Convention of 1949 regarding the protection of civilian people in wartime, but still designate respect and implementation of human rights in conflict zones as concerns deriving from "the violation of human rights in Arab territories occupied by Israel, (…) the disregard of fundamental freedoms and human rights in occupied territories, (…) acts of destroying homes of the Arab civilian population inhabiting areas occupied by Israel". In response, the United Nations called upon the Israeli government

> to respect and implement the Universal Declaration of Human Rights and the Geneva Conventions of 12 August 1949 in occupied territories, (d) affirmed the unalienable rights of all inhabitants who have left their homes as a result of the outbreak of hostilities in the Middle East to return home, resume their normal life, recover their property and homes, and rejoin their families according to the provisions of the Universal Declaration of Human Rights.[65]

By the same token, Resolution 2444 recognizes the necessity of applying basic humanitarian principles in all armed conflicts, such as the prohibition "to launch attacks against the civilian population" and the distinction between people "taking part in the hostilities and members of the civilian population to the effect that the latter be spared as much as possible". To fulfill the "need for additional humanitarian international conventions or other appropriate legal instrument to ensure the better protection of civilians, prisoners and combatants in all armed conflicts", the Final Act of the International Conference on Human Rights in Teheran is held as a legal instrument for human rights respect in armed conflicts.[66] In sum, even during periods of armed conflict, principles of humanity must prevail, either by international humanitarian law or by human rights law.

65 G.A. Res. 2443 (XXIII), *Respect for and implementation of human rights in occupied territories*, U.N. Doc. A/RES/2443/XXIII (Dec. 19, 1968).

66 G.A. Res. 2444 (XXIII), *Respect for human rights in armed conflicts*, U.N. Doc. A/RES/2444/XXIII (Dec. 19, 1968).

5 The interplay between international humanitarian law and human rights law

Initial thoughts

In international legal order there are innumerable bodies of law that belong to the web of human rights law. International humanitarian law, for its part, also has some statutory instruments under its wing. As was discussed in chapter 2, all bodies of law pertain to the general and complex international legal system, with its crucial traits of unity, wholeness and coherence. Nevertheless, each branch of international law covers specific aims. While HRL always deals with the inherent rights of the person to be protected against abusive and arbitrary actions, the IHL regulates the conduct of parties in an armed conflict.

Since human rights law applies at all times, it is based on a principle of universality and therefore possesses, at first glance, a *lex generalis* character. International humanitarian law has a narrower scope of application, concerning only factual cases within the spectrum of armed conflict, thus acquiring a sense of *lex specialis*. Although inherently distinct from one another, their respective rules are not necessarily inconsistent, and it is taken for granted today that international humanitarian law and international human rights law maintain multiple subtle relationships between their respective bodies, with one branch of the law complementing, strengthening or filling the other's gaps. From a theoretical standpoint, both branches of the law have some shared or common legal ground on which they can interact.[1]

After all, both share the essential principle of humanity. Human rights and humanitarian law share a common ideal – protection of the dignity and integrity of the person – and many of their guarantees are identical, such as the protection of the right to life, freedom from torture and ill treatment, the protection of family rights, economic, and/or social rights.[2] While human rights law has been fairly recently developed and contains a lot of national, cultural and religious

1 Robert Kolb, *Human Rights Law and International Humanitarian Law Between 1945 and the Aftermath of the Teheran Conference of 1968*, in Research Handbook on Human Rights and Humanitarian Law 35, 35 (2013).

2 Cordula Droege, *The Interplay between International Humanitarian Law and International Human Rights Law in Situations of Armed Conflict*, 40 Israeli Law Review no. 2, 310, 312 (2007).

DOI: 10.4324/9781003170778-5

antecedents, humanitarian law has served as "an important historical foundation for the development of human rights law, resting on the notions of protection of human dignity inherent" in the law of armed conflicts.[3] The United Nations Charter preamble is thus addressed to all international bodies of law, including humanitarian law and human rights law. It says that one of the four key purposes of the United Nations is "to reaffirm faith in fundamental human rights, in the dignity and worth of the human person, in the equal rights of men and women and of nations large and small".

The question consequently arises, as we seek to analyze the possible ways in which the interplay between human rights law and humanitarian law works in practice, whether there is conflict and tension or synergy between these regimes. There is some dispute over the matter, even though legal authorities of international law overwhelmingly hold that human rights law is applicable alongside international humanitarian law in combat situations on the basis of their being harmoniously convergent bodies of law. Two main concepts inform their interaction: complementarity between their norms in most cases, and the prevalence of the more specific norm when there is contradiction between the two. The question is which body of law is the more specific for the situation.

Accordingly, the ICJ has held that, while the human rights prohibition on arbitrary deprivation of life also applies in hostilities, the test of what constitutes arbitrary deprivation of life in the context of hostilities is determined by IHL, which is the *lex specialis* specifically designed to regulate such situations. Similarly, the question of whether the internment of a civilian or a prisoner of war by a state that is party to an international armed conflict amounts to arbitrary detention prohibited under human rights law must be determined based on the Third and Fourth Geneva Conventions, which constitute the *lex specialis* specifically designed to regulate internment in such situations.[4] *Lex specialis* sets the priority norm, and that would be respect for life regarding the targeting of combatants. IHL, as a special regime, overlaps HRL, according to the advisory opinion on the Legality of the Threat or Use of Nuclear Weapons.

However, some years later, the ICJ provided a different understanding in the advisory opinion on the Legal Consequences of the Construction of a Wall in the Occupied Palestinian Territory, rejecting the Cartesian view of human rights law governing in peacetime and humanitarian law governing in wartime and arguing that, as *lex specialis,* humanitarian rules override human rights law. The Court now holds that human rights are duly protected in situations of armed conflict in line with the standards of human rights law, and the actions of the perpetrators must be justified by both humanitarian law and human rights law. Therefore, the *lex specialis* serves to evaluate whether human rights violations are arbitrary or not, particularly taking into consideration the military necessity and proportionality of

3 Laurie R. Blank and Gregory P. Noone, International Law and Armed Conflicts: Fundamental Principles and Contemporary Challenges in the Law of War 27 (2013).

4 Legality of the Threat or Use of Nuclear Weapons, Advisory Opinion, 1996 I.C.J. §25 (July 8).

actions. In this sense, "the Court considers that the protection offered by human rights conventions does not cease in case of armed conflict".[5] And in the case concerning Armed Activities on the Territory of the Congo, international human rights prevailed, especially with respect to Congo's civilian population, in order to condemn Uganda as negligent in its international legal obligations.[6]

In summary, the Court outlines three possible situations coming out of the interplay between these two branches of law: some rights may be exclusively matters of international humanitarian law; others may be exclusively matters of human rights law; and others may be matters of both these branches of international law.[7] The separation between the branches mainly takes into account the difficulties of a shift from a military-oriented law to a protected person-oriented law. Therefore, the analysis is made rule by rule and context by context, and not broadly as a whole body of law prevailing over another. As such, there are no longer any doubts regarding the co-application of IHL and HRL. However, the grey zone that exists between both bodies of law in deciphering how this co-applicability functions in the day-to-day judicial realm remains unsettling, challenging and ongoing.

Regarding the United Nations Resolution 2444 of 19 December 1968, human rights are officially inserted in the legal order of armed conflicts. The Final Act of the International Conference on Human Rights in Teheran upheld that the "primary aim of United Nations in the sphere of human rights is the achievement by each individual of the maximum freedom and dignity". Furthermore, it urges

> all peoples and governments to dedicate themselves to the principles enshrined in the Universal Declaration of Human Rights and to redouble their efforts to provide for all human beings a life consonant with freedom and dignity and conducive to physical, mental, social and spiritual welfare.[8]

Specifically regarding human rights in armed conflicts, the Final Act in provision XXIII says:

> *Considering* that peace is the underlying condition for the full observance of human rights and war is their negation, *Believing* that the purpose of the United Nations Organization is to prevent all conflicts and to institute an effective system of peaceful settlement of disputes, *Observing* that nevertheless armed conflicts continue to plague humanity, *Considering,* also, that the widespread violence and brutality of our times, including massacres, summary

5 Legal Consequences of the Construction of a Wall in the Occupied Palestinian Territory, Advisory Opinion, 2004 I.C.J. §§105–106 (July 9).
6 Case Concerning Armed Activities on the Territory of the Congo (Democratic Republic of the Congo v. Uganda), 2005 I.C.J. §§217–220 (December 19).
7 Legal Consequences of the Construction of a Wall in the Occupied Palestinian Territory, Advisory Opinion, 2004 I.C.J. §106 (July 9).
8 United Nations, Final Act of the International Conference on Human Rights, Teheran, 22 April to 13 May 1968, A/Conf.32/41, Sales No. E68.XIV.2, 04–05 (1968).

> executions, tortures, inhumane treatment of prisoners, killing of civilians in armed conflicts and the use of chemical and biological means of warfare, including napalm bombing, erode human rights and engender counter-brutality, *Convinced* that even during the periods of armed conflicts, humanitarian principles must prevail.[9]

The United Nations Teheran Conference of 1968 on human rights in armed conflicts, Resolution 2444, and the two covenants of 1966 – on civil and political rights (Covenant II) and on social, economic and cultural rights (Covenant I) – turn human rights law into a full-fledged positive law. The question of the application of this branch of law in times of armed conflict now appears at this level of positive law. These factors, along with others, inspire a convergence and shape cooperation between both branches of the law.[10]

On December 9, 1970, the United Nations General Assembly enacted Resolution 2675, which, with clear connections to Resolution 2444, establishes basic international principles for the protection of civilian populations in armed conflicts "to ensure the better protection of human rights in armed conflicts of all types". Eight principles have been issued: (1) fundamental human rights fully applied in situations of armed conflict; (2) distinction between people actively taking part in the hostilities and civilian populations; (3) precaution and maximum effort in military operations to spare civilian populations from ravages of war and eschew injury, loss or damage to them; (4) civilian population should not be the object of military operations; (5) places and installations inhabited by civilians should not be the object of military operations; (6) places or areas designated for the protection of civilians or refugees should not be the object of military operations; (7) civilians, collectively or individually, should not be the object of reprisals, forcible transfer or other assaults on their integrity; and (8) the provision of international relief to civilians "is in conformity with the humanitarian principles of the Charter of United Nations, the Universal Declarations of Human Rights and other international instruments in the field of human rights".[11]

It is clear that all the aforementioned principles are already embedded in international humanitarian law theory except the first and the last. The first calls for the full application of human rights in armed conflicts and is underpinned by previous instruments and resolutions. However, the last one unambiguously encompasses the shared principle of humanity and all provisions and concepts tailored in the Charter of United Nations and Universal Declarations of Human Rights. International humanitarian law and human rights law are hitherto living a biological symbiosis or, shall we say, mandatory mutualism.

9 United Nations, Final Act of the international Conference on Human Rights, Teheran, 22 April to 13 May 1968, A/Conf.32/41, Sales No. E68.XIV.2, 18 (1968).

10 Robert Kolb, *Human Rights Law and International Humanitarian Law Between 1945 and the Aftermath of the Teheran Conference of 1968*, in Research Handbook on Human Rights and Humanitarian Law 35, 45 (2013).

11 G.A. Res. 2675 (XXV), *Basic principles for the protection of civilian populations in armed conflicts*, U.N. Doc. A/RES/2675/XXV (Dec. 09, 1970).

In biology, mandatory mutualism (or symbiosis) occurs when two different species create an interspecific relationship in such a way that both species depend on the other's metabolism and start to need the other for the benefits of this association. Differences between mutualism and symbiosis are drawn, though, as mutualism is considered the relationship where both species benefit from the association, and symbiosis has a broader meaning that also entails commensalism, where only one of the species benefits from the association.[12]

As once enlightened by Edward Wilson, it is always profitable in human science to make biology juxtapositions, since humanity today is like a waking dreamer, "caught between the fantasies of sleep and the chaos of the real world".[13] With this in mind, from now on we shall refer to the fusion and co-applicability between international humanitarian law and human rights law as mandatory mutualism because it is for the benefit of both branches and, above all, the principle of humanity and pursuit of peace by mankind.

In 1977 the United Nations held a diplomatic conference where two further protocols were added to international humanitarian bodies of law. These protocols deal mostly with human rights guarantees and proceedings during armed conflict situations. Even today, however, there remains a grey zone regarding the details of their mutual interaction since none of these protocols were sufficiently clear on human rights enforcement of humanitarian law provisions. The adoption of the Fourth Geneva Convention and two Additional Protocols have progressively broadcast a new conception of law, creating common ground for the protection of the human being based on the fundamental principle of humanity. Any gap left by international humanitarian law is now filled by human rights law, offering perfect harmony among bodies of law within the international legal system.

In this vein, the complementarity born from the mutualism between the two branches of international law reflects a method of interpretation enshrined in Article 31(3)(c) of the Vienna Convention on the Law of Treaties that allows for an interpretation that takes into account "relevant rule of international law applicable in the relations between the parties." As previously mentioned, this provision contains the idea that international law is a coherent system that observes unity and exhibits wholeness between its legal sources. It sees international law as a regime in which different sets of rules are in harmony and are mutually beneficial. Thus, human rights can be interpreted in the light of international humanitarian law, and vice versa.[14]

Article 72 of Additional Protocol I of the Geneva Conventions already stresses that humanitarian law provisions are supplementary to any other applicable rule of international law relating to the protection of fundamental human rights during

12 LIBRETEXTS LIBRARY, https://bio.libretexts.org/Bookshelves/Human_Biology/Book%3A_Human_Biology _(Wakim_and_Grewal)/24%3A_Ecology/24.04%3A_Community_Relationships (last visited September 2, 2019).

13 EDWARD O. WILSON, THE SOCIAL CONQUEST OF EARTH 07–10 (2012).

14 Cordula Droege, *The Interplay between International Humanitarian Law and International Human Rights Law in Situations of Armed Conflict*, 40 ISRAELI LAW REVIEW, no. 2, 310, 337 (2007).

armed conflicts, international or non-international. Yet, the Inter-American Commission on Human Rights elucidates that it is because of their mandatory mutualism and the fact that "both normative frameworks are based on common core principles and values" that international human rights law and humanitarian law "can provide reciprocal influence and reinforcement". Therefore, the conclusion is that "international human rights law can be interpreted in the light of international humanitarian law and the latter, in turn, can be interpreted in the light of international human rights law, if required".[15] Moreover, the mandatory mutualism is applied entirely in cases of belligerent occupation. As alien occupation is also a matter of humanitarian law, according to the Hague Regulations and Fourth Geneva Convention, the enjoinment of human rights law stands, especially to protect civilian populations. It is not just the ICJ[16] that has reached this resolution, but the European[17] and Inter-American courts[18] as well.

Relationship to human dignity

As previously noted, the international legal system is a complex one which contains multiple sources of law and open clauses in order to provide law with its dynamics and ductility for settling hard cases and embracing new traits of law regarding the civilization process and rapid development of science. Therefore, regarding human rights law, human dignity is applied in international courts either as a right or as a value, mostly in difficult cases where we might find some apparent conflict of legal provisions of international bodies of law. This moral contribution from human rights law gives the law of war a more humane contour, something often called a humanization process.

Thus, it is largely conceived that the law of war, or law of armed conflict, shall be appropriately referred to as international humanitarian law, since it shares the same values and morals – i.e. the same essence – as human rights law. Hence, many people endorse a mandatory bond between them in order to indicate their mutualism and the benefits for both sides. Furthermore,

15 *Jose Isabel Salas Galindo and Others v. United States,* Case 10.573, Inter-Am. Comm'n H.R., Report No. 121/18, OEA/Ser.L/V/II.169, doc. 138, §328 (2018); same conclusion at *Franklin Guillermo Aisalla Molina, Ecuador v. Colombia,* Case IP-02, Inter-Am. Comm'n H.R., Report No. 112/10, OEA/Ser.L/V/II.140, doc. 10, §121 (2010).

16 Case Concerning Armed Activities on the Territory of the Congo (Democratic Republic of the Congo v. Uganda), 2005 I.C.J. §§172–173 (December 19); and Legal Consequences of the Construction of a Wall in the Occupied Palestinian Territory, Advisory Opinion, 2004 I.C.J. §178–179 (July 9).

17 *Al-Skeini and Others v. The United Kingdom [GC],* no. 55721/07 Eur. Ct. H.R., §§90–91, 142 (2011) and *Ilascu and Others v. Moldova and Russia [GC],* no. 48787/99 Eur. Ct. H.R. §370 (2004).

18 *Case of the "Mapiripán Massacre" v. Colombia*, Merits, Reparations and Costs, Inter-Am. Ct. H.R. (ser. C) No. 22, §238 (September 15, 2005); and *Norín Catrimán et al (Leaders, members and Activists of the Mapuche Indigenous People) v. Chile*, Merits, Reparations and Costs. Inter-Am. Ct. H.R. (ser. C) No. 279, §197 (May 29, 2014).

> the essence of the whole corpus of international humanitarian law as well as human rights law lies in the protection of the human dignity of every person, whatever his or her gender. The general principle of respect for human dignity is the basic underpinning and indeed the very *raison d'être* of international humanitarian law and human rights law.[19]

The strength that human dignity exercises in this mandatory mutualism is thus undeniable, both as a right and a value.

The main point to stress here is that, as either a right or a value, international law and jurisprudence on human rights have made human dignity a centerpiece of human rights law. This means that human dignity is held as a "supervalue" – the core from which all provisions on human rights emanate and develop their constitution and comprehension. This irradiation process can be seen in several international bodies of law – expressly – or contextualized within jurisprudence semantics and rationale as part of the provision referred to.

Examining the international scenario, we shall shed light on some relevant bodies of law where human dignity is expressly conceived of, if not in the preamble, in the provisions. Even when appearing in a preamble based on moral grounds, the human dignity supervalue embraces the applicability of all human rights provisions, chiefly through the rationale of jurisprudence. The positive treatment of human dignity in international law, and in the majority of modern national constitutions, represents a high degree of ideological latitude as well as different extents and shapes of likely realization, but it is undeniable that human dignity has reached general acknowledgement in the international community. Although we have experienced some setbacks along the way, this cannot be allowed to dwindle or compromise the main goal: to increasingly enforce respect for human dignity and to substantiate its content in an irreversible manner.[20]

The aforementioned United Nations Resolution 2444 of 19 December 1968, which puts human rights law at the center of the legal order for armed conflicts, presents the Final Act of the International Conference on Human Rights in Teheran as a symbol of human rights. In provision XXV, giving publicity to the Universal Declaration of Human Rights, it expressly recognizes that "in order to make effective use of human rights, everyone must understand the nature of these rights and his responsibility to exercise and defend them in fulfillment of the dignity of man".[21] We have explored the nature of human rights and the responsibility they represent in previous chapters, so might assert that we understand perfectly.

Besides the international statutes we looked at in chapter on human rights law (chapter 3), let us recall some core references for the sake of congruency in our

19 *Prosecutor v. Anto Furundzija [Trial Chamber]*, Case No. IT-95–17/1-T, 1998 I.C. T.Y. §183 (December 10).

20 Peter Harbele, *A Dignidade Humana como Fundamento da Comunidade Estatal*, in Dimensões da Dignidade 89, 150–152 (2005).

21 United Nations, Final Act of the International Conference on Human Rights, Teheran, 22 April to 13 May 1968, A/Conf.32/41, Sales No. E68.XIV.2, 19 (1968).

discourse. The United Nations, via the Charter of the United Nations and Universal Declaration of Human Rights, issued Resolution 1904, the Declaration on the Elimination of All Forms of Racial Discrimination, which states very clearly that racial segregation and discrimination hamper "respect for the dignity of the human person" and must therefore be considered an "offense to human dignity".[22] Furthermore, the realization of economic, social and cultural rights lies at the center of efforts to realize all human rights since an existence containing human dignity is only possible if both categories of rights – civil liberties and social rights – are fully enjoyed.[23]

All regional conventions on human rights also turn on human dignity and, regardless of whether solely expressed in the preamble or not, the characterization of values and rights falls within the orientation set by Article 31 of the Vienna Convention of 1969, whereby "a treaty shall be interpreted in good faith in accordance with the ordinary meaning to be given to the terms of the treaty in their context and in the light of its object and purpose". Furthermore, the treaty's preamble also serves the purpose of interpretation. According to the Inter-American Commission on Human Rights, the application of Article 31 is bound to work towards mandatory mutualism between international human rights law and international humanitarian law.[24]

It is also interesting that despite the fact that the European Convention on Human Rights does not explicitly refer to human dignity, either as value or right, the later Protocol 13 and Article 4 of Protocol 4 appear to embrace human dignity as a principle of law – for instance, when banning the death penalty. And the European Court of Human Rights has already recognized human dignity as a value, with an interpretation that allows for full applicability of international legal order with unity, coherence and wholeness. Human dignity "has been taken into account when interpreting the Conventions and substantive judicial decision-making has been produced".[25] In *Bouyid v Belgium* and *Khlaifia and Other v. Italy*, the recognition of human dignity was understood as a civilized value closely bound to respect. Any act that humiliates or debases an individual, shows lack of respect for or diminishes his/her human dignity shall be forbidden. Thus, "respect for human dignity forms part of the very essence of the Convention".[26] *Parrilo v. Italy* went far beyond – it recognized the dignity of an unborn human life,

22 G.A. Res. 1904 (XVIII), *United Nations Declaration on the Elimination of All Forms of Racial Discrimination*, U.N. Doc. A/RES/18/1904 (Nov. 20, 1963).

23 E.S.C. Report on the Thirty-Sixth Session, Official Records, 1980, Supplement No. 3, U.N. Doc. E/1980/13, E/CN.4/1408, §116 (February 4–March 14, 1980).

24 *Jose Isabel Salas Galindo and Others v. United States,* Case 10.573, Inter-Am. Comm'n H.R., Report N° 121/18, OEA/Ser.L/V/II.169, doc. 138, §328 (2018); same conclusion at *Franklin Guillermo Aisalla Molina, Ecuador v. Colombia,* Case IP-02, Inter-Am. Comm'n H.R., Report No. 112/10, OEA/Ser.L/V/II.140, doc. 10, §121 (2010).

25 Christopher McCrudden, *Human Dignity and Judicial Interpretation of Human Rights*, in INTERNATIONAL LAW AND JUSTICE WORKING PAPERS 2008/8, 57 (2008).

26 *Bouyid v. Belgium [GC]*, no. 23380/09 Eur. Ct. H.R., §§81–89 (2015); and *Khlaifia and Other v. Italy [GC]*, no. 16483/12 Eur. Ct. H.R., §158 (2016).

embracing the notion of ontological disrespect of human nature in a way that means working to save human lives through genetics is not acceptable.[27]

The Inter-American Court has maintained a broad perspective regarding connections between human dignity and personal integrity. Citing articles 5 and 11 of the Inter-American Human Rights Convention, the Court held that we shall find human dignity embedded in the provision that sets personal integrity as a fundamental right, since "all persons deprived of their liberty shall be treated with respect for the inherent dignity of the human person" and "everyone has the right to have his honor respected and his dignity recognized".[28] Besides that, human dignity is turned into an *erga omnes* international obligation for American states, which means that rights to life, personal integrity, honor and dignity not only need to be respected (negative obligation) but also require all states to adopt appropriate measures to enforce and guarantee them to every individual (positive obligation).[29]

Derogation of human rights in times of emergency

Although there is mandatory mutualism between international humanitarian law and human rights, it is well known that some human rights can be derogated during times of emergency following a state-party request made through a human rights convention. This is relevant here because armed conflict usually falls within an arguable area of exception, one that invites the use of exceptional law in order to avoid a state of complete collapse. After all, a moral legal order, just like contemporary international law, does not allow for moral abstention or neutrality, not even when breakdown is threatened.[30]

As Carl Schmitt grasped, the state of exception is called upon when the political unity of the state is under threat and its very existence put at risk. The system requires decision-making, and only the sovereign in power is entitled to do this because he is the chief of state. Sovereignty here does not mean monopoly of

27 *Parrilo v. Italy [GC]*, no. 46470/11 Eur. Ct. H.R., §47 (2015).

28 *Case of the Members of the Village of Chichupac and neighboring communities of the Municipality of Rabinal v. Guatemala*, Preliminary Objections, Merits, Reparations and Costs, Inter-Am. Ct. H.R. (ser. C) No. 328, §124 (November 30, 2016); *Caso Velásquez Paiz y Otros v. Guatemala*, Excepciones Preliminares, Fondo, Reparaciones y Costas, Inter-Am. Ct. H.R. (ser. C) No. 307, §173 (Noviembre 15, 2015); and *Case of Barrios Altos v. Peru*, Merits, Inter-Am. Ct. H.R. (ser. C) No. 83, §52 (March 14, 2001).

29 *Velásquez Paiz y Otros v. Guatemala*, Excepciones Preliminares, Fondo, Reparaciones y Costas, Inter-Am. Ct. H.R. (ser. C) No. 307, §106 (Noviembre 15, 2015); *Caso Gonzales Lluy y otros Vs. Ecuador*, Excepciones Preliminares, Fondo, Reparaciones y Costas, Inter-Am. Ct. H.R. (ser. C) No. 298, §168 (Septiembre 1, 2015); *Caso Defensor de Derechos Humanos y otros Vs. Guatemala*, Excepciones Preliminares, Fondo, Reparaciones y Costas, Inter-Am. Ct. H.R. (ser. C) No. 283, §138 (Agosto 28, 2014); and *Velásquez Rodríguez Vs. Honduras*, Fondo, Inter-Am. Ct. H.R. (ser. C) No. 4, §163, 165–166 (Julie 29, 1988).

30 Vladimir Jankélévitch, O Paradoxo da Moral 05 (2008).

coercion or domination, but the taking on the burden of decision that emerges as the necessary tool to reestablish security and public order. The sovereign can then suspend the rule of law as a political maneuver for the preservation of the state and its subjects. Every order, consequently, rests on a decision – which is why this doctrine is often called political decisionism – leaving the state in a situation of anomie. It is only when the threat has been eliminated and the abnormality ended that legal order can be restored and all rules reinforced.[31] To him, the chief of state is the guardian of the Constitution and the law, and nowadays Schmitt is a controversial figure in international law and social theory, his contributions denounced as ideological and propagandistic Nazi bric-a-brac.[32] Following the Nuremberg trials, this theory of international law has become completely untenable.

International law no longer covers the total absence of rights – especially human rights – in a regime. Such a situation is different from anarchy and chaos where, from a legal perspective, order still exists. Modern understanding on state of exception is far from being a legal loophole – rather, it is an international law provision that has its own exception clauses inside the legal system.[33] This exceptional situation solely allows a partial fulfillment of human rights and hence is viewed as a special application of the law out of general provisions and applicability in which interpretations shall be as restricted as possible.[34]

The international human rights conventions call these exceptions of law derogation clauses. Article 15 of the European Convention on Human Rights enables all but the absolute rights of the Convention to be suspended in "time of war or other public emergency threatening the life of the nation" provided this is "strictly required by the exigencies of the situation". Nevertheless, human rights interference must be "proportionate to the legitimate aim pursued and that this will vary from case to case, the background circumstances, the right in question and the type of interference concerned".[35] In turn, Article 27 of the American Convention on Human Rights enables all but the absolute rights in the Convention to be suspended in "time of war, public danger, or other emergency that threatens the independence or security of a State Party, (…) to the extent and for the period of time strictly required by the exigencies of the situation". Article 30 also envisions and strengthens the submission to necessity and proportionality for adopting such exceptional measures.[36]

Accordingly, most human rights can be derogated in time of public emergency, which includes situations of armed conflict. Nevertheless, it is a common

31 Carl Schmitt, Teologia Política, 11–16 (Belo Horizonte: Del Rey, 2006); and Carlos A. Fernández Pardo, Carl Schmitt en la Teoría Política Internacional 25–28 (2007).

32 China Miéville, Between Equal Rights: a Marxist Theory of International Law 27 (2006).

33 Giorgio Agamben, Estado de Exceção 39–54 (2004).

34 Carlos Maximiliano, Hermenêutica e Aplicação do Direito 183 (2006).

35 Steven Greer, The Exceptions to Articles 8 to 11 of the European Convention on Human Rights 15 (1997).

36 Comissión Inter Americana de Derechos Humanos, Informe sobre Terrorismo y Derechos Humanos, par. 360 (2002).

misconception to dismiss the application of human rights in armed conflict situations, because derogation is understood as an entire suspension of rights, which is not what international law says.[37] It is lawful to detain suspects and keep them imprisoned to prevent the risks they represent. However, some fundamental juridical guarantees must be left for them, such as the right to a counselor and judicial review of their detention, since their restriction of rights is limited and temporary and does not simply open a "black hole" in the law.[38]

Likewise, the American Commission on Human Rights has held that the Convention's derogation clause gives room for continental deliberations about times of emergency, which does not signify the explicit suspension or restriction of human rights. These deliberations, by the way, must observe the requisites of proportionality, necessity and distinction before accepting that there exists a very grave situation of armed conflict in which the state's order and safety is really threatened.[39] While any state-party may have this legal prerogative to derogate human rights, the international court has deemed this option incompatible with the scope and aims of the human rights convention and therefore it is strictly forbidden.[40]

Both the European and American conventions – articles 15 and 27, respectively – and also Article 4 of the International Covenant on Civil and Political Rights (ICCPR) set limits to the derogation clauses, permitting activities only to the extent strictly allowed by the exigencies of the situation, provided that such measures are not inconsistent with states' other obligations under international law and do not involve discrimination solely on the grounds of race, color, sex, language, religion, or social origin. Nevertheless, we now know that even in an armed conflict situation, there are some rights that are not susceptible to derogation since such derogation would imply an incompatibility with the very existence of protective bodies of human rights law. Such inderogable rights belong to *jus cogens*, as an international peremptory norm.[41] Some scholars struggle with the idea of all human rights being considered *jus cogens*, but regarding those chosen as inderogable by international law there is really no dispute.[42]

37 Cordula Droege, *The Interplay between International Humanitarian Law and International Human Rights Law in Situations of Armed Conflict*, 40 Israeli Law Review no. 2, 310, 318 (2007).

38 Michael Ignatieff, The Lesser Evil: political ethics in an age of terror 29–30 (2004).

39 Comissión Inter Americana de Derechos Humanos, Informe sobre Terrorismo y Derechos Humanos, pars. 50–51 (2002).

40 Restricciones a la Pena de Muerte (artículos 4.2 y 4.4 Convención Americana sobre Derechos Humanos), Opinión Consultiva OC-3/83, Inter-Am. Ct. H.R. (ser. Fallos y opiniones) No. 3, §61 (September 08, 1983).

41 Tania Gabriela Rodríguez huerta, Tratado sobre Derechos Humanos: el sistema de reservas 58 (2005).

42 Rodolfo E. Piza Escalante, *El Valor Del Derecho y La Jurisprudencia Internacionales de Derechos Humanos en el Derecho y la Justicia Internos – El Ejemplo de Costa Rica*, in 1 Liber Amicorum, Héctor Fix-Zamundio, 169, 185 (Corte Interamericana de Derechos Humanos, 1998).

The European Court has recognized these inderogable rights as *jus cogens* in cases brought before the court. They are judged to be *jus cogens* because of the importance of the values they protect.[43] Meanwhile, the Inter-American Court has a wider sense of *jus cogens* norms, considering human rights in general.[44] Besides being *jus cogens*, these inderogable rights are treated differently from European and American law, the latter having a wider spectrum of human rights protection than the former. The European Convention selects only four rights as inderogable: life, prohibition of torture, prohibition of slavery or servitude and no punishment without law. The American Convention selects these rights: to juridical personality; to life; to humane treatment; freedom from slavery; freedom from *ex post facto* laws; freedom of conscience and religion; of the family; to a name; of the child; to nationality; to participate in government; and to the judicial guarantees essential for the protection of such rights.

Later, Article 2 of Protocol 6 of the European Convention made an adjustment to the right to life in order to permit any state to "make provision in its law for the death penalty in respect of acts committed in time of war or of imminent threat of war", but this permission was then withdrawn from Protocol 13, articles 1 and 2, where the death penalty is abolished completely and no derogation is accepted. Moreover, the European Court of Human Rights has even widened the protection of life, maintaining that states must not only refrain from the intentional and unlawful taking of life but also take appropriate steps to safeguard the lives of those within its jurisdiction.[45] Meanwhile, the European Court has put great emphasis on torture, enshrining the prohibition of torture as one of the most fundamental values of democratic societies. "Even in the most difficult circumstances, such as the fight against terrorism and organized crime, the Convention prohibits in absolute terms torture and inhuman or degrading treatment or punishment", tolerating no "exceptions and no derogation from it is permissible under Article 15", even in the event of a public emergency threatening the life of the nation, the inderogability is in absolute terms,[46] no matter the evil perpetrated by the enemy in an armed conflict.[47] Even the deportation of the individual to a country where the belief that he/she would be subjected to torture or any inhuman or degrading treatment remains clearly impermissible under the convention's provisions. In such cases, the European Convention of Human Rights implies an obligation not to deport the individual.[48]

43 *Al-Adsani v. The United Kingdom [GC]*, no. 35763/97 Eur. Ct. H.R., §§60–62 (2001).

44 Juridical Conditions and Rights of Undocumented Migrants, Advisory Opinion OC-18/03, Inter-Am. Ct. H.R. (ser. A) No. 18, §101 (September 17, 2003); *Expelled Dominicans and Haitians v. Dominican Republic*, Preliminary Objections, Merits, Reparations and Costs, Inter-Am. Ct. H.R. (ser. C) No. 282, §264 (August 28, 2014); and *Norín Catrimán et al. (Leaders, members and activists of the Mapuche Indigenous People) v. Chile*, Merits, Reparations and Costs. Inter-Am. Ct. H.R. (ser. C) No. 279, §197 (May 29, 2014).

45 *L.C.B. v. the United Kingdom [GC]*, no. 23413/94 Eur. Ct. H.R., §36 (1998).

46 *Chahal v. the United Kingdom*, no. 22414/93 Eur. Ct. H.R, §79 (1996).

47 *Labita v. Italy*, no. 26772/95 Eur. Ct. H.R, §119 (2000).

48 *Saadi v. Italy*, no. 37201/06 Eur. Ct. H.R, §125 (2008) and *Salah Sheekh v. the Netherlands*, no. 1948/04 Eur. Ct. H.R, §135 (2007).

To the main four inderogable rights, Article 4 of the ICCPR added three more, which are still less than American provisions: the rights to juridical personality, to not be imprisoned merely on the grounds of an inability to fulfil a contractual obligation, and to freedom of thought, conscience and religion. The European Court in turn has acknowledged the broader scope of inderogability in observance of international law unity, wholeness and coherence, giving instructions for states to observe the additional criteria of temporality outlined by ICCPR, combined with necessity and proportionality.[49] Moreover, such derogation can only be conceived of when previously and formally submitted by the state-party before the regional court able to grant it (Article 4, ICCPR; Article 15, ECHR and Article 27, ACHR). Additionally, the European Court of Justice, in *Kadi v. Council of the European Union and Commission of the European Communities*, moves the mutualism of international humanitarian law and human rights law away from prevailing state-centricity and toward anthropocentricism, declaring the guidance of human rights law as fundamental principles of the Union and the sole condition of the lawfulness of Community acts, as emphasized: "*It is also clear from the case-law that respect for human rights is a condition of the lawfulness of Community acts* (…) *and that measures incompatible with respect for human rights are not acceptable in the Community*".[50]

On the other side, the Inter-American Court of Human Rights has understood that Article 27 of the Convention enjoins limits to state power for suspending rights and liberties. In this view, some suspensions are not tolerated under any circumstances, with no offer of judicial guarantees to pursue them under human rights protection. Judicial guarantee and proceeding to ensure human rights are indispensable in armed conflicts or emergency situations.[51] The control over legality of perpetrated acts in armed conflicts by an impartial and autonomous judicial organ is a key requirement to establish the state of exception as legal.[52] Consequently, other than the guarantee of due process of law, habeas corpus is the major guarantee to enforce human rights protection on liberty and personal integrity.[53] In sum, the Inter-American Court takes human rights violations very seriously. No state can justify human rights violations while declaring a state of exception.[54]

49 *A. and Others v. The United Kingdom [GC]*, no. 3455/05 Eur. Ct. H.R., §178 (2009).

50 Case C-402/05 P and C-415/05 P, Kadi v. Council of the European Union and Commission of the European Communities [GC] 2008 E.C.R. §§284, 344.

51 El hábeas corpus bajo suspensión de garantías (artículos 27.2, 25 y 8 Convención Americana sobre Derechos Humanos), Opinión Consultiva OC-8/87, Inter-Am. Ct. H.R., §§23, 28 (January 30, 1987).

52 Garantías Judiciales en Estados de Emergencia (arts. 27.2, 25 y 8 Convención Americana sobre Derecho Humanos), Opinión Consultiva OC-9/87, Inter-Am. Ct. H.R., §21 (October 06, 1987).

53 *Loayza-Tamayo v. Peru,* Merits, Inter-Am. Ct. H.R. (ser. C) No. 33, §§46–52 (September 17, 1997).

54 Juridical Conditions and Rights of Undocumented Migrants, Advisory Opinion OC-18/03, Inter-Am. Ct. H.R. (ser. A) No. 18, §§89–101 (September 17, 2003).

Notwithstanding the regional conventions on human rights, the content of common Article 3 of the Geneva Convention constitutes a minimum legal guidance that is applicable to any type of armed conflict. Thus, with respect to armed conflict, it is not possible to draw a conclusion from the absence of derogation clauses that the respective treaty does not apply. Today, human rights law is an integral part of international law for the common welfare of humanity and represents common values that no state may revoke, even in times of war. The mandatory mutualism follows the objective of protecting and safeguarding individuals in all circumstances.

In sum, despite their common ground, the core and legal processes of IHL and HRL are quite diverse, and such diversity brings an endless debate about the precision of their mutual complementarity and enforcement. We deal with this grey zone on a daily basis, there being a permanent struggle to define where the HRL should prevail and overlap with the military-based rationale of the IHL, or vice versa. Notwithstanding, since the end of the 1960s, especially after the two covenants, the HRL became mandatory worldwide, except for a restricted and temporary suspension-clause claim from a state in a time of emergency, according to procedural and substantive safeguards regarding the declaration and implementation of such a state of exception – as stated in Article 4 of the International Covenant on Civil and Political Rights, Article 15 of the ECHR and Article 27 of American Convention on Human Rights.

Today's assessment by court precedents

Regarding public emergency and situations of state of exception in contemporary international law, we have a lot of new kinds of armed conflict. We have seen armed conflicts, international and non-international, in Ukraine, Russia, Turkey and elsewhere. However, one intriguing model of armed conflict has profoundly shaped the way we conceive of mandatory mutualism, particularly in respect to human dignity and personal rights: the war on terror. We are not focusing on terrorism in this work. Rather, we focus on breaches and understanding the mutation they have provoked over the years, which can be seen in international jurisprudence on the part of the international community that is intimately engaged in the type of war carried out by belligerent groups, not states; unidentified, because they are all mixed up with civilians; with no political agenda but to inflict terror and nihilism; they do not recognize or follow international and civilized moral standards of combat, principally those related to principles of distinction and humanity; and their acts are artfully and creatively cruel, eroding any moral identity.

It is imperative, by this token, that some jurisprudential recognition of this particular and exceptional situation must be expressed. Karl Laurenz identifies this method of law pragmatism as "jurisprudence of interests" – not in a demeaning sense, but as an instrument for refurbishing concepts according to specific situations. It is the logical submission of facts for juridical concepts where the "interests" point to priority values, and these values must be linked to some idea of justice.[55] Therefore, the European Court of Human Rights has generally recognized the application of the European Convention in situations of international armed conflict, following in the footsteps of the International Court of Justice in *The Construction of a Wall* and *Congo v Uganda* precedents. However, we can sense a setback in recent jurisprudence of the court. In *Hassan v. The United Kingdom*, the European Court of Human Rights regarded the precedents set by the ICJ as evidence of the continued application of human rights law within armed conflict, but added a side note saying that it does not work in a formal or absolute way, and the exception that war represents cannot be overlooked when determining what standards should be used to judge behavior in those exceptional circumstances. The formal or absolute predominance of human rights law would consequently be "too idealistic, bearing in mind the speciality and persistence of armed conflict". Humanitarian law is related to today's reality, while human rights law is related to tomorrow's promise, for which the Court needs to ensure "the survival of a State".[56]

The twist in all of this is that the United Kingdom requested the Court to not apply its obligations under Article 5 of the European Convention on Human Rights (right to liberty) without filing a formal derogation request under Article 15 or Article 4, ICCPR (derogation in time of emergency). Yet, even when not requesting the suspension clause, as in *Hassan*, the Court made clear its constant practice of interpreting human rights law in the light of the rules set out in the 1969 Vienna Convention on the Law of Treaties that, according to its terms, when interpreting a treaty, such as the European Convention on Human Rights, it is necessary to take into account any relevant rules of international law applicable in international affairs.

In this respect, the Court has noted that it is not the practice of a state to derogate from their Article 5 obligations in order to detain persons on the basis of the Third and Fourth Geneva Conventions during international armed conflicts. Moreover, the human rights law has to be interpreted in harmony with the rules of international law as a whole, of which it forms part, and applied equally to the rules of international humanitarian law, such as those set out in the four Geneva Conventions of 1949. The Court considered that, even in situations of international armed conflict, the human rights safeguards continue to apply, albeit interpreted against the background of the provisions of humanitarian law. But, by reason of the co-existence of the safeguards provided by humanitarian law and by human rights law in times of armed conflict, the grounds of permitted deprivation of liberty set out under the human rights regime should be accommodated as far as possible, with the taking of prisoners of war and the detention of civilians who pose a risk to security under the Third and Fourth Geneva Conventions.

In this vein, the Court upheld that the exercise of the derogation clause in times of emergency is not mandatory in situations of international armed conflict, which fall under the Geneva Conventions' broad powers, amazingly overruling its

55 Karl Larenz, Metodologia da Ciência do Direito 163–164 (3rd ed. 1997).
56 *Hassan v. The United Kingdom [GC]*, no. 29750/09 Eur. Ct. H.R., §38 (2014).

previous case *A. and others v. The United Kingdom.* [57] Therefore, Hassan's capture and detention had been consistent with the powers available to the UK under the Third and Fourth Geneva Conventions, which was not unlawful given that the Court upheld an analogous case that happened a couple of years before, in *Al-Jedda*, where imprisonment or preventive detention without intention to bring criminal charges is deemed lawful within a reasonable period of time.[58]

The catch in *Al-Jedda* was the argument by the UK government that since the state was part of the United Nations Security Council task force in the war on terror, according to Resolution 1546 of June 8, 2004, the rules of engagement in war were already issued by the UNSC, which nullifies any petition before the European Court asking to apply the derogation clause. Nevertheless, the court dismissed the argument, noting that the ICJ had already held in its advisory opinion on the Legal Consequences for States of the Continued Presence of South Africa in Namibia that "the relevant Security Council resolutions are couched in exhortatory rather than mandatory language and that, therefore, they do not purport to impose any legal duty on any State nor to affect legally any right of any State".[59] Also, in the case concerning Armed Activities on the Territory of the Congo, the ICJ has vividly established that occupying forces shall fall within Article 43 of the Hague Regulations of 1907, which demands respect and full observance of international human rights law to protect civilian populations of occupied territory[60] – which was the case of the United Kingdom in *Al-Jedda*. Hence, in *Al-Jedda*, the protection of civilians was maintained by international law.[61]

Additionally, it is important to note that in the aftermath of the 9/11 terrorist attacks, the UK government had requested a derogation clause from the secretary general of the Council of Europe pursuant to Article 15 of the ECHR in order to engage in the war against terror. In this regard, the Council of Europe Parliamentary Assembly enacted the Resolution 1271 (2002), of which paragraphs 9 and 12, respectively, resolve that "in their fight against terrorism, Council of Europe members should not provide for any derogations to the European Convention on Human Rights", so all member states should "refrain from using Article 15 of the European Convention on Human Rights (derogation in time of emergency) to limit the rights and liberties guaranteed under its Article 5 (right to liberty and security)". Dealing with this, the European Court of Human Rights, in *A. and Others*, had also considered the British exercise of the derogation clause disproportionate and discriminatory under human rights commitments,[62] which

57 *A. and others v. The United Kingdom [GC]*, no. 3455/05 Eur. Ct. H.R. (2009).
58 *Al-Jedda v. The United Kingdom [GC]*, no. 27021/08 Eur. Ct. H.R., §100 (2011).
59 Legal Consequences for States of the Continued Presence of South Africa in Namibia (South West Africa) notwithstanding Security Council Resolution 276 (1970), Advisory Opinion, 1971 I.C.J. §114 (June 21).
60 Case Concerning Armed Activities on the Territory of the Congo (Democratic Republic of the Congo v. Uganda), 2005 I.C.J. §§178–180 (December 19).
61 *Al-Jedda v. The United Kingdom [GC]*, no. 27021/08 Eur. Ct. H.R., §107 (2011).
62 *A. and others v. The United Kingdom [GC]*, no. 3455/05 Eur. Ct. H.R., §§ 144, 172–190 (2009).

agreed with the general understanding provided in *Bouyid v. Belgium* and *Khlaifia and Other v. Italy*, where it was emphasized that respect for human dignity forms part of the very essence of the Convention, alongside human freedom. Yet, the general purpose of the Convention's provisions was to protect "a person's dignity and physical integrity" and to prevent "serious interferences with human dignity".[63] In *Khlaifia,* the Court added that "even in the event of a public emergency threatening the life of the nation or in the most difficult circumstances, such as the fight against terrorism and organized crime, irrespective of the conduct of the person concerned", the core of human dignity must prevail.[64]

By the same token, the United Nations Security Council issued Resolution 1373, in 2001, that called upon all states to comply with all obligations under international law, including human rights law and humanitarian law, meaning recognition of the fact that upholding human rights and protecting the public from terrorist acts are not antithetical, but complementary responsibilities of states.[65] Nevertheless, Resolution 1373 also *decided* that all states must take "the necessary steps to prevent the commission of terrorist acts".[66]

Regarding the experience in *Al-Jedda*, the UK government did not build its case upon the derogation clause in *Hassan*: "in the present case, the United Kingdom did not purport to derogate under Article 15 from any of its obligations under Article 5".[67] Set as a leading case, the Court emphasized that this "is the first case in which a respondent State has requested the Court to disapply its obligations under Article 5 or in some other way to interpret them in the light of powers of detention available to it under international humanitarian law".[68] So, the argument has mutated from *Al-Jedda*, which proved no obstacle at all before the Court. Rather, it observed the necessity to interpret and apply HRL in a manner that is coherent with the framework under international law, via the scope of Article 31 of the Vienna Convention of 1969.

Following the *Hassan* case, some court proceedings examined the mandatory mutualism in the light of the rules set out in the Vienna Convention on the Law of Treaties of 23 May 1969, Article 31. The Court therefore holds that judicial interpretation shall maintain harmony with other rules of international law of which it forms part. Emphasizing the mutualism, it says that the "four Geneva Conventions of 1949, intended to mitigate the horrors of war, were drafted in parallel to the European Convention on Human Rights and enjoy universal ratification" and were also designed to protect captured "civilians who pose a security threat". Thus, the interpretation is that in armed conflict situations, the right to life (Article 2 of the European Convention) follows the rule of international

63 *Bouyid v. Belgium [GC]*, no. 23380/09 Eur. Ct. H.R., §§89–90 (2015).
64 *Khlaifia and Other v. Italy [GC]*, no. 16483/12 Eur. Ct. H.R., §158 (2016).
65 Robert K. Goldman, *Extraterritorial Application of the Human Rights to Life and Personal Liberty, including Habeas Corpus, during a Situation of Armed Conflict*, in Research Handbook on Human Rights and Humanitarian Law 104, 104–105 (2013).
66 S.C. Res. 1373 (2001), U.N. Doc. S/RES/1373, 2(b) (September 28, 2001).
67 *Hassan v. The United Kingdom [GC]*, no. 29750/09 Eur. Ct. H.R., §98 (2014).
68 *Hassan v. The United Kingdom [GC]*, no. 29750/09 Eur. Ct. H.R., §99 (2014).

humanitarian law – not human rights law – which plays "an indispensable and universally accepted role in mitigating the savagery and inhumanity", and, for the same reason, the right to liberty (Article 5) falls within the same context.[69]

An interesting finding in *Hassan* is that the court had acknowledged the mandatory mutualism between international humanitarian law and human rights law for a long time, even following in the footsteps of the ICJ's prior advisory opinions on Nuclear Weapons and The Construction of a Wall. *Hassan*'s rationale makes reference to *Varnava and Others v. Turkey*, where people who were in government custody went missing during armed conflict and claims over the right to life and liberty were submitted before the court. There, the mutualism was acknowledged and it was established that the right to life follows the rule of international humanitarian law, which plays "an indispensable and universally accepted role in mitigating the savagery and inhumanity". However, the court found a violation of the right of life under the European Convention, Article 2, considering the lack of obligation from the government "to account for the whereabouts and fate of the missing men". A violation was also found regarding the right to liberty, Article 5, under the European Convention.[70] Thus, the mutual benefit from both branches was duly co-applied on that occasion.

On the other hand, in *Hassan* the court overrules *Varnava and Others* and other precedents. It extinguishes the mandatory mutualism to recognize a mandatory commensalism instead, where only international humanitarian law benefits from the union of two branches. Recalling the advisory opinion of The Legal Consequences of the Construction of a Wall in the Occupied Palestinian Territory, there are three possibilities that come from the interplay between international humanitarian law and human rights law: "some rights may be exclusively matters of international humanitarian law; others may be exclusively matters of human rights law; yet others may be matters of both these branches of international law".[71] The mutualism is represented by the third option, an understanding that prevailed until the *Hassan* case.

Arguing that the court's interpretation propitiates a consistency to the framework under international law, it accepts the UK's inobservance of the obligations of formalizing derogation under Article 15 of European Convention and Article 4 of ICCPR and holds that this proceeding is forfeited before international humanitarian law provisions. The court now understands that the obligation of formal derogation is applied in peacetime only. In situations of armed conflict, consequently, safeguards of human rights continue to apply, although it will always be interpreted "against the background of the provisions of international humanitarian law". So from now on, in times of armed conflict, the grounds of permitted deprivation of liberty should be matched, as far as possible, with those governing

69 *Hassan v. The United Kingdom [GC]*, no. 29750/09 Eur. Ct. H.R., §102 (2014).

70 *Varnava and Others v. Turkey [GC]*, nos. 16064/90, 16065/90, 16066/90, 16068/90, 16069/90, 16070/90, 16071/90, 16072/90 and 16073/90 Eur. Ct. H.R., §§185–186, 208 (2009).

71 Legal Consequences of the Construction of a Wall in the Occupied Palestinian Territory, Advisory Opinion, 2004 I.C.J. §106 (July 9).

the detention of civilians who pose a risk to security under the Third and Fourth Geneva Conventions. International humanitarian law becomes the governing rule for possessing "broad powers", while human rights law adheres as a subsidiary source. "This means that the detention must comply with the rules of international humanitarian law" and Article 5 comes into play only to protect individuals from arbitrariness, which is absent following the periodical review of the imprisonment allowed by Articles 43 and 78 of the Fourth Geneva Convention.[72]

Mandatory commensalism overrides mutualism in European international law. Prior precedents that had enshrined the enforcement of human rights were overlooked. Once the court stressed that human rights embedded in the European Convention and bodies of law constitute first and foremost a

> system for the protection of human rights, the Court must interpret and apply it in a manner which renders its rights practical and effective, not theoretical and illusory. The Convention must also be read as a whole, and interpreted in such a way as to promote internal consistency and harmony between its various provisions.[73]

That was not held in *Hassan*, apparently. In summary: "the Court does not consider it necessary for a formal derogation to be lodged, the provisions of Article 5 will be interpreted and applied in the light of the relevant provisions of international humanitarian law".[74] This hindsight overrules a former ruling that the civilian imprisonment in wartime shall fall within the scheme of deprivation of liberty upon the exercise of the derogation clause (Article 15, ECHR, and Article 4, ICCPR). Conversely, human rights law ought to be interpreted as permitting the exercise of broad powers in humanitarian law. The Court even diminishes the human rights content and value behind Article 5 when it states that the right to liberty, at first glance, seems the most relevant provision. However, "there does not need to be any correlation between security internment and suspicion of having committed an offence or risk of the commission of a criminal offence". Therefore, the court considers that it would not be appropriate to hold that this form of detention of civilians as prisoners of war falls within the scope of Article 5's right to liberty.[75]

Underneath these arguments, the ECtHR has established a threshold of proceedings and application of the two bodies of law. In doing so, the Court demonstrated a remarkable perspective about enjoining the unbinding obligations of human rights in armed conflicts, namely those concerned with civilians. The Vienna Convention directives recall, in a certain way, the old separatism once

72 *Hassan v. The United Kingdom [GC]*, no. 29750/09 Eur. Ct. H.R., §§103–106 (2014).

73 *Demir and Baykara v. Turkey [GC]*, no. 34503/97 Eur. Ct. H.R., §§65–66 (2008); and *Stec and Others v. The United Kingdom*, nos. 65731/01 and 65900/01 Eur. Ct. H.R., §§47–48 (2006).

74 *Hassan v. The United Kingdom [GC]*, no. 29750/09 Eur. Ct. H.R., §107 (2014).

75 *Hassan v. The United Kingdom [GC]*, no. 29750/09 Eur. Ct. H.R., §97 (2014).

mitigated in the international arena and open a whole new path of international lawyering and decision-making. Although the rationale embeds an easy-going approach regarding objections to civilians' right to liberty, its grounds might go further in order to reach other conflicts of values and dilemmas within the grey zone between international humanitarian law and human rights law.

Now arriving at the primary scope of this work, targeting civilians is what concerns us in the remainder of this thesis. If we consider Article 2 of European Convention, which stresses the right to life, we hereinafter link it to the Fourth Geneva Convention and Additional Protocol I, particularly Common Article 3. As previously mentioned, the recent interpretation of the Court is that in situations of armed conflict, the right to life follows the rule of international humanitarian law – not human rights law – which plays "an indispensable and universally accepted role in mitigating the savagery and inhumanity",[76] overruling some other precedents.[77]

It is worth noting that, nationally, the idea of human rights, particularly the right to life, is balanced against actions perpetrated under "absolute necessity". In *McCann and Others v. The United Kingdom*, the Court details that the human right to life ranks as one of the most fundamental provisions in the Convention, enshrines one of the basic values of democratic societies, and lays out the circumstances when the deprivation of life may be justified. Then, the Court's emphasis: "indeed one which, in peacetime, admits of no derogation under Article 15". The Convention describes situations when it is permitted to "use force", which may result, as an unintended outcome, in the deprivation of life and must be no more than "absolutely necessary" for the achievement of the defence of any person from unlawful violence, to effect a lawful arrest, to prevent an escape of someone lawfully detained or in an action lawfully taken for the purpose of quelling a riot or insurrection. The term "absolutely necessary", then, indicates that the principle of necessity must be more compelling than the usual necessity employed in normal application from a state action as "necessary in a democratic society".[78]

In 2011, in *Al-Skeini and Others v. The United Kingdom*, the court took into account civilian deaths caused by British soldiers during the invasion of Iraq by the Coalition of armed forces led by the United States and approved by the United Nations Security Council Resolution 1441, issued on November 8, 2002. Civilians died during the belligerent occupation of Iraq, where international humanitarian law and human rights law are applicable under articles 42 to 56 of the Hague Regulations, articles 27 to 34 and 47 to 78 of the Fourth Geneva Convention and Additional Protocol I. In this case, when military necessity is at stake in the rules of engagement, the court acknowledges that the civilian deaths happened during a

76 *Hassan v. The United Kingdom [GC]*, no. 29750/09 Eur. Ct. H.R., §102 (2014).

77 For example, *Varnava and Others v. Turkey [GC]*, nos. 16064/90, 16065/90, 16066/90, 16068/90, 16069/90, 16070/90, 16071/90, 16072/90 and 16073/90 Eur. Ct. H.R., §§185–186, 208 (2009).

78 *McCann and Others v. The United Kingdom [GC]*, no. 18984/91 Eur. Ct. H.R., §147–149 (1995).

period when crime and violence were endemic and bring up arguments of "absolute necessity" crafted for domestic crisis, in *McCann and Others.* [79]

Likewise, in *Al-Skeini and Others* it is stressed that Article 2, the right to life, ranks as one of the most fundamental provisions of the Convention, enshrines one of the basic values of democratic societies, and sets out the circumstances when the deprivation of life may be justified. Consequently, the court matches the prior understanding and adapts it to the international law framework, in which no derogation is permitted under Article 15, "except in respect of deaths resulting from lawful acts of war". In this regard, Article 2 covers both intentional killing and also the situations in which it is permitted to use force which may result, as an unintended outcome, in the deprivation of life, and any use of force must be no more than "absolutely necessary" for the achievement of one or more purposes set out, just as previously held in *McCann.* [80]

It is paramount to highlight that in *Al-Skeini and Others* the court still had the understanding of mandatory mutualism, which means that the full applicability of Article 2, right to life in armed conflict situations, was recognized. This understanding, as stated above, was overruled three year later, in *Hassan*. An excuse using Article 2 from human rights law was admitted as a principle of necessity from international humanitarian law – the principle of supreme military necessity. But this mutual relationship between human rights and humanitarian law held in *Al-Skeini and Others* no longer endures. Although the court established mandatory mutualism, which would waive charges on unlawful deprivation of life because of supreme military necessity in armed conflict, the case had no conclusion on the matter because of a lack of procedural measures. Uncertain whether civilian killings were an outcome of arbitrariness or supreme necessity, the court did not judge the facts found, and affirmed the violation of the procedural duty to review and investigate the lawfulness of the use of lethal force by the state under Article 2 of the Convention.[81]

In contrast, the Inter-American Commission and Court have strictly retained the general conception of mandatory mutualism and equal cooperation, as well as benefits between humanitarian law and human rights law regarding the American Declaration on the Rights and Duties of Man and the American Convention on Human Rights. It is almost perceived as dogma that multilateral treaties of the traditional type made to accomplish the reciprocal exchange of rights for the benefit of states do not follow modern human rights law, particularly the American Convention. The purpose of human rights law is the protection of basic rights of human beings, and states can be deemed to submit themselves to a legal order within which they, for the common good, assume various obligations to mankind. These views about the distinct character of humanitarian law and the consequences to be drawn

79 *Al-Skeini and Others v. The United Kingdom [GC]*, no. 55721/07 Eur. Ct. H.R., §161 (2011).
80 *Al-Skeini and Others v. The United Kingdom [GC]*, no. 55721/07 Eur. Ct. H.R., §162 (2011).
81 *Al-Skeini and Others v. The United Kingdom [GC]*, no. 55721/07 Eur. Ct. H.R., §§163–177 (2011).

therefore apply with even greater force to the American Convention, in which the preamble vehemently reaffirms the consolidation of a "system of personal liberty and social justice based on respect for the essential rights of man"; and recognizes these rights as essential and "based upon attributes of the human personality, and that they therefore justify international protection".[82]

Taking a step forward, the Inter-American Court, despite its limited reach over applicable human rights bodies of law, has also applied humanitarian law by interpreting the American Convention on Human Rights in light of the Geneva Conventions because of their mandatory mutualism.[83] Likewise, the Inter-American Commission has used the prerogative of expressly assigning itself the competence to apply humanitarian law: "the Commission's competence to apply humanitarian law rules is supported by the text of the American Convention, by its own case law, as well as the jurisprudence of the Inter-American Court of Human Rights".[84]

It is held in *Abella v. Argentina* and *Coard et al v. United States* (and also in some posterior analysis), that human rights bodies of law and the Geneva Conventions share a common nucleus of inderogable rights and a "common purpose of protecting human life and dignity". There is an "integral linkage between the law of human rights and humanitarian law". Moreover, human rights law applies both in peacetime and during situations of armed conflict, while international humanitarian law generally does not apply in peacetime. Although one of the purposes of human rights law is to prevent warfare, none of its provisions were designed to regulate such situations and, at same time, the purpose of humanitarian law is to place restraints on the conduct of warfare in order to diminish the effects of hostilities.[85] Hence, common Article 3 of the Geneva Conventions and Article 1 of the American Declaration of the Rights and Duties of Man share humanity as a core, which makes resorting to humanitarian law in situations of armed conflicts indispensable, but with an interpretation that makes possible the application of the American Declaration "with due consideration for the specific characteristics of this situation". Even following Article 27 of the American Declaration and Article 4 of ICCPR, it is impossible "to suspend the validity of the Convention in its entirety".[86]

82 The Effect of Reservations on the Entry into Force of the American Convention on Human Rights (Arts. 74 and 75), Advisory Opinion OC-2/82, Inter-Am. Ct. H.R. (ser. A) No. 2, §§29–31 (September 24, 1982).

83 *Bámaca-Velásquez v. Guatemala*, Merits, Inter-Am. Ct. H.R. (ser. C) No. 91, §§207–210 (November 25, 2000).

84 *Juan Carlos Abella v. Argentina*, Case 11.137, Inter-Am. Comm'n H.R., Report No. 55/97, OEA/Ser.L/V/II.95, doc. 7 rev. at 271, § 162 (1997).

85 *Juan Carlos Abella v. Argentina*, Case 11.137, Inter-Am. Comm'n H.R., Report No. 55/97, OEA/Ser.L/V/II.95, doc. 7 rev. at 271, §§ 158–159 (1997); *Coard et al v. United States*, Case 10.951, Inter-Am. Comm'n H.R., Report No. 109/99, OEA/Ser.L/V/II.106, Doc. 6 rev, §39 (1999); and Report on Terrorism and Human Rights, Inter-Am. Comm'n H.R., OEA/Ser.L/V/II.116, doc. 5 rev. 1 corr., §108 (2002).

86 *Jose Isabel Salas Galindo and Others v. United States*, Case 10.573, Inter-Am. Comm'n H.R., Report No. 121/18, OEA/Ser.L/V/II.169, doc. 138, §§323–324 (2018).

On the occasion of mandatory mutualism, the Commission believes that Article 29(b) of the American Convention, the so-called "most-favorable-to-the-individual clause", shall give full legal effect to co-apply humanitarian law properly. Thus, there is no scenario in which human rights become restricted within the Commission's landscape. Where there are differences between legal standards governing the same or comparable rights in human rights law and humanitarian law, the Commission is duty bound to give legal effect to the provision with the higher standard applicable to the right or freedom in question. It is this interplay that authorizes the Commission to vigorously apply humanitarian law where and when relevant.[87] According to Article 27 of the American Convention and Article 4 of ICCPR, the Commission is also duty bound to analyze the state's obligations under human rights law in light of the standards of international humanitarian law that apply as *lex specialis* for the purpose of interpretation under Article 31 of the Vienna Convention, being "advisable to address both systems [while] simultaneously striking a balance between the interpretation and application of the *lex specialis* and international human rights law so that humanitarian considerations and military needs are respected". Thus, the establishment of humanitarian law as *lex specialis* by precedents from the ICJ does not mean that human rights are inapplicable. Just the opposite, it means that applying human rights law under its mandate may and sometimes must turn to international humanitarian law "for the purpose of interpretation as the more specific normative framework that governs situations in armed conflict".[88]

When reviewing the legality of derogation measures taken by a state, the Commission should not resolve this question solely with reference to the text of Article 27 of the American Convention or Article 4 of ICCPR. It must also determine whether the rights affected by these measures are similarly guaranteed under applicable humanitarian law. If it finds that the rights in question are not subject to suspension under humanitarian law, the conclusion shall be that the derogation measures are in violation of the state's obligations under both human rights law and the relevant humanitarian law treaties. "It is also worth noting that the Inter-American Court of Human Rights has viewed with approval the Commission's practice of applying sources of international law, other than the American Convention."[89] Furthermore, the Commission can manage the rules of international humanitarian law as a concrete legal framework in order to give more specific application to the contents of human rights law when defining state's obligations. In addition, when dealing with this mandatory mutualism, the

87 *Juan Carlos Abella v. Argentina*, Case 11.137, Inter-Am. Comm'n H.R., Report No. 55/97, OEA/Ser.L/V/II.95, doc. 7 rev. at 271, §§ 164–168 (1997).

88 *Franklin Guillermo Aisalla Molina, Ecuador v. Colombia*, Case IP-02, Inter-Am. Comm'n H.R., Report No. 112/10, OEA/Ser.L/V/II.140, doc. 10, §122 (2010); and *Jose Isabel Salas Galindo and Others v. United States*, Case 10.573, Inter-Am. Comm'n H.R., Report No. 121/18, OEA/Ser.L/V/II.169, doc. 138, §§325–329 (2018).

89 *Juan Carlos Abella v. Argentina*, Case 11.137, Inter-Am. Comm'n H.R., Report No. 55/97, OEA/Ser.L/V/II.95, doc. 7 rev. at 271, §§ 170–171 (1997).

interpretation and application of international law must take into account the general framework of the legal system, while preserving its unity, coherence and wholeness.[90]

Regarding the right to life applied to civilians in armed conflicts, as stated in previous analysis, the Inter-American Commission makes no concession over its absolute and inderogable value. Quite different from the evolutive argumentation developed by the European Court of Human Rights in *MacCann and Others, Al-Skeini and Others* and, finally, *Hassan*, to undermine and displace human rights protection on life, the Inter-American international legal order, besides recognizing the mandatory mutualism of human rights law and humanitarian law, conveys that the arbitrary deprivation of life is completely forbidden even in situations of armed conflict. Nevertheless, the analysis of the case performed by the Commission or the court shall comply with principles of proportionality and necessity in the use of force, making attempts to limit the suffering of civilians and unnecessary loss of life.[91] It is imperative that whether in times of peace, emergency situations or armed conflict, the right to life governs the use of lethal force by states and their agents by prohibiting the arbitrary deprivation of life and summary executions. The contours of the right to life may change in the context of an armed conflict, but the prohibition of arbitrary deprivation of life remains absolute, since this right cannot be suspended under any circumstances, including armed conflicts and legitimate states of emergency.[92]

The mutualism is preserved in the Inter-American legal system because all cases and reports merge international humanitarian law and human rights law into one guidebook. Prior cases brought to the Inter-America Commission on Human Rights have appreciated the interplay between the two branches of international law in detentions and restrictions of liberty, like the central right grappled with in *Hassan*. In *Coard et al v. United States*, therefore, the primary idea is the shared benefit of mutualism, which human rights law has not been designed to apply in absolute terms. Conversely, some permissible and non-permissible limitations must be monitored in accordance with humanitarian law.[93] Considering the right to life, the Commisssion, in its Report on Terrorism and Human Rights, takes note that, even if the right is an absolute right, the use of lethal force when strictly unavoidable to protect oneself or other persons from imminent threat of death or serious injury, or to otherwise maintain law and order, is permissible where strictly

90 *Franklin Guillermo Aisalla Molina, Ecuador v. Colombia*, Case IP-02, Inter-Am. Comm'n H.R., Report No. 112/10, OEA/Ser.L/V/II.140, doc. 10, §124 (2010); and *Jose Isabel Salas Galindo and Others v. United States*, Case 10.573, Inter-Am. Comm'n H.R., Report No. 121/18, OEA/Ser.L/V/II.169, doc. 138, §§330–331 (2018).

91 *Jose Isabel Salas Galindo and Others v. United States*, Case 10.573, Inter-Am. Comm'n H.R., Report No. 121/18, OEA/Ser.L/V/II.169, doc. 138, §§338–339 (2018).

92 Report on Terrorism and Human Rights, Inter-Am. Comm'n H.R., OEA/Ser.L/V/II.116, doc. 5 rev. 1 corr., §§86, 106 (2002).

93 *Coard et al v. United States*, Case 10.951, Inter-Am. Comm'n H.R., Report No. 109/99, OEA/Ser.L/V/II.106, Doc. 6 rev, §§38–50 (1999).

necessary and proportionate.[94] The Court has explained that, in such circumstances, states have the right to use force, "even if this implies depriving people of their lives".[95]

All in all, it would be too simple to say that while humanitarian law has an underlying realistic philosophy based on military necessity, human rights law is idealistic and inappropriate for situations of hardship. The application of human rights to situations of armed conflict is compatible with the drafting and wording of human rights treaties and of the two Additional Protocols of the Geneva Conventions.[96] Besides, this mandatory mutualism combined with international jurisprudence on interpretation and application of human rights is an outcome of international law evolution in general terms, which tames states' obligations toward human rights law and international humanitarian law.[97]

The burden of morality

It seems evident today that the essential point in international law is the full protection of human rights, either individual or collective. After the Second World War international human rights became extremely significant, envisaging a modern utopia. Morality became the worldwide aspiration of mankind, and was a heavy burden for two main reasons. First, its purely moral content has great antipolitical potential; and second, in order to survive, human rights had to build a political agenda with enough programmatic scope to inject morality into foreign policy, which is initially contradictory to the antipolitical position of the utopian viewpoint. The profound moral quandaries faced by human rights today point to the very meaning of a utopia, which is its moral survival in a moment of history when all other utopias have died. Therefore, human rights were compelled to define the "good life" and offer a plan to keep them pulsing in the international community in accordance with their suprapolitical birth.[98]

Besides the understanding shown in *Hassan* and many other cases that provide support in times of emergency and the following derogation of human rights law, it is undeniable that international law has changed to embrace a broader perception of armed conflicts and emergency situations. Looking at moral compliance, some scholars and international precedents argue that international humanitarian law, as *lex specialis*, prevails in the conduct of hostilities that come under international law, because humanitarian law is the more refined body of law. On the

94 Report on Terrorism and Human Rights, Inter-Am. Comm'n H.R., OEA/Ser.L/V/II.116, doc. 5 rev. 1 corr., §§87, 112 (2002).

95 *Neira-Alegría et al. v. Peru*, Merits, Inter-Am. Ct. H.R. (ser. C) No. 20, §74 (January 19, 1995).

96 Cordula Droege, *The Interplay between International Humanitarian Law and International Human Rights Law in Situations of Armed Conflict*, 40 ISRAELI LAW REVIEW no. 2, 310, 324 (2007).

97 COMISSIÓN INTER AMERICANA DE DERECHOS HUMANOS, INFORME SOBRE TERRORISMO Y DERECHOS HUMANOS, par. 46 (2002).

98 SAMUEL MOYN, THE LAST UTOPIA: HUMAN RIGHTS IN HISTORY 213–214 (2010).

other hand, human rights law represents more refinement than domestic law enforcement. "Thus, the closer a situation is to the battlefield, the more humanitarian law will prevail over human rights law, whereas for law enforcement, human rights law prevails."[99] This idea is exactly what we attempt to overturn in this work.

First, we need to clarify why such a notion is current in doctrine and jurisprudence. Both contemporary domestic and international law share the values of human dignity to endorse and reinforce human rights. However, as we have seen in previous chapters, the smaller the social structure, the easier it is to maintain a common grasp of human dignity, because the values congregated in such a social body are less plural and more homogenic. Conversely, the larger the social body, the wider the understanding of human dignity has to be, in a process identified as generalization of values. As a society becomes more plural, its values grow more generalized and broader. For this reason, human rights are easier to enforce domestically than internationally. Today's humanitarian law, however, is a branch of law crafted with principles of humanity and designed to operate internationally, containing broader notions of law in accordance with its wider range of cover. Humanitarian law, albeit based on the principle of humanity, possesses other rules that do not converge on human dignity, unlike human rights law, which maintains human dignity as its axial value.

Therefore, it is commonly assumed that in some cases, international humanitarian law and human rights law are incompatible because of inner divergence: the former prioritizes social value, while the latter has at its core individual value. Something we have learned from human history is that violence has a tendency to perpetuate itself, like an autonomous process, and historically its power condemns all participants to impotence. Hence, no serious effort to change quasi-institutionalized conditions of violence can limit itself to such factors as insight and means-ends rationality or personal morality and values like the one supported by human dignity and its Kantian roots.[100]

Paying due heed to the conditions and phases of violence in armed conflicts, we want to put forward an opposing idea related to targeting civilians. There is space for arguing that some adaptation of mutualism may provide mutual reinforcement by standing on the back of morality: "to address both systems simultaneously striking a balance between the interpretation and application of the *lex specialis* and international human rights law so that humanitarian considerations and military needs are respected".[101] Juridical perspectives eventually face moral dilemmas, which happens because international law does not provide a precise account of moral behavior enforced by law, as the natural sciences usually do. What shall be demonstrated is a balance in the moral argument to push the action forward, in

99 Cordula Droege, *The Interplay between International Humanitarian Law and International Human Rights Law in Situations of Armed Conflict*, 40 Israeli Law Review, no. 2, 310, 344 (2007).

100 Hans Joas, War and Modernity 193–194 (2003).

101 *Jose Isabel Salas Galindo and Others v. United States,* Case 10.573, Inter-Am. Comm'n H.R., Report No. 121/18, OEA/Ser.L/V/II.169, doc. 138, §326 (2018).

order to reasonably justify the perpetration of such conduct. Thus, the incongruence between morality and law shall be lifted, since the morality behind any act may differ according to the individuals or communities involved.[102]

When we deal with social values in the decision-making process, we bring to light social goals that are based on reasoning related to individual and collective welfare. Morality and welfare merge on common ground. The conventional philosophy of social science has asserted that the task of the social scientist is the production of law-like generalizations, as they have to foresee the outcomes of alternative policies that derive from knowledge of law-like generalizations. MacIntyre inserts an interesting comparison into the debate when he considers that chemical equations relating pressure, temperature and volume of gases have a very well defined set of counterfactual conditionals, as does natural science, in a way that law-like generalizations do not. Natural science has universal quantifiers that do not serve in law-like generalizations of social science. Although we have universal values, they mutate from case to case depending on probabilities and social phenomena. Pure contingency is a social modifier; even trivial contingencies can powerfully influence the outcome of great events.[103]

This is interesting because one of the most amazing things about gases that we learned in our high school days is that, in spite of wide differences in chemical properties, all gases obey the laws that deal with how they behave in respect to temperature and pressure – that is, the famous NTP, or STP (Normal Temperature and Pressure, or Standard Temperature and Pressure), which represent the normal conditions that allow gas laws to form patterns. Since temperature and air pressure vary from place to place, a standard reference is necessary for comparing the measurement and documentation of chemical and physical outcomes. Thus, the International Union of Pure and Applied Chemistry (IUPAC) has established the pattern as "air at 60°F (520°R, 15.6°C) and 14.696 psia (1 atm, 1.01325 bara)",[104] which means that when conditions of temperature and pressure are at 60°F and 1 atm, the gases will always behave the same way. If conditions of temperature and pressure change, gases' properties alter according to the appropriateness of the new conditions.[105] Again, STP is the regular base for the outcome of reactions of gases but, eventually, exceptional conditions arise which provoke continuous natural adjustments during moments of irregularity. When conditions return to normal, normal physical properties are back in place.

MacIntyre's assessment using the chemistry rationale is interesting because natural science works with logic and patterns and looks for different results where stabilization and normality can be found, no matter how the original conditions shift. In social science, as in international law, the logic that can be applied in natural science is not entirely enough because we have social elements that

102 Heidi M. Hurd, O Combate moral 21 (2003).
103 Alasdair MacIntyre, After Virtue 88–100 (3rd ed. 2007).
104 The Engineering ToolBox, www.engineeringtoolbox.com/stp-standard-ntp-normal-air-d_772.html (last visited September 21, 2019).
105 The Pennsylvania State University, http://chemistry.bd.psu.edu/jircitano/gases.html (last visited September 21, 2019)

overload the equations in such a way as to produce multiple answers to the same scenario and standard conditions. Thus, natural science rationale is resourceful to set binary results, like cost-benefit analysis and decisions on social public policies where the generalization of values must be considered. The social science analysis, therefore, needs to improve the formula to model social elements from case to case and provide appropriate answers for social quandaries.

As argued by Michael Rosen, to treat human beings as an end begs questions that remain unanswered by the formula of humanity, particularly since Kant does not prohibit treating humans as a means totally but as a *means only*, from which arises a variety of semantic differences in a grey zone of uncertainty about what is and is not morally permissible regarding human rights.[106] However, since we can apply human rights law in peacetime – i.e. when there is political stability and social normality, or "normal conditions" – some useful knowledge may be gathered using this for comparison. Under certain standard conditions, the conclusion to ensure and protect human rights – to fully respect and endorse human dignity in the general sense – shall be repeatedly the same. Furthermore, on occasions where we experience political instability and social abnormality, the answer may not be the same if the main goal becomes the reestablishment of the *status quo*, stability and normality.

Scholars and international jurisprudence accept this notion that human rights law is comfortably applied in peacetime, which is why their response is the overall predominance of international humanitarian law as *lex specialis* over human rights law. They see human rights law as STP, or the answer for our social pattern at 60° F and 1 atm, while humanitarian law is the answer for unbalanced conditions – the social contingencies – until normality is restored. Obviously, it was learned over the course of time that international humanitarian law and human rights law do not exclude each other, but instead have a common nucleus – the principle of humanity – which cannot be set apart, and is the reason why the mutualism theory was developed in ICJ precedents and reproduced in regional human rights courts.

Even with the recognition of mandatory mutualism in certain cases such as targeting civilians in wartime, the understanding of the court is to displace human rights law in order to open the pathway for international humanitarian law, the rules of which are more appropriate to certain unbalanced conditions since it carries the existential paradox of inserting moral and legal restriction into a scenario typified by a lot of aggression and violence. When human rights law lodges in domains of humanitarian law, there are some who believe this leads to unavoidable respect for human dignity as a minimum and essential core to rule humanity; others point to the longstanding lessons of Emer de Vattel and argue that morality is sacrificed for the sake of keeping the state's political system stable, making justice bound to necessity.[107]

Thus, human dignity does not always serve international law and the international community and, as it is seen as an immovable core of human rights law and

106 Michael Rosen, Dignity: its history and meaning 83–86 (2012).
107 Ruti G. Teitel, Humanity's Law 47–74 (2011).

morality, the solution to fulfill certain conditions and justify actions aimed at the reestablishment or maintenance of public order is usually commensalism: the withdrawal of human rights for the sole benefit of international humanitarian law. After all, men do whatever it takes to save themselves and their community, so morality is generally detached from law during wartime.[108] Therefore, there are moments – such as public emergencies and states of exception – when we lose our normal and stable social conditions (the STP analogy) and the "hive switch" occurs, which means that collective values based on intersocial grounds are fully and temporarily applied and we reach the realm of "*sacred*, where the self disappears and collective interests predominate", guided by a "very notion of an objective moral order" that is essential for the political survival of the community. This temporary moral law is founded on social duty, which means the renunciation of self-interest for the sake of the community's spiritual existence, which represents the consistency of mankind's values.[109]

Also, the communitarianism trait of contemporary international law represents an embodiment of common shared values of a collective nature. In this regard, the more heterogenous the community, the greater the need for overarching values (generalization of values). The embodiment process, then, drains individual morality in order to strengthen collective morality. This is the *hive switch*. By assimilation, international community members make seeking the greatest good for the greatest number a golden rule.[110]

Notwithstanding court decisions, for the sake of Habermas's communicative action theory and Joas's creativity action theory of law, we present a different formula, one in which human rights law does not need to be kept aloof from or frozen within mandatory mutualism for its full application of mutual benefits for both branches of law. Nevertheless, as a rule, it regards some military acts towards civilians as rational actions that retain legality and certainty of moral acceptance. The unbalanced conditions of instability and abnormality described in Article 4 of ICCPR, Article 15 of ECHR and Article 27 of ACHR, change human rights law's STP response regarding human moral dignity to utilitarianism as a metamorality – overarching shared value – for the sake of normality and recovering stability. As required by the United Nations, these new conditions of abnormality must be of exceptional and temporary nature and their unbalanced features well defined by the United Nations as a "public emergency which threatens the life of the nation, and the State party must have officially proclaimed a state of emergency" pursuant to the main goal of regaining normality, noting as well that "not every disturbance

108 Michael Walzer, Just and Unjust Wars 03–21 (4th ed. 2006).

109 Jonathan Haidt, The Righteous Mind: why good people are divided by politics and religion 226–241 (2012).

110 Amitai Etzioni, The New Golden Rule: community and morality in a democratic society 195–197 (1997); Bernard Williams, Moral: uma introdução à ética 117–134 (2005); Hans Joas, The Sacredness of the Person: a new genealogy of human rights 179–182 (Alex Skinner trans., 2013); Jonathan Haidt, The Righteous Mind: why good people are divided by politics and religion 223 (2012); and Joshua Greene, Moral Tribes: emotion, reason, and the gap between us and them 306–345 (2013).

or catastrophe qualifies as a public emergency which threatens the life of the nation".[111]

Earlier it was mentioned that the international legal framework embraces a plurality of values that go through a process of generalization. This means that all beliefs, opinions and thoughts can exist peacefully in the international community. Consequently, in order to apply the concept of metamorality to human dignity, a shared value must exist as common currency. Plurality of thoughts, opinions and values acknowledge justice as a common currency, very well represented by endeavoring to achieve the greatest good for the greatest number. This utilitarian conception of justice as a social value is indisputably a common currency in a plural international society that seeks to solve moral quandaries and controversies while concurrently keeping all members of society united by a common goal. Therefore, metamorality functions as a second moral compass triggered by the "hive switch", and comes into action when the first moral compass, human dignity, fails to deliver solutions to controversies. The second moral compass, due to its pragmatic nature, is more suitable for delivering satisfactory answers,[112] and its predominance is temporary and contemplates the renunciation of self-interest for the sake of a community's political survival and a constitution of values for mankind.

The utilitarian morality that temporarily surpasses human dignity also raises social values to the realm of *sacred*, where the self disappears and collective interests preponderate, overriding the realm of the *profane* and the ordinary day-to-day values that govern our lives in normality and stability, under STP conditions. The realm of the profane is overshadowed by something higher and nobler. And all this happens not to annul the cardinal *self* value of human dignity, but rather to uphold a sociologically informed standpoint related to the creation of a community that pulls people up from a lower level (the profane) to a higher level (the sacred).[113]

As already mentioned, today it is global terrorism that plays the role of *hostis humani generis*. We are not talking about terrorism against alien occupation, colonial domination or racist regimes, which is largely accepted by United Nations resolutions.[114] Rather, *hostis humani generis* is the nihilist terrorism that purports to destroy the morale of a nation or a group of people by adopting a random method of murdering innocent people and undercutting any sign of solidarity.

111 C.C.P.R. General Comment No. 29, *States of Emergency (Article 4): International Covenant on Civil and Political Rights*, U.N. Doc. CCPR/C/21/Rev.1/Add.11, §§2–3 (August 31, 2001).

112 Joshua Greene, Moral Tribes: emotion, reason, and the gap between us and them 290–292 (2013).

113 Jonathan Haidt, The Righteous Mind: why good people are divided by politics and religion 247–248 (2012).

114 G.A. Res. 1514 (XV), *Declaration on the Granting of Independence to Colonial Countries and Peoples*, U.N. Doc. A/RES/1514 (XV) (Dec. 14, 1960); and G.A. Res. 2908 (XXVII), *Implementation of the Declaration on the Granting of Independence to Colonial Countries and Peoples*, U.N. Doc. A/RES/2908 (XXVII) (Nov. 02, 1972).

The actions of revolutionary terrorism, like those of the IRA, display a modicum of honor. As Walzer narrates, IRA bombing maneuvers avoided the unnecessary suffering of children, for example. "Even in destruction there is a right way and a wrong way, and there are limits." Children, policeman and pedestrians are like civilians in wartime, and they are innocent politically just as civilians are innocent militarily. It is precisely these people that contemporary terrorists aim to kill. There is a moral difference between aiming at particular people because of things they have done or are doing and aiming at whole groups of people, indiscriminately, because of who they are.[115]

There are moments of extremity and crisis when the state's rights and human rights have to be violated for the greater good of all. For these extreme moments, the conventions of war do not provide an answer; these extremes lie beyond the reach of conventional provision. The greater the justice of the cause, the more rules I can violate for the sake of the cause – though some rules, like *jus cogens,* are always inviolable (like torture[116]). The same argument can be put in terms of outcomes, so the greater the injustice that is likely to result from my defeat, the more rules I can violate in order to avoid defeat.[117] For this, we have to look at the principle of necessity. One criterion of lawful necessity is submitting the enemy to the least possible expenditure of time, life and money. According to this point of view (and the theory of double effect), military necessity determines whether the civilians involved are attacked or not. In actual humanitarian law, we need to balance military necessity against protection of life (respecting the principle of war that noncombatants cannot be attacked at any time) in such a way that the war can be considered justly fought (there is a moral distinction between people who can and people who cannot be killed in a war), and this constant tension between winning and fighting well is a major modern challenge.

In this regard, the restoration of normality, and STP's answer, would be political stability and social normality in peacetime, in which public emergency and threats to the life of the nation are absent – and under such conditions, the reaction of international law shall also be predictably normal. Thus, normality supports the duty to respect human dignity, which, by international human rights law, is conceived of as respect-as-observance. According to our discussion some chapters ago, the legal duty of respect-as-observance human dignity presupposes the existence of human rights, and the respect comes formally and bound by the law in such a manner that we respect a person just as we respect the speed limit by driving below a certain speed. This is exactly the legal force generated by the postwar human rights bodies of law and Common Article 3 of the Geneva Conventions.[118] Thus, the moral reasoning for judgement moves from duties, as fixed

115 Michael Walzer, Just and Unjust War 199–200 (2006).

116 *Prosecutor v. Anto Furundzija [Trial Chamber],* Case No. IT-95-17/1-T, 1998 I.C. T.Y. §153 (December 10); *Demir and Baykara v. Turkey [GC],* no. 34503/97 Eur. Ct. H.R., §73 (2008); and *Neira-Alegría et al. v. Peru,* Merits, Inter-Am. Ct. H.R. (ser. C) No. 20, §§74–75 (January 19, 1995).

117 Michael Walzer, Just and Unjust War 221–229 (2006).

118 Michael Rosen, Dignity: its history and meaning 57–60 (2012).

in Kantian deontology of categorical morality, to ends, consequences of actions, teleologically secured in consequentialist morality.

Graphically, it would be something like the representation below, meaning that in peacetime, when we face STP conditions of normality and stability, the universe of international humanitarian law in contemporary international law is completely submersed in and dependent on human rights law, while in armed conflict situations, when we face abnormality and instability provoked by public emergency and state of exception, the universes of international humanitarian law and human rights law are concentric and isomorphic.

As we can see, in any apparent conflict between the provisions of international humanitarian law and human rights law in peacetime, human moral dignity must prevail, since it is the value and right highly appreciated by both democratic societies and the international community. It is the cardinal value – the super-value – of the whole legal system. Therefore, commensalism on behalf of human rights signifies the civilized commitment to respect, endorse and guarantee individual rights. Conversely, in wartime, the two branches of law equalize and human moral dignity no longer transcends the apparent conflicts and moral quandaries, which therefore require a metamorality with values common to both branches and capable of providing the benefits of mutual application. Peter Singer's expanding circle of morality includes utilitarianism as the common currency of all nations in a cosmopolitan environment such as the international community.[119] Following the

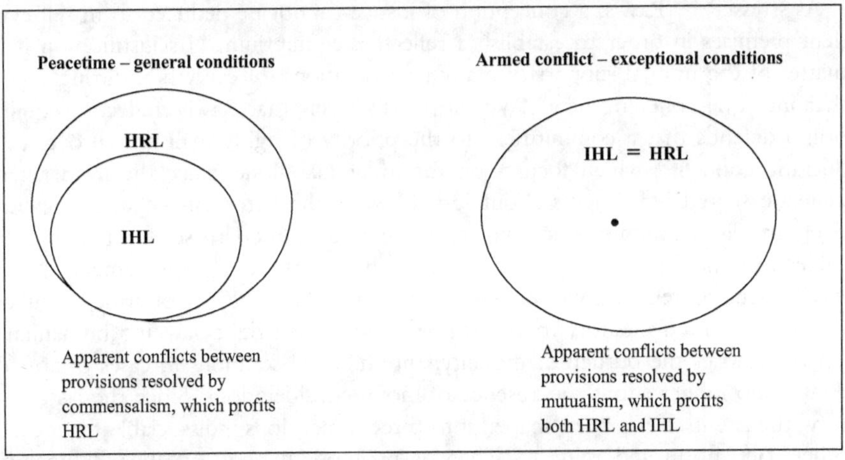

Figure 5.1 Representation of the two bodies of law considered, international humanitarian law (IHL) and human rights law (HRL), and their interaction in peacetime and armed conflict situations. In peacetime, HRL has a broader reach than IHL, while in armed conflict situations the two share the same reach and become concentric.

119 Peter Singer, The Expanding Circle 118–123 (2011); and Peter Singer et Renata Singer, The Moral of The Story: an anthology of ethics through literature 401 (2005).

Aristotelic teleological reasoning, only by living in a polis and partaking in politics do we fully realize our nature as human beings, by essence meant to live in a political community that exists by nature and comes before the individual. Human beings are not self-sufficient without a political community.[120] What is being defended here is an international community in which the international legal system is designed to protect the lives and liberties of the members of that community – as in the Latin phrase cited by Walzer, *fiat justicia ruat coelom*: "Do justice even if the heavens fall." Walzer adds: "Do justice unless the heavens are really about to fall," recalling the extreme necessity that characterizes a supreme emergency.[121]

Courts, or international governmental organizations such as the United Nations, can identify a supreme emergency and make it international. As we have seen, the international legal system allows the use of general legal clauses that might be filled by interpretation and application of international law (Article 31, Vienna Convention). Moreover, this law-making process via its decision-making rationale has to take into account the unity, coherence and wholeness of the entire legal system, brought together by a systematic and teleological interpretation. By this token, the mandatory mutualism between international humanitarian law and human rights law complies with international law standards. The utilitarian meta-morality can deal with the imminent danger of high impact when targeting civilians might appear necessary and proportional as a side effect of coping with the supreme emergency.

As stressed by Rawls, a conception of justice cannot be deduced from self-evident premises in order to establish a reflective equilibrium: "Its justification is a matter of the mutual support of many considerations, of everything fitting together into one coherent view". We can boldly assert that Rawls' reflective equilibrium defends that a commitment to the priority of rights shall prevail over the Socratic good life, which focuses on the individual alone, since the former can generate shared judgements about justice, while the latter cannot. It is imperatively true in peacetime, when we can theorize on a modern society building its values to uphold political stability, equality and social moral improvement.[122] All in all, then, contemporary international law, principally the law of armed conflict that follows the mandatory mutualism between human rights law and humanitarian law, carries the burden of morality. International solutions in cases of armed conflict no longer admit the absence of moral considerations. Since the last century, the law itself has been shaped into three dimensions indissociable from each other: fact, norm and value.[123] There is no modern body of law of humanity devoid of moral values, so the burden of morality and moral justification is a constant reality. Therefore, the rationale we are developing of using utilitarianism

120 Peter Singer, Ética Prática 21 (3rd ed. 2002); Alasdair MacIntyre, After Virtue 148 (3rd ed. 2007); and Michael Sandel, Justiça: o que é fazer a coisa certa 54–55 (2012).

121 Michael Walzer, Just and Unjust War 230–231 (2006).

122 John Rawls, Uma Teoria da Justiça 70–88 (3rd ed. 2008).

123 Miguel Reale, Teoria Tridimensional do Direito 124–126 (5th ed. 1994).

as metamorality to overcome moral quandaries of human rights law in reference to targeting civilians in armed conflict situations complies with the contemporary burden of morality and also has some social rules of applicability, value of community and social harmony.[124]

Utilitarianism is a theory of both personal morality and social justice.[125] Applying utilitarianism as metamorality does not mean human moral dignity is forfeited. Utilitarianism not only has personal morality within its walls, but a Durkheimian version also recognizes that human flourishing requires social order and embeddedness, all tied up in a social notion of justice.[126]

While social justice prevails in exceptional situations of armed conflict, particularly those with moral dilemmas related to targeting civilians. As abnormality and instability remove normal conditions of legal interpretation and application, social justice trumps personal morality, such as it did in overruling *Parrilo v. Italy*'s hold on human moral dignity as an impediment to using human embryos for the sake of genetic developments in cures and saving human lives.[127] It is just a pragmatic morality whereby principles are put forward tentatively in the expectation that they will be shaped and modified by our responses to practical problems – in which adjustments, by the way, also support Rawls' rationale of reflective equilibrium, since utilitarianism as metamorality underpins our judgment of community seeking a greater good cooperatively.[128]

As stated by Joshua Green, utilitarianism is a fine idea with a bad name in politics and moral philosophy despite being a great answer to promoting a community's social values of liberty and security, delivering the best outcome to the greatest number of members of society. Therefore, when we have a clash of values, or an apparent conflict of legal provisions (which is how we have expressed it since the beginning of the book), utilitarianism serves the purpose of pointing a way out based on rationality and morality that preserves human values and interests. As we have an international community based on generalized and plural values, utilitarian metamorality also serves as *common currency* among nations, since everyone can easily understand the value of promoting a greater good for the survival and continuity of society, while weighing it against unintended losses in the context of a significant victory or advantage.[129] Working as a common currency, utilitarian metamorality must surpass two moral truths we have been working on: morality in God and morality in Reason. As we explored extensively in chapter 3, conceptions

124 Xiaorong Li, *"Asian Values" and the Universality of Human Rights*, in THE PHILOSOPHY OF HUMAN RIGHTS 397, 403–405 (2001).

125 RICHARD A. POSNER, THE ECONOMICS OF JUSTICE 51–52 (1996).

126 JONATHAN HAIDT, THE RIGHTEOUS MIND: WHY GOOD PEOPLE ARE DIVIDED BY POLITICS AND RELIGION 272 (2012).

127 *Parrilo v. Italy [GC]*, no. 46470/11 Eur. Ct. H.R. (2015).

128 JONATHAN GLOVER, HUMANITY: A MORAL HISTORY OF THE 20TH CENTURY 06 (2nd ed. 2012); and JOSHUA GREENE, MORAL TRIBES: EMOTION, REASON, AND THE GAP BETWEEN US AND THEM 328 (2013).

129 JOSHUA GREENE, MORAL TRIBES: EMOTION, REASON, AND THE GAP BETWEEN US AND THEM 106–107, 175 (2013).

of human rights rely immensely on both, one through Christian values and the other through Kant's breakthrough.

Barack Obama once said in a lecture that the biblical episode where Abraham takes his only son to the top of a mountain to sacrifice him in the name of God to prove his faith is a good story to show an audience that treating a person as a means to an end is divinely wrong, since God had to personally interfere to teach us the importance of human dignity. However, if nowadays any of us saw Abraham taking his son out of the church to sacrifice him in the name of God in the middle of the street, we would call the police or personally intervene, whether or not Abraham had followed the Bible's orientation. The analogy may fit in the sense that it is safer for us to act according to what we see and hear – that is, according to our perception of the current facts – as a common inherited right or even as basic rationality.[130] The point is that morality in God has its reasons and rationality – all valid – but it does not serve as a common currency for the international community. Thus, if we are against abortion for reasons based on God and we believe we are right, we have to defend the idea on different grounds before those who do not believe in the same God or in any God at all. Morality from Judeo-Christian precepts cannot serve as common currency in a plural society.

Morality of reason, in most Western cultures, rests on Immanuel Kant's shoulders, recalling his moral groundwork and practical pure reason. Kant departs from an immanent sense of morality rooted in our humanity, which is a universal and self-evident feature. All of us share these traits regardless of our personal inclinations. From humanity emerges the element of morality that leads to two characteristics that only human reason provides: dignity and autonomy. Thus, the first human value is dignity of the human person. Only after this are other values defined, and this process is developed by human autonomy. From this point of view, the human being has dignity because moral law lives within – it is embodied in the person – which is why he praises a universal and self-evident morality. Also, reason enjoins us to obey two imperatives: universal law and humanity as an end. The former proposes that we "act only on that maxim whereby you can at the same time will that it should become a universal law". The latter insists that all humanity "has in itself an absolute value … an end in itself … . I say that man, and in general every rational being, exists as an end in himself, not merely as a means for arbitrary use by this or that will."[131] As discussed in chapter 3, a lot of practical and real-life problems come into being because of Kant's morality of human dignity, which transcends the human person to become a universal imperative. It is more theoretical than pragmatic, while utilitarianism is just the opposite. Besides not being unanimously shared as the best conception of justice or true universal value of morality, Kantian terms are also unfit as universal common currency.

130 Barack Obama, *Obama's 2006 Speech on Faith and Politics* (June 28, 2006), www.nytimes.com/2006/06/28/us/politics/2006obamaspeech.html (last visited Oct. 2, 2019).

131 Immanuel Kant, Fundamentação da Metafísica dos Costumes 62–70 (2006).

In moral science, however, justice is goodness and the fulfilment of good deeds by men. Justice as value requires an endless reinterpretation so that its meaning might realize new ideals and their unfulfilled potential pursue new social achievements.[132] Neither human dignity nor utilitarianism are moral dogmas, and there is no such thing in moral philosophy. Yet, when we talk about shared values obtained by a generalization process, utilitarian morality serves quite well as common currency. The pursuit of a greater good coincides with restraints on freedom, life and property. Utility, here, is the combination of good life experiences, which as a notion accessible to all mankind makes utilitarianism a common currency and metamorality. And as a metamorality, when utilitarianism makes the greatest good the desirable end, it allows us the international community to compromise in order to evolve and be morally better. There is no need to be morally perfect.[133]

Human moral dignity is fully endorsed as the prevailing moral compass for leading human rights law and international law in peacetime, an ideal scenario where social STP is found normal and politically stable. Once configured as the state of exception, utilitarianism works as metamorality of human rights law and, even though human dignity plays a secondary role when contrasting actions toward civilians with necessity, proportionality and the mandatory configuration of targeting are side effects, which makes those monstrous and theoretical examples have little tangible weight in a pragmatic approach. Complementarily, Michael Walzer says it is wrong to believe that the fight to enforce and endorse universal values and principles shall always be fought the same way. It is wrong because universal values have multiple concrete applications.[134]

Doctrine of double effect and utilitarianism

The factual scenario of targeting civilians mentioned above, to be morally acceptable in this work, has to contain its epistemological limits within the doctrine of double effect. It is morally permissible to perform an act that has both a good and an evil effect so long as the intended good effect outweighs the evil effect, which is simply foreseen rather than intended. In essence, the double effect is a way of reconciling the absolute prohibition against attacking noncombatants and the legitimate conduct of military activity. Even before the modern formulation of proportionality in Additional Protocol I, the laws of war incorporated these notions,[135] and its applicability looms in actions against nonstate actors as well.[136]

It is paramount that the evil consequence is not intended as an end in itself, but is in pursuit of a greater good as an end by neutral or good means, even if a lesser

132 Hans Joas, The Sacredness of the Person: A New Genealogy of Human Rights 135 (2013).
133 Joshua Greene, Moral Tribes: Emotion, Reason, and the Gap Between Us and Them 280–284 (2013).
134 Michael Walzer, Just and Unjust Wars 117 (4th ed. 2006).
135 Laurie R. Blank and Gregory P. Noone, International Law and Armed Conflicts: Fundamental Principles and Contemporary Challenges in the Law of War 52 (2013).
136 Ruti G. Teitel, Humanity's Law 122 (2011).

evil is a certain and anticipated side effect in which there is no other way to achieve the greatest good. Therefore it is important to highlight a subtle detail in this formula, which is intentional and targeted. The morally acceptable doctrine of double effect is one where the intention is good but the aim contains a certain evil consequence. Acts that have both evil intention and aim are not the focus of this work since they are incompatible with all moral advancement achieved in international law and would advocate the annulation of human moral dignity, the heart of human rights law.

As made clear above, utilitarianism works as metamorality – overarching shared value – and while human moral dignity is still there, it is in the background. Although the subjective content is intentional, practice and pragmatism advise its identification by evidence collected on a case-by-case basis. The power of the state to act and target civilians is not unlimited, nor may the state resort to any means to attain its ends.[137] Thus, it is important to analyze the intentional character of human actions – that is, the specific corporeal dimensions and the original social nature of the human capacity for action.[138]

The doctrine of double effect is relevant because it morally distinguishes the terror of bombing civilians in armed conflicts from – for example – the bombing of military targets with predictions of certain civilian casualties from collateral damage. The former is unacceptable since its intention is evil, while the latter might be acceptable. This doctrine is thus deeply related to morality in wartime. Two things must be taken into consideration: the action is itself a means to the greatest good while bearing an evil effect, and the greatest good must outbalance the evil effect. The principle of proportionality also adds the aspect that this foreseen evil ought to be the lesser evil possible. Thus, "it may be permissible to produce a lesser evil as a side effect only if we are pursuing a greatest good as a final end".[139] For instance, if we bomb a munitions factory, civilians are going to die as a side effect, but it does not mean we target their deaths. Then, to be permissible, the greatest good must outbalance this evil effect, seeing that munitions are necessary to kill people in war and the reduced ability to have munitions equals a greater number of people being alive, while civilian deaths represent the lesser evil. Furthermore, resorting to the lesser evil is not an immorality.[140]

Likewise, Jonathan Glover stresses that armed conflicts allow some actions that have foreseen but unintended consequence as a side effect. To tolerate innocent people being targeted, the good must be sufficient to outweigh the harm. So long as the numbers are not disproportionately large, some foreseen but unintended civilian targets can be morally acceptable. The doctrine of double effect then causes acts that have both good and bad effects. The morality of the acts is tied to

137 Report on Terrorism and Human Rights, Inter-Am. Comm'n H.R., OEA/Ser.L/V/II.116, doc. 5 rev. 1 corr., §§89, 107 (2002); and *Neira-Alegría et al. v. Peru*, Merits, Inter-Am. Ct. H.R. (ser. C) No. 20, §75 (January 19, 1995).

138 Hans Joas, War and Modernity 191 (2003).

139 Frances Myrna Kamm, The Moral Target: aiming at right conduct in war and other conflicts 28–33 (2012).

140 Vladimir Jankélévitch, O Paradoxo da Moral 30 (2008).

whether the bad effect is merely foreseen or actually intended. A merely foreseen bad effect may be permissible so long as the badness is not out of proportion to the good being pursued. After all, intention is important in moral thinking – even teleological consequentialist moral reasoning. To many of us, there is an important moral difference between unintentionally killing civilians in a raid on the ball-bearing factory and deliberately bombing a housing estate.[141]

Justice in this scenario comes from fighting justly, which the utilitarian outlook drawn from international humanitarian law and human rights law gives a twofold aspect. Basically, in the conduct of armed conflict it is not permitted to do any mischief that does not materially lead to the end of the hostility or a significant gain in strategy towards its end, as maximization of utility. Therefore, excessive harm and evil intentions are prohibited. This requires determining the utility of military necessity and analyze proportionality of mischief done on targeting civilians, weighing it according to not only the immediate harm to individuals but also any injury to the permanent interests of mankind against the contribution that mischief makes to the end of hostilities.

The limits of utility and proportionality are very important. Utilitarianism applied to armed conflicts invites soldiers to calculate costs and benefits up to a point, and at that point it establishes a series of precise rules governing moral barricades that can only be breached at great moral cost. The utilitarian argument here is that victory or great advantage will end the conflict or reduce the probability of future combats or even eschew immediate and horrifying consequences. It all sets the interests of individuals and of mankind at a lesser value than the victory or advantage that is being sought, which follows utilitarian morality of the greatest good for the greatest number.[142]

After all, the rationality of armed conflict and the nature of its necessity are to compel the submission of the enemy with the least possible expenditure of time, life and money. Military necessity can determine whether the civilians involved are attacked or not. Generally, they must not be attacked if their activities can be stopped or their products seized or destroyed in some other way and without significant risk. They can never be the objects or targets of military activity. Nevertheless, because of civilian proximity to a conflict zone, the doctrine of double effect does not require that the battle be stopped, but rather that some degree of care be taken not to harm civilians, which commonly implies that we recognize their rights as best as we can within the context of armed conflict.

This doctrine is closely related to our ordinary ways of thinking about moral life; it is a way of reconciling the absolute prohibition against attacking non-combatants and the legitimate conduct of military activity,[143] and it is far and away more complex than the simple statement of solving international issues "on the basis of arithmetical considerations". This banalization would be contrary to

141 Jonathan Glover, Humanity: A Moral History of the 20th Century 84 (2nd ed. 2012).

142 Henry Sidgwick, The Methods of Ethics 75–79 (2012).

143 Michael Walzer, Just and Unjust Wars 144–152 (4th ed. 2006).

the idea of human nature and the purpose of the international humanitarian law and human rights law mutualism.[144]

Combatants, on the other hand, can be hit deliberately or as a side effect. Targeting individual enemy combatants in war is accepted as both legal and moral.[145] International humanitarian law does not prohibit the targeting or killing of enemy combatants who have not laid down their arms or been placed *hors de combat*, and the death of a combatant under these circumstances does not constitute a violation of the right to life.[146] Nevertheless, noncombatants can only be attacked as a side effect, or collateral damage. The mandatory mutualism between international humanitarian law and human rights law, regarding military necessity on targeting, can be synthetized as below.

Notwithstanding, international humanitarian law has been interpreted as permitting deliberate harming of civilians in a supreme emergency where there is a necessity to overcome an imminent catastrophe and win, with the principle of humanity put aside to some degree. The bombings in the Second World War fit this perspective because, besides the elevated number of civilian deaths, the greater good of defeating worldwide Nazism overshadowed those civilian casualties. In 1939, when atomic energy became a serious possibility, the United Kingdom and United States were concerned about the German atomic program and the danger of a Nazi bomb. In Germany, large quantities of heavy water from Norway were being used for experiments on the possibility of a chain reaction that pertained to the Norsk Hydro plant at Rjukan. Suddenly, the Nazis decided to dismantle the plant and transport the heavy water to Germany.

Glover tells us that it was vital to stop the heavy water from reaching Germany, but there was no time for a full-scale raid on the plant in Rjukan as there were no troops nearby to undergo a successful attack to destroy the plant. The water would go by train, crossing a lake by rail-ferry. The train would be hard to blow up and would be crowded with civilians. The ferry carried fewer people but blowing it up would still kill civilians. However, the results were important enough to justify these losses, so those concerned aimed to minimize the effects of hitting civilians as much as possible. The plant's transport engineer supported the plan and he sent the water on a relatively uncrowded Sunday ferry. Afterwards the

Table 5.1 Targeting combatants and civilians

Target	*Combatant*		*Civilian*
Harm	deliberate	side effect	side effect

144 *Khlaifia and Other v. Italy [GC]*, no. 16483/12 Eur. Ct. H.R., partially dissenting opinion of Judge Serghides, §52 (2016).

145 William Shawcross, Justice and the Enemy: Nuremberg, 9/11, and the Trial of Khalid Sheikh Mohammed 193 (2011).

146 Report on Terrorism and Human Rights, Inter-Am. Comm'n H.R., OEA/Ser.L/V/II.116, doc. 5 rev. 1 corr., §100 (2002).

ferry was blown up, killing 26 of the 53 people on board and sending all the heavy water to the bottom of the lake. It was the end of German heavy water production in Norway, and the Germans could not resume the heavy water project, which contributed hugely to their failure to achieve a self-sustaining atomic reactor before the end of the war. Post facto studies and scientific analysis indicate that, without this attack, Germany would have completed its atomic bomb project in three to four more years, a frightening hindsight considering the Nazi atomic program would have come out ahead of the Manhattan Project.[147]

The case of the ferry carrying the heavy water from Norway illustrates the abstract calculation that decision-makers face, and these are the kind of indicators that legitimately guide the decision-making process in international law.[148] If the heavy water had reached Germany, a Nazi atomic bomb would not have been certain, but it would have been more likely. Letting Hitler have an atomic bomb would have risked a huge number of deaths and perhaps a Nazi victory, a fictional scenario depicted in an acclaimed TV show.[149] With so much at stake, that evaluation made it seem worth paying a substantial price to keep the chance of a Nazi atomic bomb as low as possible. On this occasion the doctrine of double effect was quite welcome. Considering that the deaths of the ferry passengers were not intentional and the sinking was permitted, civilian deaths were a side effect. It is not morally perfect, but it is morally acceptable.

In this regard, Michael Walzer also agrees that the rights of innocent people can be overridden for the sake of the political community. He stresses that "individuals cannot kill other individuals to save themselves, but to save a nation we can violate the rights of a determinate but smaller number of people".[150] Alasdair MacIntyre believes the same, and for him, loyalty and cosmopolitism should govern the decision-making around supreme emergencies. The survival and freedom of political communities are the highest values of international society.[151] Thus, the prohibition in international humanitarian law and human rights law is not absolute; there is a threshold that may be permissibly overridden even if it involves infringing the rights of civilians. For that, Kamm adds, the supreme emergency must involve a "dilemmatic situation" in which the deliberate killing of civilians is a wrong and not killing them is also wrong, and the lesser evil should prevail. Standard *jus in bello*, however, rules out (most) deliberate targeting of civilians despite the fact that some military operations may expect civilian casualties as collateral damage.[152]

Fiction allows us to have a great account of what this theory might represent in real life. In the movie *Ender's Game*, the world is at war with an alien race called Formics, a storyline that ultimately provides us with complex philosophical insight.

147 Jonathan Glover, Humanity: A Moral History of the 20th Century 89–92 (2nd ed. 2012)
148 Scott Sigmund Gartner, Strategic Assessment in War 33–36 (1997).
149 The Man in the High Castle (Amazon Studios 2015–).
150 Michael Walzer, Just and Unjust Wars 232–254 (4th ed. 2006).
151 Alasdair MacIntyre, After Virtue 152 (3rd ed. 2007).
152 Frances Myrna Kamm, The Moral Target: Aiming at Right Conduct in War and Other Conflicts 85, 93 (2012).

Ender Wiggin, the main character, is playing battles at a futuristic facility in something that looks like a videogame. All his military training takes place in these videogame battles, and he is informed that they are simulations.

Long story short, at the end of the movie – spoiler alert – Ender engages in the final battle of his simulated training, which no military student had ever won before. Somehow Ender finds a solution that completely ends the war, annihilates the enemy and gives his army victory. Everyone is astonished and congratulates him so emphatically that he suddenly realizes the war was real. As he mourns the decision that wiped out the whole Formic race – despite being rational and teleologically aimed at an acceptable end, victory – his general offers consolation and justification, "Son, you are going to be remembered as a hero because you put an end to the war," and Ender replies, "No, I am going to be remembered as a murderer." To end the discussion, the general answers, "We won, that is all that matters," while Ender concludes, "The way we win is what really matters."[153]

Of course, it is a fictional situation and too extreme for our purpose of endorsing utilitarian metamorality on targeting civilians. Even so, the example serves because Ender's military target was the entire enemy planet and he intended the annihilation of all Formic soldiers with Formic civilians as side effect. However, there was no prior cost-benefit calculation, or an attempt to minimize civilian casualties. Second, there is a clear disproportionality in the maneuver, since he wiped out the whole race in a moral vacuum, which is absurd for the development of utilitarian metamorality. The equivalent solution for world war would be to blow up all of Germany and Japan. This is not conceivable, but it is worth noting the rationale employed in Ender's decision-making process. It was purely teleological, as his only goal was to end the war. Pure rationality is saved by its own open-endedness, but it is not acceptable when detached from moral boundaries.

This movie helps me to didactically defend utilitarianism as metamorality and the imposition of mutualism for the benefit of both international humanitarian law and human rights law because it demonstrates the underlying presence of human rights morality on dignity. It shows that utilitarian metamorality trumps human moral dignity in order to teleologically achieve an end, but it does not entirely remove human moral dignity from the equation because, as Ender said, *the way* we win also matters. *How* we do what we have to do counts.

Ender's concern was not for the victory he won but rather for his having denied the Formics their dignity, which was not even a considered element in his equation of cost-benefit analysis. There was no estimation of proportionality in this regard, and he believed this should have occurred whether or not he knew it was a real fight. There is plausibility in his view because if an action is morally the best one available to us, then we are not morally worse for carrying it out. This is an appeal of symmetry. It is not just about winning – some moral grounds must remain to keep our perpetrated actions morally admissible.[154] Some people would

153 Ender's Game (Summit Entertainment, 2013).

154 David Rodin and Henry Shue, Just and Unjust Warriors: the moral and legal status of soldiers 12–15 (2008).

challenge this, but they would still accept that it is relevant that the alleged action was morally the best – or least bad – of all possibilities assessed. Therefore, utilitarian metamorality applied in international humanitarian law and human rights law mutualism is not just rationality and mere mathematic calculation of cost-benefit. Moral deontology plays its supporting role through principles of proportionality and necessity.

Returning to examples of the Second World War bombings, the Allied atomic bomb project had started in response to German development in the area. After fulminating over the German project, the Manhattan project took aim at Japan. The object was to end the war quickly, because a long-lasting war would have terrible human costs: the Japanese occupation of Asian countries was bloody and cruel and a military cost-benefit analysis of an invasion of Japan by Allied armies showed there would be enormous casualties on both sides and the period of armed conflict would be even longer, with further cost in terms of American and Japanese lives. Hence, on August 6, 1945, the Enola Gay dropped the atomic bomb called "Little Boy" on Hiroshima, causing 140,000 deaths, a number that, five years later, amounted to 200,000. On August 9, 1945, an American bomber dropped "Fat Man" on Nagasaki, killing 70,000 people. Five years later that total amounted to 140,000.

Considering Ender's conundrum, could the war against Japan have been stopped by other means? And, if there were no alternative ways of stopping the war, would the dropping of bombs remain justifiable? Maybe there was no certain way of ending the war without the use of the bomb. Nevertheless, in the light of what happened to the people of Hiroshima and Nagasaki, the thought is unavoidable that the quest for an alternative should have at least been tried. Today we suppose that using the bomb was the only way of shortening the war. Glover narrates a leading study undertaken at Oxford University in 1956 that indicated that, under the circumstances of war with Japan, dropping the bomb probably saved many lives, but pointed out that the terms included the Allies' demand for unconditional surrender and their disregard of Japan's known desire for a negotiated peace. The justification for the bombings was that they reduced the risk of a far greater evil.[155]

All the same, a party launching an attack against a legitimate military objective must always seek to avoid or minimize foreseeable civilian casualties and damage to civilians. An attempt to minimize the damage inflicted on civilians must exist. While the distinct nature of the principle of proportionality applicable under international humanitarian law must be recognized, it is considered a general rule that excessive foreseeable damage or injury to certain people or objects is prohibited in peacetime as well as in armed conflict.[156] The European Court of Human Rights has already asserted that it is paramount to examine whether an

155 Jonathan Glover, Humanity: a moral history of the 20th century 97–107 (2nd ed. 2012).

156 Report on Terrorism and Human Rights, Inter-Am. Comm'n H.R., OEA/Ser.L/V/II.116, doc. 5 rev. 1 corr., §110 (2002).

operation was planned and controlled by the authorities so as "to minimize, to the greatest extent possible, recourse to lethal force. The authorities must take appropriate care to ensure that any risk to life is minimized" and "a balance must be achieved between the aim pursued and the means employed to achieve it".[157]

As cited above, Resolution 1373 of the United Nations Security Council calls on states to work together to prevent and suppress terrorist acts, and also requires states to take "the necessary steps" to prevent the commission of terrorist acts.[158] The war in Afghanistan, which commenced right after and in compliance with Resolution 1373, has witnessed aerial bombardment and a high number of civilian casualties. The aerial bombardment has been justified on the "necessity" grounds as being "essential" to NATO's efforts to clear out Taliban insurgents. According to an annual report issued by the United Nations in Afghanistan in 2010, there was a significant growth in human cost, "2,777 civilian deaths in 2010, an increase of 15 per cent compared to 2009", but "2,080 deaths (75 per cent of total civilian deaths) were attributed to Anti-Government Elements, up 28 per cent from 2009. Suicide attacks and improvised explosive devices (IEDs) caused the most civilian deaths, totaling 1,141 deaths (55 per cent of civilian deaths attributed to Anti-Government Elements)".[159] As terrorism has grown in the international arena and become a real threat to the values of our international community, Resolution 2249 came to be enacted, with the same purpose as prior ones, but with updates on recent global tragedies and enemies.[160]

Taking a pragmatic stance, let's work on some variables to illustrate this foreseeable assessment of military necessity to achieve a good consequence with the cost of an evil consequence as side effect. As a military action finds acceptance and moral justification in utilitarianism, the harm on targeted civilians is deemed the lesser evil, and a greater good is reached teleologically. Decision-making elements can be predicted to allow proper planning and coordination of necessary actions, and we are going to follow Richard Posner's formula on cost-benefit analysis to predict the proportionality and assurance of lesser evil.[161] As was mentioned in chapter 4, the use of drones has been used constantly in military operations to fight enemies of the global commonwealth.

Let us now imagine that a terrorist plot from an ISIS cell hidden on a farm near Brussels is discovered to be planning an attack not on a military target but on a shopping mall in London that has the largest movie theater in town premiering the final Harry Potter film at 5:00 p.m. (I chose Harry Potter because William Shawcross says in his book that Harry Potter books are by far the most read books by the inmate population at Guantanamo Bay[162]). Let's say that 1000 people are

157 *Isayeva v. Russia [Former First Section]*, no. 57950/00, Eur. Ct. H.R. §§175, 181 (February 24, 2005).

158 S.C. Res. 1373 (2001), U.N. Doc. S/RES/1373 (September 28, 2001).

159 United Nations, Afghanistan Annual Report on Protection of Civilians in Armed Conflicts 2010, Executive Summary (March, 2011).

160 S.C. Res. 2249 (2015), U.N. Doc. S/RES/2249 (November 20, 2015).

161 Richard A. Posner, Frontiers of Legal Theory 37 (2001).

162 William Shawcross, Justice and the Enemy: Nuremberg, 9/11, and the trial of Khalid Sheikh Mohammed (2011).

expected to be in the mall for the premier. A task force under Resolution 2249/UNSC then discovers the plot and plans a preventive drone attack on this cell hidden on a farm near Brussels, since the danger against the Harry Potter audience is imminent (eliminating, as well, the chance of an alternative plan). The strike by drone must therefore be performed immediately, there will be no other opportunity. The task force then receives the information that civilians unrelated to the evil terrorist plan are on the premises. Counting children, women and farm workers, we estimate there are 100 civilians near the target that could be harmed as a side effect. In sum, the imminent danger posed to those 1,000 London citizens can be avoided by this military action that will eliminate the terrorists who are plotting the attack – primary targets duly intended – while possibly also harming 100 civilians as collateral damage, constituting an unintended but inevitable secondary target (considering there is no other military maneuver at their disposal).

Let's do some math to analyze the cost-benefit of the attack, the result of which will support the double effect argumentation and validation of utilitarian morality. First, we need to ascertain for readers that this is an anticipated calculation, which means that it entails probabilities of occurrences, and is exactly the predictability exercise that militaries do in rules of engagement. In sequence, let's identify the formula's elements. The evil consequence of the terrorist attack is the harm of 1,000 people that might happen with the probability *TA* (for terrorist attack). So, the cost of not acting against the terrorists is the Harry Potter's fans' human lives, which we call *HL* (for human lives). The possibility of eliminating such an attack would impose a cost on our action, which we call perpetrator burden *PB*, and would be the 100 civilians targeted as a side effect of a drone assault on the farm. The harm of targeting these civilians is called *PB* (for perpetrator burden) in this equation. Therefore, the cost of avoiding the attack *TA* is *PB*, and to be morally acceptable in utilitarian terms, as metamorality, it must be less than the expected cost of *HL* (or benefit of avoiding the attack) multiplied by the probability of the attack happening *TA*. The formula is therefore $PB < TA*HL$.

Now we have the formula, let's run some numbers. Let's say that the UNSC task force estimates the probability of the attack happening at 100 per cent. This would make the representation of *TA* in our formula 1,0. $PB < TA*HL$ equals $100 < 1{,}0*1{,}000$, giving us the outcome 100 < 1,000. If the mathematical statement portrays reality, military necessity passes the cost-benefit analysis and lesser evil scrutiny; the former explains the teleological rationale in seeking a good end regardless of means (which was solely applied in *Ender's Game*), while the latter seeks to comply with moral argumentation of proportionality and all efforts converged to mitigate the loss, in order to let utilitarian morality trump human moral dignity morality as little as possible (this is Ender's conundrum grasped in "the way we win matters").

During this second analysis of lesser evil and mitigating the loss, attempts to minimize the number of civilians targeted on the farm are considered (such as creating a detour on the farm access road so ten workers would not be there at the moment of the strike, which is similar to the ferry explosion in Norway case, when the engineer selected a Sunday route to transport the water because it had fewer passengers). Nevertheless, independent of the final outcome, the greatest good must outweigh the evil outcome of civilian collateral damage. In this nexus, the doctrine of double effect is morally acceptable and connects to mutualism benefits, both to international humanitarian law and human rights law (with the latter underlying utilitarian metamorality as a primary moral compass during emergency).

In contrast, if the probability of occurrence of terrorist attack is 10 per cent, then the formula is *100 < 0,1*1,000*, giving us the outcome 100 < 100. This mathematical statement is false, and therefore the drone strike is not morally acceptable or legally justified. A graphic exposition of our thesis is synthetized in the figure below.

The rationale of utilitarianism offers solutions to socio-political problems while satisfying the greatest number of interests possible. Individual interests are considered in the equation despite being considered secondary to the maximization of general welfare of international society. The good promoted collectively in utilitarian rationality follows the best path to quantity and quality in the welfare outcome. Obviously, not all utilitarian solutions satisfy all individual interests. However,

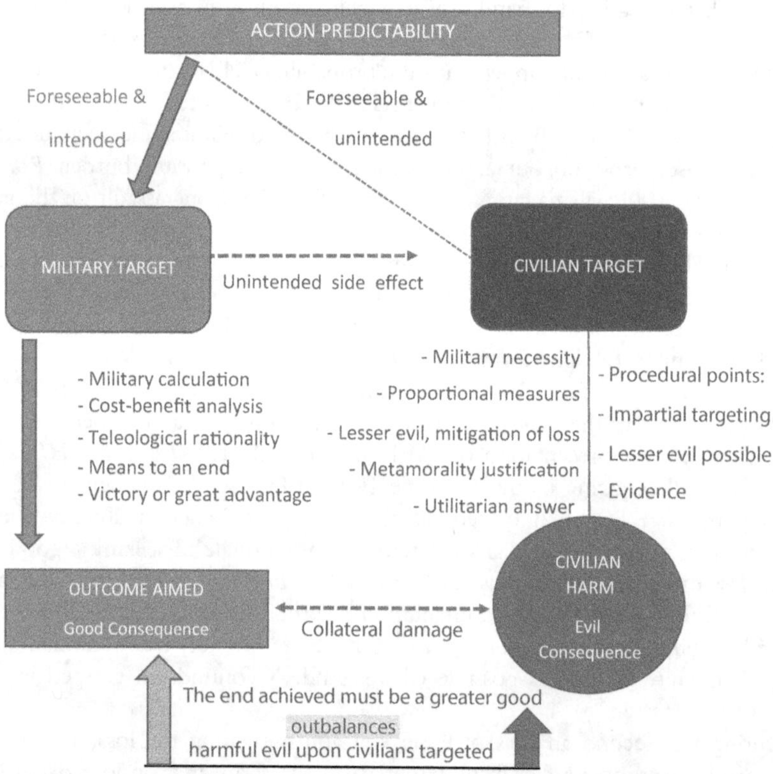

Figure 5.2 A representation of the author's theory on targeting civilians as a result of a supreme emergency justified by the mandatory mutualism between international humanitarian law and human rights law.

justice, as a social value cherished by the international community, is met in the form of the favorable measurement to the collective body.[163] The doctrine of double effect is invoked to permit some acts that will predictably target innocent civilians. When these harms are foreseen but not intended, and where they are not out of proportion to the good aimed at, the act is morally permissible. The doctrine of double effect is crucial in work on international regulation of armed conflicts because it provides moral identity instead of moral emptiness.

Nevertheless, regarding the preconditions of necessity and proportionality, cost-benefit analysis must also be carried out and, in practical life, all law procedures must be observed as well. Thus, all information on unintentionally targeting civilians as side effects, attempts to minimize the harm on civilians, lack of military alternative to achieving the end pursued and the configuration of the lesser evil must demonstrate that the greatest good achieved outweighs the evil consequence, and must be confirmed with evidence – since international investigations cannot always rely on proof[164] – and impartiality, which is closely linked to unintentionality of action, which indicates an action performed without any motive of discrimination or prejudice.[165]

Finally, all requirements of moral background and rational reasoning have been examined in this work. Pragmatically departing from a factual scenario of supreme emergency, which separates us from the normal regular conditions we face in peacetime and social STP, we recognize a mutation in international law that is able to provide answers to overcome the crisis. Therefore, the mandatory mutualism between international humanitarian law and human rights law remains untouched with respect to inner interplay and considerations. The important shift in their applicability occurs as utilitarian morality trumps human moral dignity and functions as metamorality to solve pragmatic problems in armed conflicts. It must be highlighted though that human moral dignity is not removed. Rather, while not the primary moral compass, it becomes the secondary moral compass, leaving the leading role to utilitarian metamorality.

As a consequence, the rationale of deontology attached to human moral dignity universally enjoins that always treating people as an end and never as a means is surpassed by teleological rationality, which is attached to utilitarian morality and, conversely, accepts treating people as a means to seek the greatest good for the greatest number. Regarding civilian targeting in situations of armed conflicts, which is the scope of this work, it is only permitted as a side effect when the good outcome outbalances the evil consequences of the harm inflicted on civilians. More than that, proportionality and the justification of the lesser evil as a duty to minimize the losses or the harmful impact on civilians are the moral considerations to comply with human rights rationale whose mutual benefit derives from the fulfillment of social values for victory or an advantage toward the end pursued.

163 Daniel Sarmento, Livres e iguais: Estudos de Direito Constitucional 56–57 (2006).

164 Jonathan Glover, Humanity: a moral history of the 20th century 84 (2nd ed. 2012) and Michael Walzer, Just and Unjust Wars 231–232 (4th ed. 2006).

165 Joshua Greene, Moral Tribes: emotion, reason, and the gap between us and them 200–204 (2013).

Yet, human dignity still plays a supporting role in utilitarian metamorality when forbidding *jus cogens* violations like, for example, torture. Even in the face of utilitarian metamorality, human dignity plays an important role that makes us conclude, at first glance, that there is no predictable good consequence that outweighs the evil consequence of eroding a *jus cogens* value. We believe it is accurate in utilitarian terms that the erosion of *jus cogens* could, in the long run, irreparably harm mankind's ability to flourish and the development of human values.

6 Conclusion

According to Ricardo Guibourg, the purpose of human knowledge for the study of law is generally threefold: (i) identify the right in question so that it is possible to discuss its content and controversies; (ii) observe and define the way society responds to the conduct that is under the lens of the law; and (iii) decide whether, after examining the facts, the right in question, the law and its social content, justice has been served.[1] We can now say we have considered all three aspects.

Building the theory from the very bottom, over time, international society has been shaped politically and legally by wars. Even at the beginning of the last century some improvements were made in the international arena, but after two world wars, the scale of human loss in frightful atrocities, the terrible banalization of evil and the powerlessness of the international framework to deter such dreadful events, the world came together in a spirit of cooperation to build the system anew.

Following the sociological footsteps, the establishment of core values came first, to be then put into practice and safeguarded by reliable institutions. The foundation of values for the international community was drafted in universal language that had the scope to reach every individual on the planet. When we think about international society, it is crucial to build a fabric of moral capital that can sustain and unify a moral community, since social cohesion is key.

First in the sequence was the development of human rights and its links with natural law and the rebirth of this thinking in the rebuilding process of international community and law design. Following these trails, the roots of human rights reveal its basis in morality, rationalizing human emotions and convictions which turn on the sacredness of human life, an ethos of love and universal respect. Human dignity then takes its place at the center of all human rights law and the corresponding international framework, becoming a crucial watchword. Respect for human dignity irradiates as both value and right, committing all international actors to obey, enforce and endorse. Divergence as to its practical applicability arises in international courts, leading to some sort of incommensurability diagnosis and an emphasis again on plurality of values. An embracing value generalization is applied to meet plurality and community welfare, carrying the promise of peace

1 Ricardo A Guibourg, Derecho, Sistema y Realidad 12 (2010).

DOI: 10.4324/9781003170778-6

and an end to human cruelty. Moreover, a vast body of jurisprudence is generated, and the judicial decision-making of international courts gradually transforms international society and law into a living body, permanently breathing and active.

Coexisting with human rights bodies of law, the complex international legal system harbors multiple other primary sources of law that may appear to conflict with human rights provisions. International humanitarian law represents the effort to resolve quarrels in armed conflict situations, which may contradict human rights law that was initially conceived for peacetime regulation only. Nevertheless, international legal understanding started to add some contemporary values to the law of war – values that were formally put in place during the reform of international society that motivated the Geneva Conventions (and further protocols) to implant the principle of humanity in warlike regulation in order to humanize behavior in armed conflicts.

Interchangeability between HRL and IHL then took place. Alongside humanity, principles of necessity, proportionality and distinction have been commonly applied to alleviate the horrors of war while taking civilians firmly into account. Subsequently, legal material was drafted to protect civilians and strengthen civilian immunities, even though armed conflicts inevitably place civilians in danger.

Despite the moral duty to minimize the horrors associated with the course of hostilities, only the mitigation of dangers to which civilians are exposed can be ascertained. Meanwhile, a new species of war has arisen, one that poses an immense danger and threatens the life of all nations, risking the destruction of values so strenuously fought for in human history. Furthermore, this cowardly new engagement, terrorism, becomes the contemporary *hostis humani generis* – the enemy of mankind. To maintain order, international welfare and the survival of society, treaties have been modified and new resolutions added to international organizations and official documents and, most important of all, the judicial decision-making that serves as auxiliary sources and instruments of international law.

In the first wave, international decisions established the union of international humanitarian law and human rights law, determined that they should not be two independent branches of law with different scopes of applicability – war and peacetime, respectively. From that historical moment there has been interplay between international humanitarian law and human rights law, and this interaction takes place within legal systems that has to interpret and apply the law regarding the apparently colliding provisions of these two branches – with the former being *lex specialis*, the latter *lex generalis*. In any apparent collision between the provisions of these two branches, the humanitarian provision prevails. As we have seen throughout this work, new understandings upheld by international courts, particularly human rights courts, have significantly developed international law.

The mutual influence between international humanitarian law and human rights law has become mandatory and has fostered developments in the interpretation and application of legal concepts and values in international law. It is now well understood that there are many instances in which human rights law and humanitarian law do not contradict each other but rather regulate different aspects of a situation or regulate a situation in more or less detail and are therefore mutually reinforcing.

From this understanding of the interplay between the two branches of law comes a better appreciation of what it means in practical terms and the daily decision-making process. From biology we borrowed the analogy of living organisms that work together in a symbiotic relationship, leading to one of two situations: mutualism, where both organisms benefit from the symbiotic relationship and share the duties and gains of the union; and commensalism, where one organism takes a leading role, coordinates actions and exclusively benefits from the union. A mandatory mutualism is the regime we recognize in the intertwined relation of international humanitarian law and human rights law. The umbilical cord between them is the principle of humanity, which, from the perspective of human rights, is enriched with the moral evaluation of human dignity.

The second wave, then, is the formal observance of human dignity's roots in armed conflict situations, which provides guidance in case-law solutions brought before international courts of human rights. In this regard, both the Inter-American Court and Commission and the European Court and Council deliver a considerable number of precedents that recognize values of human dignity as a limitation on state agency in relation to the adversary – which on many occasions has been terrorist groups that deny all international rules of war and refuse to follow any moral code regarding their deeds. States often claim the derogation clause in human rights conventions to get round the international obligation on human rights in the war on terror, but it is not granted as it would overturn the safeguards and guarantees on human rights established in conventions and jurisprudence. Taken piecemeal, especially in the European Court, where the fight is constant, it becomes clear that human moral dignity represents an obstacle in warzones and enemy engagement – which brings us to the third and current wave, established openly in the *Hassan* case.

The rationale in *Hassan* is fruit of a process which amounts to the piling of precedents – some cited above – that lead to this (disputable) conclusion: the interplay between international humanitarian law and human rights law is no longer mutualism, but rather commensalism, with the former taking the leading role, under *lex specialis*, and determining what is permissible or not. For example, not even the derogation claim is needed in accordance with Article 4 of ICCPR, Article 15 of ECHR and Article 27 of ACHR since it is a human rights disposition that, in situations of armed conflict, has no command over ongoing facts.

This leading case formally recognizes commensalism, showing human rights law as having no benefit from its interwoven relationship with humanitarian law. Rather, it has a supporting role in the *jus cogens* value of human rights such as the prohibition of torture – at least for now. This understanding of the *Hassan* case is here reshaped since I hold that human rights cannot be overruled or be given a subordinate role, even in times of crisis.

It is said that each person possesses an inviolability founded on justice that even the welfare of society as a whole cannot override. This is not entirely true. Human dignity is founded on justice, but it does not constrain justice. As grasped in *Hassan* and other background cases, the legal framework of wartime is formally and substantially different from the peacetime framework. The statement of individual inviolability makes perfect sense for peacetime, as the European Court states in their new commensalist understanding of the interplay between IHL and HRL, saying that the latter is only fully applicable in non-conflict situations – as stressed in the *Hassan* case.

While I do not agree with the Court's affirmation, I hold on to its central idea, which is the notion of separating the use of law in peacetime – when there is normality and political stability – and its use in a crisis such as an emergency, a state of exception or war – when there is abnormality and political instability. The goal of the former is to keep the legal order functional as part of endeavouring to leave society better off, while the goal of the latter is to recover normality and stability as soon as possible, since the more we persist in crisis, the more damage we do to society.

Therefore, under normal conditions of political stability without threat to the very existence of society and international community as we know it, it is accurate to say that each person possesses an inviolability founded on justice that even the welfare of society as a whole cannot override. When we are experiencing abnormal conditions of political instability that threaten to erode the very existence of society and international community as we know it, the welfare of society *must* override individual rights until normality has returned. The main focus of legal order shifts, especially regarding the branches of law involved in mandatory mutualism, but without giving space to anomie. The nature of mutualism mutates from deontology to teleology in order to restore the status quo. And for that, we do not need to step aside from justice, or distance ourselves from human rights law.

For justice to be meaningful, we ought to pin it down to a value other than individuality, and to grasp human rights we ought to grapple with a morality that overlaps human moral dignity, which means we have to bring a metamorality that fits the rule of law. After all, incommensurability of values in a pluralistic society requires reason for justifying actions while leaving some conceptual room for explaining a wrongful act, for which teleology and the end pursued might be considered a rightful action.

To be able to act according to necessity, the perpetrator must judge the nature of the situation. Besides cost-benefit analysis, it is necessary to evaluate the type of situation in which it is appropriate to proceed with targeting people and accepting collateral damage. Pragmatism revealed in real cases explains why situations of armed conflict are not merely a neutral field of activity for intentions conceived of beyond that situation. Rather, it calls for certain actions already in our perception that are suitable to replace the deontology of means-ends as a primary basic category of international law. The relationship between action and the examined situation is not one-sided, but involves teleological interpretation as well.

Human agency makes judgements regarding abnormality and exceptional situations, taking into account cost-benefit analysis and moral perceptions of values aimed to a certain end. The following actions then become teleological and constitute, as far as possible, a way out of moral dilemmas. This dialogue between deontology and teleology is a reciprocal process that regulates a complex legal order based on incommensurable pluralistic values.

Teleology shows us that the end pursued justifies the means employed, and that the law, in general terms, national or international, is aimed at social greater good. Human agency is set to accomplish things and always has a goal to attain. Human behavior is teleologically aimed at an end and governed by values. The ultimate components of meaningful human action are initially bound to the categories of "ends" and "means". Reasoning about purpose and ends is an unavoidable feature of arguing about justice. The link between justice and "the good" is unavoidable, and principles of justice get their justification from the moral worth or intrinsic good of the ends. There is a certain legitimacy to heavy attacks on military and industrial targets that makes the targeting of civilians inevitable. But there must be an acceptable balance between the means employed and the purpose achieved.

For instance, it was crucial in *Hassan* that the denial of his liberty was justified by overriding good for others, since his liberty posed a risk to the welfare of others and society. Therefore, his right became instrumental for the advancement of some end held to be a precedent, some social moral capital that is the common good and the welfare of society and international community. As remarked by Michael Sandel, it has been assumed that universal morality can be described in binary terms: either you respect human dignity or you treat human beings as a means (i.e. as things), not an end. However, this duality no longer pertains.[2] There is something between humanity as an end and humanity as a means. For this reason, the argument that human rights are entirely unfit for the context of armed conflicts is misleading.

The justice pursued by human rights law and international humanitarian law is rightly measured in terms of the treatment and protection of persons, peoples and the community of nations (or community of communities). Many defenders of moral philosophy on rights think individual rights morality and social welfare morality are incompatible, but they are not. They actually coexist harmoniously. To understand utility, as social welfare, and to set boundaries according to necessity and proportionality, a cost-benefit analysis must be employed. With its persuasive pragmatic scope, cost-benefit analysis targets deep issues and designs to assist people in making complex judgements where multiple goods are involved. However, cost-benefit analysis cannot be the only tool used in the decision-making process. Some values must be attached to it, some reasons why proportionality and necessity are part of the rationale behind the principle of humanity.

It is relevant to highlight that human dignity remains a moral axis of human rights; it remains present, albeit working as a secondary enjoinment in some situations. Utilitarianism is a theory of both personal morality and social justice, and the absence of human moral dignity within utilitarian metamorality would engender all sort of asocial traits, such as cruelty and intentional evil deeds. Instead, utilitarianism serves the international community as an overarching shared value whose content is embodied in international law and values.

2 Michael Sandel, The Case Against Perfection: ethics in the age of genetic engineering 126–127 (2007).

A creative dimension of human action shall be incorporated into this conceptual structure to enrich its content, since social order establishes a valid nexus between creativity and action, and it becomes clear that an emphasis on rationality is a normative orientation, just as much as it is for dignity. Therefore, with utilitarian value applicable as metamorality, the overarching shared value to maintain endorsable human rights in mandatory mutualism in armed conflicts is, in essence, that the creative model is superior to the normativist model because it leads to the examination of two questions that would otherwise remain unanswered. The first is the question of how norms and values are to be applied to specific situations, and the second is the question of how the values that guide our behavior arise in the first place.

Contemporary armed conflicts have shown us that it is not always possible to deduce how values should be applied in particular situations. Instead, the opposite occurs, as particular situations call for independent creative specifications of these values. In this equation, which is very far from our sense of social normality and political stability (the STP analogy), a commitment to specific values does not arise through intention, but through powerful experiences. Not all experiences come from enthusiasm; rather, they can be the product of powerlessness – for example, exposure to terrorist attacks or violence – that causes trauma and opens up a space where there is scope for this third model of creative action and the reshaping of positive universalistic values as common currency.

Thus, the achievement of collective good – the greatest good for the greatest number – is a positive universalistic value that incorporates utilitarian morality and underpins community values. By this token, teleology can be understood as a form of action that rationalizes ends, values and consequences, which remains ideal for situations of armed conflict because universal values mutate from case to case. Only teleology can rationally galvanize the probabilities and social phenomena involved in military necessity and proportionality in an action where civilians are targeted as a side effect.

Utilitarian morality comprehends a normativist theory of social order that implies decision-making, and people often have to make decisions under conditions of profound uncertainty with multiple contingencies. However, some decision-making elements can be predicted to afford proper planning and coordination of necessary actions. When we deal with social values in the decision-making process, we shed light on social goals that are based on reason towards individual and collective welfare. Morality and welfare merge on a common ground, becoming a common currency.

The conventional philosophy of social science has asserted that the contemporary task of the social scientist is the production of law-like generalizations to foresee the outcomes of alternative policies, themselves deriving from knowledge of such law-like generalizations. In this regard, utilitarianism, by the equation of the greatest good for the greatest number, trumps human moral dignity, serving dilemmas of armed conflicts, such as targeting civilians for military necessity, as metamorality.

Ruti Teitel, reporting a UN Conference held in 2004, *A More Secure World: Our Shared Responsibility*, lists six clusters of threat which the international community must be concerned about now and in the decades ahead and that would fit the abnormal conditions that shift moral density and application, recalling the STP analogy from chemistry:

> (1) Economic and social threats, including poverty, infectious diseases and environmental degradation; (2) Inter-State conflict; (3) Internal conflict, including civil war, genocide and other large-scale atrocities; (4) Nuclear, radiological, chemical and biological weapons; (5) Terrorism; and (6) Transnational organized crime.[3]

Some criticisms of utilitarianism come from the fact that its ethics treat people as cells in the overall social organism rather than individuals, and that it has no boundary principles, except possibly sentience. Nevertheless, some objections to utilitarian ethics can be overcome by replacing wealth for utility as the maxim and interpreting wealth not in strictly monetary terms but rather as the summation of all the valued tangible and intangible objects in society.

It is just a matter of argumentative allocation. Placing utilitarian morality into judgement calls on military actions covered by the scope of mandatory mutualism does not put human rights law to one side, as *Hassan* did. Respecting the idea of mutual reinforcement, utilitarian morality fits goals of human rights law as metamorality over human dignity. This is not to say that utilitarianism displaces the central role of human dignity deontology, but it prevails as metamorality under armed conflict exceptionalism in order to achieve a good outcome for the international community and general values.

Therefore, the conflict of interests and aims between international humanitarian law and human rights law is merely apparent. In reality there is no conflict between them, no need to establish commensalism between them and thereby give international humanitarian law precedence over human rights law for its sole benefit. Again, utilitarian metamorality fits both branches, giving them both the benefit of application without erasing the broad knowledge of humanitarian law as *lex specialis* and human rights law as *lex generalis.*

What is being defended here is the international community and its bonding social moral capital which the international legal system is designed to protect just as much as the lives and liberties of the members of this community. Thus, like a Latin catchphrase, *fiat justicia ruat coelom*, "do justice even if the heavens fall", it calls for extreme necessity during an intense crisis or a supreme emergency that authorizes exceptional action to recover normality and stability. In relation to this, the identification of supreme emergency ought to be made by international courts or an international governmental organization such as the United Nations.

The international legal system allows the usage of legal general clauses that require the interpretation and application of different rationalities and outlooks of international law (Article 31 Vienna Convention). Moreover, this law-making process via the decision-making rationale has to take into account the unity,

3 Ruti G. Teitel, Humanity's Law 109 (2011).

coherence and wholeness of the entire legal system, made concrete by a systematic and teleological interpretation. The mandatory mutualism between IHL and HRL, by this token, complies with international law standards when applying utilitarian metamorality to combat imminent danger of high impact in situations where targeting civilians might appear necessary and proportional as a side effect to overcome the supreme emergency.

In such cases, international humanitarian law and human rights law intermingle through mandatory mutualism. Human moral dignity remains the primary moral compass in this mutual relationship, at least while social STP, social normality and political stability of international community are preserved. When such traits erode, an exceptional state takes over and STP morality becomes secondary for the sake of mutual integrity.

Furthermore, by using human agency to recover the status quo of the international community and defend our cherished values and cooperative fellowship, some acts deemed necessary shall be performed. We may eventually have a civilian target situation that is accommodated into a legal-moral wall since certain conditions are met. The harm that shall fall upon them must be unintended, but predicted as a side effect. For that, the primary target of military necessity shall be one properly intended objective, the defeat contributing to the overall goal of overcoming a supreme emergency, definitely or partially, or providing a great advantage in battle.

To make this operation possible, the doctrine of double effect must be argued together with the considerations of cost-benefit analysis, where all costs (including the evil consequence of harming targeted civilians as collateral damage) shall be balanced by the benefits of reaching a certain end. The path to this intended end with good consequence – the greatest good – is rationally constructed, using the teleological argument that the end justifies the means, essentially a mathematical assessment. To morally evaluate this cost-benefit analysis teleologically connected to the greatest good of the end pursued, utilitarianism provide the moral grounds to challenge the action and therefore serve as the primary moral compass during times of emergency. As the welfare of the international community is the value that will subject all action to scrutiny, moral consideration of proportionality and the duty to mitigate the harm and minimize the evil effect are established in advance of any targeting civilians situation.

Considering the formula I provided above, $PB < TA*HL$, military necessity must undergo cost-benefit analysis and lesser-evil scrutiny. The former explains the teleological rationality of seeking a good end regardless of means, while the latter seeks to comply with moral argumentation around proportionality and directing all efforts at mitigating the loss in order to let utilitarian morality trump human moral dignity to the least degree possible.

Nevertheless, independent of the final outcome, the greatest foreseeable good should outweigh the evil outcome of harming civilians as collateral damage. Thus, the doctrine of double effect is morally acceptable, as are mutualism benefits, to both international humanitarian law and human rights law, with the latter underlying utilitarian metamorality as the primary moral compass during a supreme emergency.

For this account, departing from a factual scenario of supreme emergency, which diverges from the normal regular conditions we face in peacetime and social STP, we recognized a mutation in international law that is able to provide answers for overcoming the crisis. Thus, the mandatory mutualism between IHL and HRL remains untouched with respect to their inner interplay and considerations. The important shift in their applicability is the way that utilitarian morality now trumps human dignity and functions as metamorality to solve pragmatic problems in armed conflicts. It is worth highlighting that human moral dignity is not removed, but instead of being the primary moral compass, it becomes a secondary moral compass, leaving the leading role to utilitarian metamorality.

As a consequence, the deontological reasoning attached to human moral dignity, that universally enjoins us to treat people as an end and never as a means, is superseded by teleological rationality, which is attached to utilitarian morality and, conversely, accepts treating people as a means in order to achieve the greatest good for the greatest number. Regarding the action of targeting civilians in situations of armed conflicts, it is indeed permitted as a side effect, since the good outcome outbalances the evil consequences of the harm inflicted on civilians.

More than that, proportionality and the justification of the lesser evil as a duty to minimize the losses or the harmful impact on civilians are the moral considerations to comply with human rights rationale, by which the mutual benefit derives from the fulfillment of social value for victory or a great advantage in pursuing the end. Yet, human dignity still plays a supporting role in utilitarianism metamorality when forbidding *jus cogens* violations, for example.

Even alongside utilitarian metamorality, human dignity plays an important role that makes us conclude that, at first glance, there is no predictable good consequence that outweighs the evil consequence of eroding a *jus cogens* value. We believe it is accurate in utilitarian terms in that the erosion of *jus cogens* in the long run can bring about irreparable harm to the flourishing of mankind and development of values.

That is why we agree with the *Hassan* conclusion, even if we disagree with its terms. If I had the chance, I would write a partial dissenting opinion on the *Hassan* case, preserving the conclusion but modifying the rationale. In line with the theory argued for here, human rights law should not be removed from the equation in order to give international humanitarian law all the benefits of fulfillment of international law, which we called commensalism.

Rather, in reaching the same conclusion, I would apply the rationale that permits utilitarian metamorality to fight against the *hosti humani generis* of our time, whatever form they take, that cause significant risks to the core values and social capital of our international community and the welfare of its members. The danger they pose is imminent and of high impact, which conforms to definitions of supreme emergency and endorses the mandatory mutualism between IHL and HRL, with law applications whose benefits ought to be left to both branches.

It is inconceivable that human rights law shall be put aside in order to fight abnormality as the only way to overlap with or mitigate human dignity legal prescriptivity. In turn, a metamorality underpinned by social values shall be measured in terms of its balancing of necessity and proportionality, even if civilians are targeted as a side effect, their harm not intended but foreseen during the process to achieve the greatest good. The survival, flourishing and freedom of the community are the highest values, also embedded in the human rights morality frame.

In situations of armed conflict, international society is characterized by such danger that STP social conditions are no longer assessed. The teleology and systematic interpretation that allow us to get to the end and restore social normality and political stability is morally acceptable and preserves unity of legal order, coherence and wholeness. Notwithstanding, regarding the preconditions of necessity and proportionality, cost-benefit analysis must also be carried out and all procedures properly observed.

Thus, all information regarding targeting civilians as unintentional side effect, the attempts to minimize the harm on civilians, the lack of military alternatives to achieve the end pursued and the configuration of the lesser evil all demonstrate that the greater good outweighs the evil consequence. In addition, the case of targeting civilians in accordance with mandatory mutualism between IHL and HRL must be confirmed with evidence presented in each case – since international investigations cannot only rely on proof – and impartiality – which is closely linked to unintentionality of action and indicates a conduct performed without any discriminatory motive.

Under such conditions, both substantial and procedural understandings of international law are met. Likewise, the mandatory mutualism between international humanitarian law and human rights law is wholly preserved, opening up space for their mutual relationship to thrive and develop, granting benefits to both sides. Even this consideration reaches up to utilitarian morality since it is the international community that will be better off from the continuity of interwoven interpretation and application of these two humane branches of law.

The adoption of mandatory mutualism between IHL and HRL is far better suited to international law contemporary traits and the fostering of human rights morality than the total abandonment of HRL in the armed conflict legal realm. The international legal system and its mechanisms for interpreting and applying the morality of law allow us to put forward a theory that allows human rights to reign supreme, giving even human dignity a mitigated or secondary role in face of exceptional and temporary situations where the greater good of international society shall prevail. The generalization of values embedded in the international community and the social moral capital of survival and flourishing call for the teleological use of utilitarianism as metamorality to regain threatened normality and stability.

Bibliography

Books and articles

Accioly, Hildebrando et al. *Manual de Direito Internacional Público*, 20ª edição. São Paulo: Saraiva, 2012.

Agamben, Giorgio. *Estado de Exceção*. São Paulo: Boitempo, 2004.

Amaral Júnior, Alberto do. *Curso de Direito Internacional Público*, 2ª edição. São Paulo: Atlas, 2011.

Armstrong, David, Farrell, Theo and Lambert, Helene. *International Law and International Relations*. Cambridge: Cambridge University Press, 2007.

Barcellos, Ana Paula de. *A Eficácia Jurídica dos Princípios Constitucionais: o princípio da dignidade da pessoa humana*. Rio de Janeiro: Renovar, 2002.

Barral, Weber Oliveira. *Metodologia da Pesquisa Jurídica*, 3rd edition, Belo Horizonte: Del Rey, 2007.

Blank, Laurie R. and Noone, Gregory P. *International Law and Armed Conflict: fundamental principles and contemporary challenges in the law of war*. New York: Wolters Kluwer, 2013.

Bobbio, Norberto. *A Era dos Direitos*. Trans. Regina Lyra. Rio de Janeiro: Elsevier, 2004.

Bobbio, Norberto. *Da Estrutura à Função: Novos Estudos de Teoria do Direito*. Trans. Daniela Beccaccia Versiani. Barueri: Manole, 2007.

Bobbio, Norberto. *Teoria do Ordenamento Jurídico*. Trans. Maria Celeste Cordeiro Leite dos Santos. 10ª edição. Brasília: UnB, 1999.

Borsa, Merve Ozkan. The Contribution of International Court of Justice to the Development of International Humanitarian Rules and Principles. *Public and Private International Law Bulletin*, 36(2), 83–130 (2016).

Buergenthal, Thomas. *Manual de Derecho Internacional Público*. México: Fondo de Cultura Económica, 1994.

Butler, Paul. Foreword: terrorism and utilitarianism. *Journal of Criminal Law & Criminology*, 93(1), 1–22 (2003).

Campos, German J. Bidart. Jerarquía y Prelación de Normas em un Sistema Internacional de Derechos Humanos. In *Liber Amicorum, Héctor Fix-Zamudio* Vol. I, 447–480. San José, Costa Rica: Corte Interamericana de Derechos Humanos, 1998.

Cárcova, Carlos María. *Las Teorías Jurídicas Post Positivistas*, 2ª edición. Buenos Aires: Abeledo Perrot, 2009.

Cassese, Antonio. *International Law*, 2nd edition. Oxford: Oxford University Press, 2005.

Coupland, Robin. Humanity: what is it and how does it influence international law? *International Review of the Red Cross* 83(844), 969–989 (2001).

Daly, Erin. *Dignity Rights: courts, constitutions, and the worth of the human person*. Philadelphia: University of Pennsylvania Press, 2013.

Descartes, René. Discurso do Método, in *Obras Escolhidas* 39, 41. São Paulo: DIFEL (2nd edition), 1973.

Desimoni, Luis María. *Los Derechos Humanos y La Guerra Contra el Terror*. Buenos Aires: Editorial Ábaco de Rodolfo Depalma, 2009.

Droege, Cordula. The Interplay between International Humanitarian Law and International Human Rights Law in Situations of Armed Conflict. *Israeli Law Review* 40(2), 310–355 (2007).

Durkheim, Émile. Individualism and the Intellectuals, in *Durkheim on Religion*, ed. W.S.F. Pickering, 59–73. New York: Oxford University Press, 1994.

Dworkin, Ronald. *Justice for Hedgehogs*. Cambridge: Harvard University Press, 2011.

Escalante, Rodolfo E. Piza. El Valor Del Derecho y La Jurisprudencia Internacionales de Derechos Humanos en el Derecho y la Justicia Internos: El Ejemplo de Costa Rica. In *Liber Amicorum, Héctor Fix-Zamudio* Vol. I, 169–192. San José, Costa Rica: Corte Interamericana de Derechos Humanos, 1998.

Etzioni, Amitai. *The New Golden Rule: community and morality in a democratic society*. Basic Books: New York, 1997.

Fayt, Carlos S. *Los Derechos Humanos y El Poder Mediático, Político y Económico: su mundialización en el siglo XXI*. Buenos Aires: La Ley, 2001.

Fernandes, Bernardo Gonçalves. *Curso de Direito Constitucional*, 3ª edição. Rio de Janeiro: Lumen Juris, 2011.

Fukuyama, Francis. *As Origens da Ordem Política: dos tempos pré-humanos até a Revolução Francesa*. Rio de Janeiro: Rocco, 2013.

Fuller, Lon L. *The Morality of Law*. New Haven, CT: Yale University Press, 1969.

Gadamer, Hans-Georg. *Verdade e Método* I. Trans. Flávio Paulo Meurer. Petrópolis: Vozes, 1997.

Gadamer, Hans-Georg. *Verdade e Método II*. Trans. Flávio Paulo Meurer. Petrópolis: Vozes, 1997.

Gallardo, Helio. *Teoria Crítica: matriz e possibilidade de direitos humanos*. São Paulo: Unesp, 2013.

Gartner, Scott Sigmund. *Strategic Assessment in War*. New Haven, CT: Yale University Press, 1997.

Giddens, Anthony. *Durkheim on Politics and the State*. Redwood City, CA: Stanford University Press, 1986.

Glendon, Mary Ann. *A World Made New: Eleanor Roosevelt and the Universal Declaration of Human Rights*. New York: Random House, 2002.

Glover, Jonathan. *Humanity: a moral history of the 20th century*, 2nd edition. London: Yale University Press, 2012.

Gonçalves, Joanisval Brito. *Tribunal de Nuremberg 1945–1946*, 2ª edição. Rio de Janeiro: Renovar, 2004.

Graves, Robert. *Good-bye to All That: an autobiography*. New York: Penguin, 2014.

Greene, Joshua. *Moral Tribes: emotions, reason, and the gap between us and them*. New York: Penguin, 2013.

Greer, Steven. *The Exceptions to Articles 8 to 11 of the European Convention on Human Rights*. Strasbourg: Council of Europe, 1997.

Guerra, Sidney. *Curso de Direito Internacional Público*, 5ª edição. Rio de Janeiro: Lumen Juris, 2010.

Guibourg, Ricardo A. *Derecho, Sistema y Realidad*. Buenos Aires: Editorial Astrea, 2010.

Habermas, Jürgen. *Direito e Democracia: entre facticidade e validade, volume I*, 2ª edição. Rio de Janeiro: Tempo Brasileiro, 2012.

Habermas, Jürgen. *Direito e Democracia: entre facticidade e validade, volume II*. Rio de Janeiro: Tempo Brasileiro, 2011.

Haidt, Jonathan. *The Righteous Mind: why good people are divided by politics and religion*. New York: Pantheon Books, 2012.

Harbele, Peter. A Dignidade Humana como Fundamento da Comunidade Estatal. In *Dimensões da Dignidade*, 89–154. Porto Alegre: Livraria do Advogado, 2005.

Hart, Herbert L. A. *O Conceito de Direito*, 5ª edição. Lisboa: Fundação Calouste Gulbenkian, 2007.

Hayden, Patrick. *The Philosophy of Human Rights*. St Paul: Paragon House, 2001.

Hicks, Donna. *Dignity: its essential role in resolving conflict*. New Haven: Yale University Press, 2011.

Higgins, Rosalyn. *Problems and Process: international law and how we use it*. Oxford: Oxford University Press, 2004.

Huerta, Tania Gabriela Rodríguez. *Trarado sobre Derechos Humanos: el sistema de reservas*. Porruá, México: ITAM, 2005.

Hunt, Lynn. *Inventing Human Rights: a history*. New York: W.W. Norton & Company, 2007.

Hurd, Heidi M. *O Combate Moral*. São Paulo: Martins Fontes, 2003.

Ignatieff, Michael. *The Lesser Evil: political ethics in an age of terror*. Princeton, NJ: Princeton University Press, 2004.

Jankélévitch, Vladimir. *O Paradoxo da Moral*. São Paulo: Martins Fontes, 2008.

Jellinek, Georg. *The Declaration of the Rights of the Man and Citizens*. Frankfurt: Outlook, 2018.

Joas, Hans. *The Creativity of Action*. Chicago: University of Chicago Press, 2005.

Joas, Hans. *The Genesis of Values*. Chicago: University of Chicago Press, 2000.

Joas, Hans. *The Sacredness of the Person: a new genealogy of human rights*. Washington, DC: Georgetown University Press, 2013.

Joas, Hans. *War and Modernity*. Malden, MA: Blackwell, 2003.

Jorge Junior, Alberto Gosson. *Cláusulas Gerais no Novo Código Civil*. São Paulo: Saraiva, 2004.

Kamm, F. M. *The Moral Target: aiming at right conduct in war and other conflicts*. New York: Oxford University Press, 2012.

Kant, Immanuel. *Fundamentação da Metafísica dos Costumes*. São Paulo: Martin Claret, 2006.

Keane, Fergal. *Season of Blood: a Rwandan journey*. New York: Penguin, 1996.

Kolb, Robert et al. *Research Handbook on Human Rights and Humanitarian Law*. Northampton, MA: Edward Elgar, 2013.

Korkut, Ekrem. *Turkey and the International Law of the Sea*. London: Wildy, Simmonds & Hill, 2017.

Kunz, Josef Laurenz. *La Filosofía del Derecho Latinoamericana del Siglo XX*. Buenos Aires: Lousada S.A., 1951.

Larenz, Karl. *Metodologia da Ciência do Direito*, 3ª edição. Lisboa: Fundação Calouste Gulbenkian, 1997.

Li, Xiaorong. "Asian Values" and the Universality of Human Rights. In *The Philosophy of Human Rights*, 397–408. St Paul: Paragon House, 2001.

MacIntyre, Alasdair. *After Virtue*, 3rd edition. Notre Dame, IN: University of Notre Dame Press, 2007.

Magnoli, Demétrio. *O Mundo Contemporâneo: relações internacionais 1945–2000*. São Paulo: Moderna, 1997.

Martinez, Jenny S. *The Slave Trade and the Origins of International Human Rights Law*. New York: Oxford University Press, 2012.

Maximiliano, Carlos. *Hermenêutica e Aplicação do Direito*, 19ª edição. Rio de Janeiro: Forense, 2006.

Mazzuoli, Valério de Oliveira. *Curso de Direito Internacional Público*, 5ª edição. São Paulo: RT, 2011.

McCrudden, Christopher. Human Dignity and Judicial Interpretation of Human Rights. International Law and Justice Working Papers, Institute for International Law and Justice of New York University School of Law, 2008.

Mello, Celso Albuquerque de. *Curso de Direito Internacional Público*, 15th edition. Rio de Janeiro: Renovar, 2004.

Melzer, Nils. *International Humanitarian Law: a comprehensive introduction*. Geneva: ICRC, 2016.

Mercier, Hugo and Sperber, Dan. *The Enigma of Reason*. Cambridge, MA: Harvard University Press, 2017.

Miéville, China. *Between Equal Rights: a Marxist theory of international law*. Chicago: Haymarket Books, 2006.

Moncayo, Guillermo R. et al. *Derecho Internacional Público*. Buenos Aires: Zavalia, 1990.

Moreira, Eduardo Ribeiro. *Critérios de Justiça*. São Paulo: Saraiva, 2014.

Moyn, Samuel. *Christian Human Rights*. Philadelphia, PA: University of Pennsylvania Press, 2015.

Moyn, Samuel. *Human Rights and the Uses of History*. New York: Verso, 2014.

Moyn, Samuel. *The Last Utopia: human rights in history*. Cambridge, MA: Harvard University Press, 2010.

Neff, Stephen C. *Justice Among Nations*. Cambridge, MA: Harvard University Press, 2014.

Neves, Marcelo. *Transconstitucionalismo*. São Paulo: Martins Fontes, 2009.

Nussbaum, Martha C. *Fronteiras da Justiça: deficiência, nacionalidade, pertencimento à espécie*. São Paulo: Martins Fontes, 2013.

Pardo, Carlos A. Fernández. *Carl Schmitt en la Teoría Política Internacional*. Buenos Aires: Biblos, 2007.

Pejic, Jelena. The Protective Scope of Common Article 3: more than meets the eye. *International Review of The Red Cross* 93(881), 189–225, 2011.

Piovesan, Flávia. *Direitos Humanos e o Direito Constitucional Internacional*, 8ª edição. São Paulo: Saraiva, 2007.

Posner, Richard A. *The Economics of Justice*. Cambridge, MA: Harvard University Press, 1983.

Posner, Richard A. *Frontiers of Legal Theory*. Cambridge, MA: Harvard University Press, 2001.

Rabinovich-Berkman, Ricardo David. *Derechos Humanos: una introducción a su naturaleza y a su historia*. Buenos Aires: Quorum, 2007.

Ramírez, Manuel Becerra. Las Decisiones Judiciales como Fuente del Derecho Internacional de Los Derechos Humanos. In *Liber Amicorum, Héctor Fix-Zamudio* Vol. I, 431–446. San José, Costa Rica: Corte Interamericana de Derechos Humanos, 1998.

Ráo, Vicente. *O Direito e a Vida dos Direitos*, 5ª edição. São Paulo: RT, 1999.

Rawls, John. *Uma Teoria da Justiça*, 3ª edição. São Paulo: Martins Fontes, 2008.

Raz, Joseph. *The Morality of Freedom*. New York: Oxford University Press, 1988.

Reale, Miguel. *Teoria Tridimensional do Direito*. 5ª edição. São Paulo: Saraiva, 1994.

Rieff, David. Humanitarianism in Crisis. *Foreign Affairs Magazine* 81(6), 111–121, 2002.

Rodin, David and Shue, Henry. *Just and Unjust Warriors: the moral and legal status of soldiers*. New York: Oxford University Press, 2008.

Rosen, Michael. *Dignity: its history and meaning*. Cambridge, MA: Harvard University Press, 2012.

Rosenvald, Nelson. *Dignidade Humana e Boa-fé no Código Civil*. São Paulo: Saraiva, 2005.

Sandel, Michael J. *Justice: a reader*. New York: Oxford University Press, 2007.

Sandel, Michael J. *Justiça: o que é fazer a coisa certa*. Rio de Janeiro: Civilização Brasileira, 2012.

Sandel, Michael J. *Liberalism and the Limits of Justice*, 2nd edition. Cambridge: Cambridge University Press, 1998.

Sandel, Michael J. *Public Philosophy: essays on morality in politics*. Cambridge: Harvard University Press, 2005.

Sandel, Michael J. *The Case Against Perfection: ethics in the age of genetic engineering*. Cambridge: Harvard University Press, 2007.

Sandel, Michael J. *What Money Can't Buy: the moral limits of markets*. New York: Farrar, Straus & Giroux, 2012.

Sarmento, Daniel. *Livres e Iguais: estudos de Direito Constitucional*. Rio de Janeiro: Lumen Juris, 2006.

Schmitt, Carl. *Teologia Política*. Belo Horizonte: Del Rey, 2006.

Shaw, Malcolm N. *International Law*, 6th edition. Cambridge: Cambridge University Press, 2008.

Shawcross, William. *Justice and the Enemy: Nuremberg, 9/11, and the trial of Khalid Sheikh Mohammed*. New York: Public Affairs, 2011.

Shermer, Michael. *The Moral Arc: how science make us better people*. New York: St Martin's Griffin, 2015.

Sidgwick, Henry. *The Methods of Ethics*. Cambridge: Cambridge University Press, 2012.

Simpson, A. W. Brian. *Human Rights and the End of Empire: Britain and the genesis of the European Convention*. New York: Oxford University Press, 2004.

Singer, Peter. *Ética Prática*, 3ª edição. São Paulo: Martins Fontes, 2002.

Singer, Peter. *The Expanding Circle*. Princeton, NJ: Princeton University Press, 2011.

Singer, Peter and Singer, Renata. *The Moral of The Story: an anthology of ethics through literature*. Oxford: Blackwell, 2005.

Steiner, Henry J., Alston, Philip and Goodman, Ryan. *International Human Rights in Context*, 3rd edition. New York: Oxford University Press, 2007.

Streck, Lênio. *Hermenêutica Jurídica e(m) Crise: uma exploração hermenêutica da construção do direito*, 4ª edição. Porto Alegre: Livraria do Advogado, 2003.

Orend, Brian. Kant on International Law and Armed Conflict. *Canadian Journal of Law and Jurisprudence* 11(2), 329–381, 1998.

Teitel, Ruti G. *Humanity's Law*. Oxford: Oxford University Press, 2013.

Temkin, Larry S. *Rethinking the Good: moral ideals and the nature of practical reasoning*. New York: Oxford University Press, 2015.

Tesón, Fernando R. International Human Rights and Cultural Relativism. In *The Philosophy of Human Rights*, 379–396. St Paul: Paragon House, 2001.

Trindade, Antônio Augusto Cançado. A Contribuição dos Tribunais Internacionais à Evolução do Direito Internacional Contemporâneo. In *O Direito Internacional e o Primado da Justiça*, 3–48. Rio de Janeiro: Renovar, 2014.

Trindade, Antônio Augusto Cançado. *A Humanização do Direito Internacional*. Belo Horizonte: Del Rey, 2006.

Trindade, Antônio Augusto Cançado. *Direito das Organizações Internacionais*, 5th edition. Belo Hozironte: Del Rey, 2012.
Walzer, Michael. *Just and Unjust Wars*, 4th edition. New York: Basic Books, 2006.
Williams, Bernard. *Moral: uma introdução à ética*. São Paulo: Martins Fontes, 2005.
Wilson, Edward O. *The Social Conquest of Earth*. New York: Liveright, 2012.

Internet resources

Obama, Barack. Obama's 2006 Speech on Faith and Politics, June 28, 2006. www.nytimes.com/2006/06/28/us/politics/2006obamaspeech.html (last visited October 2, 2019).
LibreTexts Library. https://bio.libretexts.org/Bookshelves/Human_Biology/Book%3A_Human_Biology_(Wakim_and_Grewal)/24%3A_Ecology/24.04%3A_Community_Relationships (last visited September 2, 2019).
Meron, Theodore. The Case for War Crimes Trials in Yugoslavia. *Foreign Affairs Magazine*, Summer 1993. www.foreignaffairs.com/articles/yugoslavia/1193-06-01/case-war-crimes-trials-yugoslavia (last visited August 15, 2019).
The Engineering ToolBox. www.engineeringtoolbox.com/stp-standard-ntp-normal-air-d_772.html (last visited September 21, 2019).
Pennsylvania State University. http://chemistry.bd.psu.edu/jircitano/gases.html (last visited September 21, 2019).

Film materials

Ender's Game, directed by Gavin Hood, based on the novel by Orson Scott Card. Summit Entertainment, 2013.
Sophie Scholl – The final days, directed by Marc Rothemund. Zeitgeist Films, 2005.
The Man in the High Castle, TV series. Amazon Studios, 2015–.
Weapons of the Spirits, documentary, directed by Pierre Sauvage. Chambon Foundation and Pierre Sauvage Productions, 1990.

International materials, international law cases

International Court of Justice

Case Concerning Armed Activities on the Territory of the Congo (*Democratic Republic of the Congo v. Uganda*), 2005 I.C.J. (December 19).
Case Concerning Military and Paramilitary Activities In and Against Nicaragua (*Nicaragua v. United States of America*), 1986 I.C.J. (June 27).
Case Concerning the Arrest Warrant of 11 April 2000 (*Democratic Republic of Congo v. Belgium), 2002* I.C.J. (February 14).
Interpretation of the Agreement of 25 March 1951 Between the WHO and Egypt, Advisory Opinion, 1980 I.C.J. (December 20).
LaGrand Case (*Germany v. United States of America*), 2001 I.C.J. (June 27).
Legal Consequences for States of the Continued Presence of South Africa in Namibia (South West Africa) notwithstanding Security Council Resolution 276 (1970), Advisory Opinion, 1971 I.C.J. (June 21).
Legal Consequences of the Construction of a Wall in the Occupied Palestinian Territory, Advisory Opinion, 2004 I.C.J. (July 9).
Legality of the Threat or Use of Nuclear Weapons, Advisory Opinion, 1996 I.C.J. (July 8).

International Criminal Tribunal for Rwanda

The Prosecutor v. Jean-Paul Akayesu [Chamber I], Case No. ICTR-96–94-T, 1998 I.C.T. R. (September 2).

Criminal Tribunal for the Former Yugoslavia

The Prosecutor v. Anto Furundzija [Trial Chamber], Case No. IT-95–17/1-T, 1998 I.C.T. Y. (December 10).

The Prosecutor v. Blaskic [Trial Chamber], Case No. IT-95-14-T, 2000 I.C.T.Y. (March 03).

The Prosecutor v. Dusko Tadic [Appeal Chamber], Decision of the Defense Motion for Interlocutory Appeal on Jurisdiction, Case No. IT-94–91, 1995 I.C.T.Y. (October 2).

The Prosecutor v. Galic [Trial Chamber], Case No. IT-98–29-T, 2003 I.C.T.Y. (December 05).

The Prosecutor v. Kupreskic et al. [Trial Chamber], Case No. IT-95–16-T, 2000 I.C.T.Y. (January 14).

The Prosecutor v. Ramush Haradinaj et al [Trial Chamber], Case No. IT-04–84-T, 2008 I. C.T.Y. (April 3).

Court of Justice of the European Union

Case C-402/05 P and C-415/05 P, Kadi v. Council of the European Union and Commission of the European Communities [GC], 2008 E.C.R.

European Court of Human Rights

A. and others v. The United Kingdom [GC], no. 3455/05 Eur. Ct. H. R. (2009).

Al-Adsani v. the United Kingdom [GC], no. 35763/97 Eur. Ct. H.R. (2001).

Al-Jedda v. The United Kingdom [GC], no. 27021/08 Eur. Ct. H.R. (2011).

Al-Skeini and Others v. The United Kingdom [GC], no. 55721/07 Eur. Ct. H.R. (2011).

Bouyid v. Belgium [GC], no. 23380/09 Eur. Ct. H.R. (2015).

Chahal v. the United Kingdom, no. 22414/93 Eur. Ct. H.R, (1996).

Demir and Baykara v. Turkey [GC], no. 34503/97 Eur. Ct. H.R. (2008).

Hassan v. The United Kingdom [GC], no. 29750/09 Eur. Ct. H.R. (2014).

Ilascu and Others v. Moldova and Russia [GC], no. 48787/99 Eur. Ct. H.R. (2004).

Isayeva v. Russia [Former First Section], no. 57950/00, Eur. Ct. H.R. (2005).

Khlaifia and Other v. Italy [GC], no. 16483/12 Eur. Ct. H.R. (2016)

Labita v. Italy, no. 26772/95 Eur. Ct. H.R. (2000).

Lambert and Others v. France [GC], no. 46043/14, Eur. Ct. H.R. (2015).

L.C.B. v. the United Kingdom [GC], no. 23413/94 Eur. Ct. H.R. (1998).

Mamatkulov and Askarov v. Turkey [GC], nos. 46827/99 and 46951/99 Eur. Ct. H.R. (2005).

McCann and Others v. The United Kingdom [GC], no. 18984/91 Eur. Ct. H.R. (1995).

Parrilo v. Italy [GC], no. 46470/11 Eur. Ct. H.R. (2015).

Pretty v. United Kingdom [Fourth Section], no. 2346/02, Eur. Ct. H.R. (2002).

Saadi v. the United Kingdom [GC], no. 13229/03 Eur. Ct. H.R. (2008)

Salah Sheekh v. the Netherlands, no. 1948/04 Eur. Ct. H.R. (2007).

Stec and Others v. The United Kingdom [GC], nos. 65731/01 and 65900/01 Eur. Ct. H.R. (2006).

Varnava and Others v. Turkey [GC], nos. 16064/90, 16065/90, 16066/90, 16068/90, 16069/90, 16070/90, 16071/90, 16072/90 and 16073/90 Eur. Ct. H.R. (2009).

Vo v. France [GC], no. 53924/00, Eur. Ct. H.R. (2004).
Von Hannover v. Germany [Third Section], no. 59320/00, Eur. Ct. H.R. (2004).

Inter-American Commission on Human Rights

Coard et al v. United States, Case 10.951, Inter-Am. Comm'n H.R., Report N° 109/99, OEA/Ser.L/V/II.106, Doc. 6 rev (1999).
Franklin Guillermo Aisalla Molina, Ecuador v. Colombia, Case IP-02, Inter-Am. Comm'n H.R., Report No. 112/10, OEA/Ser.L/V/II.140, doc. 10 (2010).
Jose Isabel Salas Galindo and Others v. United States, Case 10.573, Inter-Am. Comm'n H. R., Report No. 121/18, OEA/Ser.L/V/II.169, doc. 138 (2018).
Juan Carlos Abella v. Argentina, Case 11.137, Inter-Am. Comm'n H.R., Report No. 55/97, OEA/Ser.L/V/II.95, doc. 7 rev. at 271 (1997).
Report on Terrorism and Human Rights, Inter-Am. Comm'n H.R., OEA/Ser.L/V/II.116, doc. 5 rev. 1 corr. (2002).

Inter-American Court of Human Rights

Artavia Murillo et al. (In Vitro Fertilization) v. Costa Rica, Preliminary Objections, Merits, Reparations and Costs, Inter-Am. Ct. H.R. (ser. C) No. 257 (November 28, 2012).
Bámaca-Velásquez v. Guatemala, Merits, Inter-Am. Ct. H. R. (ser. C) No. 91 (November 25, 2000).
Bámaca Velásquez v. Guatemala, Reparaciones y Costas, Inter-Am. Ct. H.R. (ser. C) No. 91 (Febrero 22, 2002).
Barrios Altos v. Peru, Merits, Inter-Am. Ct. H.R. (ser. C) No. 83 (March 14, 2001).
Blake v. Guatemala, Fondo, Inter-Am. Ct. H.R. (ser. C) No. 36 (Enero 24, 1998).
Caesar v. Trinidad and Tobago, Merits, reparations and costs, Inter-Am. Ct. H.R. (ser. C) No. 123 (March 11, 2005).
Case of the Ituango Massacres v. Colombia, Preliminary Objections, Merits, Reparations and Costs, Inter-Am. Ct. H.R. (ser. C) No. 148 (July 1, 2006).
Case of the "Mapiripán Massacre" v. Colombia, Merits, Reparations and Costs, Inter-Am. Ct. H.R. (ser. C) No. 22 (September 15, 2005).
Case of the Members of the Village of Chichupac and neighboring communities of the Municipality of Rabinal v. Guatemala, Preliminary Objections, Merits, Reparations and Costs, Inter-Am. Ct. H.R. (ser. C) No. 328 (November 30, 2016).
Case of the Sawhoyamaxa Indigenous Community v. Paraguay, Merits, Reparations and Costs, Inter-Am. Ct. H.R. (ser. C) No. 146 (March 29, 2006).
Contreras et al. v. El Salvador, Merits, Reparations and Costs, Inter-Am. Ct. H.R. (ser. C) No. 232 (August 31, 2011).
Defensor de Derechos Humanos y Otros vs. Guatemala, Excepciones Preliminares, Fondo, Reparaciones y Costas, Inter-Am. Ct. H.R. (ser. C) No. 283 (Agosto 28, 2014).
El hábeas corpus bajo suspensión de garantías (artículos 27.2, 25 y 8 Convención Americana sobre Derechos Humanos), Opinión Consultiva OC-8/87, Inter-Am. Ct. H. R. (January 30, 1987).
Espinoza Gonzáles v. Peru, Preliminary objections, merits, reparations and costs, Inter-Am. Ct. H.R. (ser. C) No. 289 (November 20, 2014).
Expelled Dominicans and Haitians v. Dominican Republic, Preliminary Objections, Merits, Reparations and Costs, Inter-Am. Ct. H.R. (ser. C) No. 282 (August 28, 2014).

Garantías Judiciales en Estados de Emergencia (arts. 27.2, 25 y 8 Convención Americana sobre Derecho Humanos), Opinión Consultiva OC-9/87, Inter-Am. Ct. H. R. (October 06, 1987).

Gonzales Lluy y Otros vs. Ecuador, Excepciones Preliminares, Fondo, Reparaciones y Costas, Inter-Am. Ct. H.R. (ser. C) No. 298 (Septiembre 1, 2015).

Juridical Conditions and Rights of Undocumented Migrants, Advisory Opinion OC-18/03, Inter-Am. Ct. H. R. (ser. A) No. 18 (September 17, 2003).

Loayza-Tamayo v. Peru, Merits, Inter-Am. Ct. H. R. (ser. C) No. 33 (September 17, *1997)*.

Neira-Alegría et al. v. Peru, Merits, Inter-Am. Ct. H.R. (ser. C) No. 20 (January 19, 1995).

Norín Catrimán et al. (Leaders, Members and Activists of the Mapuche Indigenous People) v. Chile, Merits, Reparations and Costs, Inter-Am. Ct. H.R. (ser. C) No. 279 (May 29, 2014).

Restricciones a la Pena de Muerte (artículos 4.2 y 4.4 Convención Americana sobre Derechos Humanos), Opinión Consultiva OC-3/83, Inter-Am. Ct. H. R. (ser. Fallos y opiniones) No. 3 (September 08, 1983).

Rosendo Cantú et al. v. Mexico, Preliminary objection, merits, reparations and costs, Inter-Am. Ct. H.R. (ser. C) No. 216 (August 31, 2010).

The Effect of Reservations on the Entry into Force of the American Convention on Human Rights, Advisory Opinion OC-2/82, Inter-Am. Ct. H. R. (ser. A) No. 2 (September 24, 1982).

The Right to Information on Consular Assistance in the Framework of the Guarantees of the due Process of Law, Advisory Opinion OC-16/99, Inter-Am. Ct. H.R. (ser. A) No. 16 (October 1, 1999).

Velásquez Paiz y Otros v. Guatemala, Excepciones Preliminares, Fondo, Reparaciones y Costas, Inter-Am. Ct. H.R. (ser. C) No. 307 (Noviembre 15, 2015).

Velásquez Rodríguez vs. Honduras, Fondo, Inter-Am. Ct. H.R. (ser. C) No. 4 (July 29, 1988).

United Nations materials

C.C.P.R. General Comment No. 29, State of Emergency (Article 4 of International Covenant on Civil and Political Rights, U.N. Doc. CCPR/C/21/Rev.1/Add.11 (August 31, 2001).

E.S.C. Report on the Thirty-Sixth Session, Official Records, 1980, Supplement No. 3, U. N. Doc. E/1980/13, E/CN.4/1408 (February 4 – March 14, 1980).

G.A. Res. 804 (VIII), Question of atrocities committed by the North Korean and Chinese Communist forces against United Nations prisoners of war in Korea, U.N. Doc. A/RES/804/VIII (Dec. 3, 1953).

G.A. Res. 1514 (XV), Declaration on the Granting of Independence to Colonial Countries and Peoples, U.N. Doc. A/RES/1514 (XV) (Dec. 14, 1960).

G.A. Res. 1904 (XVIII), United Nations Declaration on the Elimination of All Forms of Racial Discrimination, U.N. Doc. A/RES/18/1904 (Nov. 20, 1963).

G.A. Res. 1312 (XIII), The Situation in Hungary, U.N. Doc. A38/49 (Dec. 12, 1958).

G.A. Res. 2443 (XXIII), Respect for and implementation of human rights in occupied territories, U.N. Doc. A/RES/2443/XXIII (Dec. 19, 1968).

G.A. Res. 2444 (XXIII), Respect for human rights in armed conflicts, U.N. Doc. A/RES/2444/XXIII (Dec. 19, 1968).

G.A. Res. 2675 (XXV), Basic principles for the protection of civilian populations in armed conflicts, U.N. Doc. A/RES/2675/XXV (Dec. 09, 1970).

G.A. Res. 2908 (XXVII), Implementation of the Declaration on the Granting of Independence to Colonial Countries and Peoples, U.N. Doc. A/RES/2908 (XXVII) (Nov. 02, 1972).

Manuel Wackenheim v. France, Communication No. 854/1999, U.N. Doc. CCPR/C/75/D/854/1999 (2002).

S.C. Res. 1373 (2001), U.N. Doc. S/RES/1373 (September 28, 2001).

S.C. Res. 2249 (2015), U.N. Doc. S/RES/2249 (November 20, 2015).

United Nations, Afghanistan Annual Report on Protection of Civilians in Armed Conflicts, 2010, (March, 2011).

United Nations, Final Act of the International Conference on Human Rights, Teheran, 22 April to 13 May 1968, A/CONF.32/41, Sales No. E68.XIV.2 (1968).

European Union materials

Council of Europe – European Court of Human Rights. Human Rights and the Fight Against Terrorism. Strasbourg, France: Council of Europe, 2005.

Inter-American Commission on Human Rights materials

Commissión Inter-Americana de Derechos Humanos, Informe sobre Terrorismo y Derechos Humanos (2002).

Foreign jurisdiction: Germany

Bundesverfassungsgericht [German Constitutional Court] December 15, 1999, Case of *Von Hannover v. Germany*, BverfGE 101, 1 BvR 653/96, 1999 (Ger.).

Index

For Product Safety Concerns and Information please contact our EU representative GPSR@taylorandfrancis.com
Taylor & Francis Verlag GmbH, Kaufingerstraße 24, 80331 München, Germany

www.ingramcontent.com/pod-product-compliance
Lightning Source LLC
LaVergne TN
LVHW021036011026
849160LV00009BA/668
9780367773205